narrative therapy

narrative therapy

An Introduction for Counsellors

MARTIN PAYNE

SAGE Publications
London · Thousand Oaks · New Delhi

SAGE Publications Ltd
6 Bonhill Street
London EC2A 4PU

SAGE Publications Inc
2455 Teller Road
Thousand Oaks, California 91320

SAGE Publications India Pvt Ltd
32, M-Block Market
Greater Kailash – I
New Delhi 110 048

British Library Cataloguing in Publication Data
A catalogue record for this book is available from the British Library
ISBN 0 7619 5782 0
ISBN 0 7619 5783 9 (pbk)

Library of Congress catalog card number 99-72916

Typeset by Type Study, Scarborough, North Yorkshire
Printed in Great Britain by Biddles Ltd, Guildford, Surrey

For Mary
valued colleague, loved partner

Contents

Foreword

This is a fascinating and important book. Martin Payne is a British counsellor who underwent his initial training and professional socialization in a person-centred tradition which emphasizes core concepts such as self, actualization, congruence, acceptance and empathy. He has subsequently found a source of meaning and influence in the work of Michael White and David Epston and their 'narrative therapy'. His book tells the story of how he has assimilated and integrated these influences into his practice, and indeed into his whole way of making sense of the world. He tells us a lot about the ways in which he has evolved an appropriately narrative-informed practice, and in doing so reveals an approach which clearly allows him to engage actively and fully with the lives of people in a highly affirming and creative manner. Towards the end of the book he also writes about his struggle to come to terms with the moral and philosophical implications of some of Michael White's ideas. Unlike the majority of counselling writing currently being published, this is a genuinely radical book. There is much to reflect on here both for those who are sympathetic to the narrative approach, and for those who would question its effectiveness. The radical and perplexing nature of narrative therapy is clearly illustrated in Martin Payne's account. As a way of responding to people who come for help with 'problems in living', his approach to narrative counselling is supportive, purposeful and well received. Yet at the same time, the therapist's conception of what he or she is trying to do is quite different from that of most contemporary counsellors and psychotherapists. At one level, this difference can be seen to generate novel techniques and interventions (for example, writing letters to clients). But, as Martin Payne clearly acknowledges, at another level letter writing and other narrative-informed methods are not merely techniques to be slotted in to a counsellor's repertoire, but are indicative of a different way of understanding what therapy is, and what it should be. My own view is that narrative therapy is *postpsychological*, and forms part of a broad movement that has recognised the extent to which psychological models and concepts have contributed not only to the diffusion of what

Kenneth Gergen has called a 'language of deficit' but also to the erosion of collective and communal forms of life and being in relationship. Martin Payne has done us all a great service in describing some of the ways in which counselling practice can be re-imagined from a more culturally and socially-oriented perspective.

John McLeod
University of Aberdeen
Dundee

Acknowledgements

I thank Lynda Dugdale for typing transcripts of sessions and for other work in connection with the production of the book, and Barrie Mencher for searching out references in F.R. Leavis's writings. Rose Battye and Peter Emerson helped me greatly by reading and commenting on early drafts of parts of the book. Freda Sharpe has been committed and untiring in sifting through much of the text and discussing nuances of wording, often suggesting excellent emendations, and making cogent general points which I was able to apply to other parts of the book. I am very grateful to all these friends.

Michael White found time in a very busy life to discuss the structure and content of the book with me and to read and comment on Chapter 9. I thank him for this, and for his general encouragement. I am grateful to John McLeod for the time he has given to reading the text and for writing a Foreword which is so sensitive to my intentions.

I owe an enormous debt of gratitude to my partner Mary Wilkinson, who introduced me to narrative therapy in the first place; read and discussed several complete versions of the manuscript; explored and clarified unfamiliar ideas; suggested many important emendations; noted many typing and spelling errors; and gave great personal support while the book was in preparation.

I thank all the members of Sage Publications staff who have been involved in the planning and production of the book, in particular Susan Worsey, Melissa Dunlop, Alison Poyner, Susie Home, Nerida Harrowing, Vanessa Harwood and Louise Wise. Their support and professionalism have been invaluable. Copyediting by Sue Ashton was meticulous, with many positive suggestions for improved layout and phrasing. The cover designers, Design Deluxe, creatively translated my suggestions into a striking and wholly appropriate visual image.

Finally, I particularly thank the persons who so willingly gave permission for their stories to appear in these pages. They did this in a generous spirit of hope that their experiences might be of assistance to therapists working with people facing similar issues. These persons have been an inspiration to me.

Introduction

Some years ago I was part-way through a diploma in counselling course based on person-centred approaches which also included a wide-ranging introduction to other 'individual' counselling psychologies and methods. I was also, informally, learning a little about family therapy, as my partner Mary Wilkinson was attending a diploma course in systemic therapy at a different training institution. I was struck by how little overlap there was in our recommended reading material and in the ideas and practices of these two courses, and I found this puzzling – many ideas in family therapy seemed exciting and stimulating. I particularly liked the idea of a person's family and social context being taken into account in the definitions of problems and the processes of therapy. I began to wonder whether ideas and practices from family therapy might be appropriate in working with individuals.

I happened to open one of Mary's books, by a family therapist I'd never heard of, and came across this description of part of a session with a 12-year-old boy and his parents:

> John suddenly remarked with surprise, 'This is the first time a definite way of defeating my fears has come up' (although he had, in the past, been encouraged on many occasions to stop his obsessive-compulsive behaviour). He now 'knew' the solution was to stop feeding the fierce friends of the fears. John and Mrs Walker began sobbing quietly with what I suspected was relief. John, with his hands over his eyes, lapsed into silence. I asked him what he was thinking, and he replied that he was worrying what I would think of him for crying. I said, 'if you are crying on the inside and not on the outside at the same time, you will drown your strength.' (White, 1989: 5)

I was struck by the compassion and imagination of the description, and moved by the sensitivity of the response being offered to the boy for his shame at crying. As I looked through the book, intrigued now, another passage leapt out at me, this time with powerful echoes from a past period in my own life:

> Externalising is an approach to therapy that encourages persons to objectify, and at times to personify, the problems that they experience as

oppressive. In this process, the problem becomes a separate entity and thus external to the person who was, or the relationship that was, ascribed the problem. Those problems that are considered to be inherent, and those relatively fixed qualities that are attributed to persons and relationships, are rendered less fixed and less restricting. (White, 1989: 97)

I had experienced clinical depression some years before, and had found myself calling it 'the Enemy'. I knew this had been helpful, but I had never really thought about why, or articulated the difference this had made to me. The passage suddenly illuminated my experience: I realized that by referring to depression by an insulting name I had been able to feel more separated from it and more in control of my life.

The book was *Selected Papers* by Michael White (1989). I began to read more of White's writing, and that of his colleague David Epston, and thus began an intellectual, professional and personal journey which has resulted in my identifying my own work as narrative therapy. I do not know how far their reputation has penetrated counselling world-wide, but I have found that, to most of my counsellor colleagues, Michael White and David Epston are unknown names. Certainly, apart from an article I contributed myself (Payne, 1993), I have never come across a reference to narrative therapy in the British Association for Counselling's journal *Counselling*, whereas references are frequent in *Context*, the newsletter of the (British) Association for Family Therapy. In family therapy circles they are major names, with narrative therapy perceived as one of the most influential and innovative therapies of our time.

Michael White is a co-director of the Dulwich Centre in Adelaide, South Australia, and David Epston is a co-director of the Family Therapy Centre in Auckland, New Zealand. They have written books and articles individually and jointly, generally published at 'local' level and available only through specialist outlets in their own countries and elsewhere. An exception is their joint *Narrative Means to Therapeutic Ends*, which was published internationally in 1990. White is perhaps the more prolific and influential of the two. They have re-thought many established family therapy ideas from Europe and North America, and drawn on recent Western philosophy of science, the history of ideas, postmodern philosophy, social psychology, feminist theory and literary theory (White, 1995a: 11–12, 61–2). Narrative therapy is now established, and being increasingly written about, in the US, Canada and elsewhere (for example, White's work is strongly featured in Parry and Doan, 1994; Parker et al., 1995; Freedman and Combs, 1996; Zimmerman and Dickerson, 1996; McLeod, 1997; Parker, 1999).

Scope and style of the book

In this book 'narrative therapy' refers to the ideas and practices developed by Michael White and David Epston. A different book could be written on the ways in which their ideas have been taken up by therapists working in many different contexts, and on therapies which share some of their assumptions and practices. White himself modestly insists that he has merely 'made a contribution to this work', that it belongs to all who identify with it, and that its actuality is embodied in the multiple day-to-day practice of many therapists (White, 1997a). However, in this introduction to narrative therapy I have made White's ideas and practice the central focus: his books, papers, published interviews and international presentations have spearheaded its development and he is, by far, the therapist most widely identified with it.

White did not initially use the term 'narrative' for his way of working. He had already published articles and books outlining some of his ideas when 'it was Cheryl White and David Epston who encouraged me to interpret my work according to the narrative metaphor, and to undertake a more specific exploration of this metaphor' (White, 1995a: 13). The term also appears in therapies which are not 'narrative therapy' in the White–Epston sense, and this can be confusing. John McLeod cautions:

> all therapies are narrative therapies. Whatever you are doing, or think you are doing, as therapist or client can be understood in terms of telling and re-telling stories. Yet there is no 'narrative therapy', no one way of doing this. To present 'narrative therapy' as a new brand-name product in the therapeutic marketplace (with accompanying training manual) is to misunderstand what this is all about. (McLeod, 1997: x)

White and his colleagues have never made claims such as these, and see their work in terms of evolving, collaborative practices, not as 'methods to be learned'. 'In my view [family therapy] is still open and pluralistic, and I think that this is perhaps its most important strength. Family therapy does not signify a "closed shop" ' (White, 1995a: 78). 'I'm still learning how to do this therapy – I'm not a Michael White therapist!' (White, 1997a).

Creators of other therapies have not, however, specifically chosen the word 'narrative' to define their work, as White and Epston have. Persons do 'tell stories' when talking with therapists who describe their work as *Gestalt*, person-centred, psychodynamic, cognitive-behavioural and so on, but it is only White and Epston who have appropriated the term, and in whose work a deliberate, sustained focus on narrative processes and concepts *is* the therapy. In describing their work I do not attempt to define a 'product', let alone offer a 'manual' for that product, but I do believe that White and Epston have developed a distinctive and coherent way of working which validates their use of 'narrative therapy' as a definition.

When I asked Michael White what he would like to see in this book, what on no account should be omitted or understated, I expected a reply along the lines of, 'Make sure you emphasize externalization' or 'Include a description of telling and re-telling.' What he said was: 'I would hope to hear your own voice, your own discoveries of this work, the ways in which this work has resonated in your own life and the ways in which your life has contributed to your participation in this work' (White, personal communication, 1997a). The book is primarily an account of what I understand to be White's 'contribution'. The account is based on my own reading, thinking and understanding or misunderstanding. To avoid its being viewed as an attempt to be authoritative or comprehensive I have incorporated elements of my own history of trying to understand and practise this therapy. Examples of practice come from my own counselling unless otherwise stated.

I have followed David Epston in his use of italic, exclamation marks, rhetorical questions and informal, sometimes colloquial, phrasing in order to avoid an academic, impersonal register, an 'expert stance', reflected in an all-knowing and remote style: 'I chose early on to allow my own "voice" to pervade and situate my account, and renounced the objective, distancing rhetoric required in scientific "writing up"' (Epston, 1989: 7). I use 'counsellor' and 'therapist' interchangeably, and follow Michael White's practice of calling people who come to therapy 'persons', not 'clients'. The pronouns he/she, her/his appear at random.

The book is intended to be read in sequence, as ideas, practices and terminology are described progressively. The exception is Chapter 2, on theory, which can either be read after Chapter 1 or saved until later – perhaps being read before Chapter 9. Chapter 1 outlines some key narrative therapy practices and Chapters 3–7 describe these in more detail, with examples from my own work. These examples are disguised and have the consent of the persons concerned. Chapter 8 presents in some detail two stories of therapy – in another approach these might be called 'case histories'. Chapter 9 returns to ideas, exploring how the post-structuralist basis of narrative therapy invites reconsideration of some 'cherished assumptions' about therapy and the counselling culture. The Appendix offers an experiental learning exercise.

My particular hope is that the book will be found sufficiently interesting as a broad introduction to narrative therapy to stimulate colleagues who work with individuals and/or couples to explore White and Epston's writings, and the writing of others who are developing and shaping the work. My further hope and belief is that colleagues who do this will, as I have, find their conceptions and assumptions about therapy both challenged and enriched.

1 An Overview of Narrative Therapy

'Thin' and 'rich' descriptions

I once had a delightful book, now lost (so unfortunately I can't give the title or author), which described the changing seasons in the English countryside in two parallel ways. One description was 'scientific', covering topics such as atmosphere, temperature changes brought about by the earth's journey round the sun, chemical changes in the soil, biochemical aspects of plant growth, and the mating and migration patterns of birds. The other description was 'evocative', describing the misty beauty of autumn fields, the starry carpeting of ditch banks by primroses, the distant call of a cuckoo. Each description was valid and yet they were utterly different. Taken together they gave a dual perspective, a more complete overall description. Two disparate narratives combined to make a richer overall narrative.

The book had illustrations, two for each season. One portrayed open landscape and the other woodland. These pictures were, in a sense, very realistic. Colours were precise and vivid and each animal, bird, plant or tree was drawn in meticulous detail. Yet one aspect was far from realistic: crowded into each scene was almost every tree, flower, plant, insect, fungus, bird, animal and reptile associated with the season! The illustrations followed a convention – the reader knew that she would never see all this wildlife gathered together in one landscape in real life, but it was convenient for the book to show them all at once in one picture. Even so, there were missing elements: in an actual landscape there are possibilities for surprise (once, in Kent, I saw an osprey diving – a bird native to Scotland). No portrayal of the typical can include variants and yet it can be the variants that make experience uniquely memorable. Narrative therapy encourages a focus on the untypical – untypical, that is, as perceived by the person. It encourages the untypical to be considered in great detail because it is through the untypical that people can escape from the dominant stories that influence their perceptions and therefore their lives. Stereotyped descriptions of experience become less fixed, certain and influential when methods of therapy assist these descriptions to be more complete. Narrative therapy encourages 'richer' narratives to emerge from separate disparate descriptions of experience, which are not conceived as 'mistaken' or 'limited' but as 'thin'.

Another reason for my analogy with the seasons book is that the outline of narrative practices included in this chapter follows a convention similar to the illustrations. It offers an overview but does not imply that all of these elements are necessarily found in any one session or indeed in any sequence of sessions. Certain practices are often found in narrative therapy sessions, but the priority is a sensitive response to the person, not the imposition of a predetermined sequence of actions. I have taken part in counselling in which almost exactly the sequence of practices described was followed, counselling where few of the practices were used, and sessions in which these particular ideas were not used at all.

The language of narrative therapy

Michael White and David Epston's writing is often clear, vivid and engaging:

> Nick had a very long history of encopresis, which had resisted all attempts to resolve it, including those instituted by various therapists. Rarely did a day go by without an 'accident' or 'incident', which usually meant the 'full works' in his underwear. To make matters worse, Nick had befriended the 'poo'. The poo had become his playmate. He would 'streak' it down walls, smear it in drawers, roll it into balls and flick it behind cupboards and wardrobes, and even taken to plastering it under the kitchen table ... the poo had even developed the habit of accompanying Nick in the bath. (White, 1989: 9)

> I purposefully mis-heard the few responses that she gave me to my questions. I often do this with nervous, shy or unwilling adolescents:

> *Neolene*: [*mumbling inaudibly in response to DE's question.*]
> *DE*: [*incredulously*] You want to buy a pumpkin?
> *Neolene*: [*looking at me in amazement*] What do you mean pumpkin?
> *DE*: I thought you said you wanted to buy a pumpkin?
> *Neolene*: [*laughing, but now perfectly audible and responsive*] No . . . what I said was . . .
> (Epston and White, 1992: 39)

The reader new to narrative therapy may find some of White and Epston's language puzzling or obscure, or discover that familiar terms are used in unfamiliar ways. Sometimes this may be because they are addressing family therapists, in language and concepts perhaps unfamiliar to counsellors trained in different traditions:

> In that the metaphor of system relates to theories of equilibrium, of the maintenance of order, of stability and so on, and in that the metaphor of pattern relates to theories of regularity or redundancy, both metaphors construct a timeless reality . . . since the criterion for verifying a pattern is the identification of a redundancy across time, then immunity or invulnerability to the effects of time is built into its very definition. (White, 1995a: 215)

On other occasions their language carries clear, specific meanings familiar to those who have read publications where the terms are defined, but which may puzzle readers new to them: 'I will present candidate questions that assist family members to select out unique outcomes, place these unique outcomes in the context of a pattern across time, ascribe significance to unique accounts, and speculate about new possibilities. These are all questions that invite, from family members, a "performance of meaning"' (White, 1989: 41). I explain narrative therapy terms when describing their place in narrative therapy practice. Their strange quality should evaporate with familiarity. All therapies develop vocabularies reflecting their ideas and assumptions, and White and Epston give particular attention to precision of language because language can blur or distort experience in the telling, can condition the ways in which we act and feel, or, on the other hand, be purposefully chosen as a therapeutic tool. Being conscious of language usage is seen by White and Epston as a central responsibility of therapists: 'We have to be very sensitive to the issue of language. Words are so import-ant. In so many ways, words are the world. So, I hope that a sensi-tivity to language shows up in my work with persons and, as well, in my writing' (White, 1995a: 30).

White is scrupulous to maintain gender- and ethnic-neutral vocabulary, but his concern goes further than these widely accepted conventions. He is particularly alert to vocabularies which have developed within institutions incorporating power-based relation-ships, where linguistic terms have transferred to other contexts where their implicit meanings may be unrecognized yet influential. He particularly avoids the 'medical model' language of some ther-apies: 'There now exists a simply fantastic number of opportunities that are available to mental health professionals for the pathologising of people's lives ... we now have at our disposal a vast array of speaking with and interacting with people that reproduce the subject/object dualism that is so pervasive in the structuring of relations in our culture' (White, 1995a: 112). White's use of 'person' instead of 'client' demonstrates, perhaps, dissatisfaction with the role implications of a word widely used and presumably widely thought to be respectful. I have not come across an explanation by White of his usage but it is present from his earliest published work. He also never refers to 'cases' or 'case histories', seeing this as an example of language which objectifies persons' lives and diminishes the sense that people bring experiences to therapy which are central to them, often painful, meshed with loving, puzzlement, joys, despairs and grieving. Such trust is not appropriately honoured when referring to people in difficult stages of their lives by the distancing and pathologizing word 'case' (White, 1997a).

A relatively simple yet telling instance of precisely chosen vocabulary comes from the opening words of a training exercise (White, 1995b: 1): 'This exercise has been developed to *assist* people to explore externalising conversations' (emphasis added). The word 'assist' perhaps feels a little formal and ponderous – would not 'help' be a more appropriate choice? But I wonder whether by using 'assist' rather than 'help' White incorporates a subtle distinction to do with power differentials between himself as 'trainer' and trainees? A *helper* offers expertise to a subordinate; an *assistant* offers to share knowledge or skills with someone who is already to a degree competent. This vocabulary is consistent with White's idea of therapist 'decentring', of attempting to ensure that the person herself is at the centre of therapy (see Chapter 9).

The organization of sessions

There is no set convention for the length of narrative therapy sessions. My own counselling tends to stay within the conventional frame of 50 minutes, but I have observed White and his colleagues hold sessions lasting over two hours, not just with families but also with individuals and couples. Intervals between sessions vary – there is no assumption that weekly sessions, or sessions set at any other predetermined interval, should be a norm. Narrative therapy is not a 'brief therapy', and some of White and Epston's descriptions are of work over many sessions, but elements such as 'outsider witnessing' and the use of 'therapeutic documents' can make the overall length of effective counselling much shorter than in some other therapies (White, 1995a: 195, 200). Their accounts often reveal that just a few sessions, sometimes at wide intervals, are enough for therapy to be effective, even with persons presenting difficulties experienced over a long period.

An outline of narrative therapy practices

The following outline of narrative therapy practices is a generalized overview, intended to orientate the reader through the rest of the book. Each element described is explored at greater length in later chapters, with references to publications or other sources; here I exclude references in order to keep the text unbroken and save the reader the interruption of continually moving away from it. Between sections I tell a 'story of therapy' to illustrate the text. Unlike elsewhere in this book, this is an invented account; I have not worked with any one person in the precise sequence, and with all the practices, described in this simplified summary. However, the 'story' does derive from actual counselling with several persons.

Practices are outlined in approximate sequence, although the therapist may, both within a single session and over a sequence of sessions, expand them, contract them, return to them or omit them altogether according to her sense of what might be of assistance to the person. They are separated here into headed sections simply for convenience of description. The variety, intricacy, sensitivity, tact and flexibility of narrative therapy are not reflected in this outline, which should not be taken as a prescription for practice. For simplicity, I have referred to working one to one, but later chapters also include examples of work with couples.

The person tells her 'story': 'problem-saturated' description
Narrative therapy, like all therapies, begins with the counsellor giving the person respectful, interested attention in a safe and uninterrupted place. The person is invited to talk about her concerns, and the therapist listens. Often, persons starting therapy tell stories that are full of frustration, despair and sadness, with few or no gleams of hope. One of White's names for such accounts is 'problem-saturated description'. A problem-saturated description embodies the person's present 'dominant story' of her life. The therapist takes this description seriously, and accepts it, while at the

same time assuming that it is not likely to be the whole or only story. Although most descriptions by persons starting therapy are 'problem-saturated', some descriptions are not, as the person may already have moved towards positioning herself differently towards the issues which concern her. In these instances the practices outlined below may be considerably modified.

Once the person has reached the end of her account, and there is a natural pause, the therapist begins to ask clarifying and extending questions, encouraging her to describe in even greater detail the ways in which she is experiencing difficulties, and the effects of these difficulties on her life. Through the person's responses both the therapist and the person gain a store of remembered and perceived experience to use as the basis of therapy. Recently, White has moved from the term 'problem-saturated description' to the term 'thin description', which reflects more accurately the idea that an initial 'story' always omits certain forgotten or unnoticed elements of lived experience.

Louise, a schoolteacher, and Jim, a machine operator, married after a whirlwind courtship. After a happy year Jim's health deteriorated and Louise nursed him for six months through a long and distressing illness until his death eight months before she came to counselling. She attributed his illness to his employers' neglect of safety precautions and to a culture of 'macho risk-taking' in the workforce. She described the circumstances of his illness and death and how her feelings were still overwhelming her; she could not sleep, her work was suffering, and she would find herself crying when shopping or driving. I invited her to describe other ways in which her life was affected, and she spoke of many other reactions, including nightmares, inability to enjoy life and a sense of hopelessness.

Naming the problem

When encouraging the person to expand her initial narrative, the therapist invites her to give a specific name or names to the problem, perhaps a single word or short phrase. If the person cannot think of a name the therapist floats possibilities, such as 'depression', 'stress in the marriage', 'abuse' and so on, until a name is provisionally agreed. This is then used, unless further description by the person suggests that a different, more precise, name might be appropriate, when another name is chosen. Naming encourages focus and precision, enables the person to feel more in control of the problem and gives a precise definition for 'externalization' of the problem (see below).

Louise named her problems as 'Grief, Frustration and Anger'. When we had looked more closely at the circumstances and cause of her husband's illness Louise changed the name 'Anger' to 'Justified Outrage'.

Using externalizing language

The therapist uses language embodying an implicit assumption that the problem is 'having an effect on' the person rather than existing within or being intrinsic to him. This linguistic device is called 'externalizing the problem'. The therapist says 'depression invaded your life' rather than 'you became depressed', or she might say 'You were both affected by stress' rather than 'You were both stressed.' Externalizing language is used throughout therapy, not just at the first session. The aim is to help the person separate from her problems and conceive them as the product of circumstances or interpersonal processes, and to avoid colluding in a view that her problems are, or are caused by, her 'psychology' or 'personality'. Externalizing language is *not*, however, used for damaging or abusive actions. Abuse and violence are bluntly named: 'He abused you over a long period' or, if the person himself is an abuser, 'You abused her over a long period.' Beliefs and assumptions used to 'justify' the abuse may be externalized: 'You were dominated by a belief that violence is acceptable.'

I used externalizing language when discussing Louise's situation, speaking, for example, of 'grief having power over your life', 'justified outrage insisting on being heard' and 'frustration invading your quiet times'.

Considering social and political issues

Narrative therapy embodies an assumption that cultural, social and political factors affect lives, and in particular that power-based relations in Western society are endemic both 'locally' (interpersonally) and more widely. Narrative therapists recognize that persons sometimes ascribe the distressing and unjust results of these social factors to themselves, as personal failures, shortcomings or faults, and that they are implicitly encouraged do so by those who hold power. Correspondingly, a force assisting persons to free themselves from the interiorization of blame and guilt can be an examination of issues of social power. For example, the 'politics' of gender interaction or of parental authority may be named and examined, and also the effects on persons' lives of institutional and governmental economic and social policies. Reading may be recommended and discussed in sessions. Therapy itself is recognized as potentially harmful when based on unrecognized power relations, and narrative therapists attempt to reduce this potential by continuous critical examination of their practice, and by regular checking-out with persons that they find the therapy acceptable.

After checking that Louise was comfortable about detailed discussion of the circumstances of her husband's illness, I encouraged her to say why she considered that his death had resulted from inadequate safety precautions at his place of work, and to explore what she might wish to do about this. She decided to bring the matter to the attention of the appropriate legal authorities, both as something worth doing in itself, and as a therapeutic activity in tribute to her husband. We also discussed the expectations of 'getting over it and moving on with your life' being placed on her by others which made her suspect that her continuing, powerful emotions of grief might indicate 'instability'. Louise concluded that in present-day Western society people are embarrassed at witnessing powerful feelings, and that the intensity of her grief was appropriate – a problem for others, not for her.

Relative influence questioning

'Relative influence questioning' elicits two descriptions: (a) the influence the problem has had and is having on the life of the person; and then, in contrast, (b) the influence the person has had, and is having, on the 'life of the problem'. White and Epston's earlier writings suggest that, after drawing out a full problem-saturated description, they would ask the person to remember occasions when she managed to get the upper hand over the problem, even if only slightly, or to remember occasions when she was able to deal to her satisfaction with similar or related issues. The person would describe these slipped-out-of-memory examples in detail and then the therapist would invite her to consider their significance. More recently, White has preferred simply to wait for such memories to emerge spontaneously from the person's 'richer' account of experience, and at that point to focus on them and explore them with her in detail. Questions at this point concern feelings, thoughts and actions, past and present, perceived by the person direct, and perceived by others. White uses Erving Goffman's (1961) term 'unique outcomes' for these significant memories which contradict the problem-saturated, dominant story.

Louise identified some unique outcomes – instances which contradicted her dominant story of being overwhelmed. She had continued with her work, she had dealt with the legal and financial aspects of her husband's death, she had continued to run a hockey team for handicapped young people and she had cut down on her drinking, which had increased considerably in the period immediately after her loss. She had also come to recognize that attempts to persuade her to 'move on in her life' were inappropriate and unhelpful. On the whole, despite occasional moments of panic when she wondered if the intensity of her feelings did indicate 'instability', she managed to hold on to a recognition that powerful grief and justified outrage were natural and appropriate.

'Deconstruction' of unique outcomes

When the person has mentioned aspects of her experience which appear to deny, contradict or modify her dominant problem-saturated story, the therapist, through questioning, invites her to expand on the circumstances and nature of these 'unique outcomes' and, by asking questions, focuses attention on how these do not fit with the story-as-told. This detailed focusing and description, or 'deconstruction', assists the second description to become a firm account rather than to dissolve away. Therapist questions continue to be wide ranging and to cover the person's feelings, actions and thoughts in the past, the present and for the future. The therapist invites speculation on how other people, important to the person, who witnessed these unique outcomes, may have understood them. Through this 'deconstructive' process the person gains a wider perspective on her experience, 'writes a richer story' and evolves unanticipated bases for preferred change.

Among the unique outcomes I deconstructed with Louise, her desire to take direct legal and political action loomed large. She recognized that outrage at what had happened to her husband was not actually a 'problem' at all but a wholly appropriate reaction, and that her determination to gain retribution for her husband was a healing element in her life. By outlining in great detail the carelessness, negligence and 'macho culture' at his place of employment, which led him to undertake work without insisting on full safety measures, she gained both a conviction that she had to act, and the energy to do so. By discussing in detail the action she intended to take, she gained a perspective of 'resistance' which contradicted her previously dominant story of being 'overwhelmed and powerless'. Her continuing to run the hockey team involved skills in organization and human relations, and she was sure that the members of the team and their parents would recognize that she had not allowed her personal situation to stand in the way of fulfilling this responsibility. In discussing all these details of continuing activity, she became aware that alongside her periods of accepting her immense grief, there was another, complementary story, of competence and 'pushing on with life'.

The person is invited to take a position

Therapy has now reached a turning point. The person can decide to remain dominated by the problem-saturated story of her life, or she can decide to take fully into account the richer story the therapist has encouraged her to tell. Dilemmas for the person might include: Is this the right time for me to take new directions or do I need more time to consider these possibilities? Is the problem still too much in charge of my life for me to challenge it safely? If it is, when might its power be reduced? How might I recognize that development? Usually persons do decide to position themselves differently in relation to the problem, but sometimes they feel this is too disturbing, painful or premature. The therapist explores with the person, in detail, the possible outcomes of these different courses of action.

After several sessions Louise gained a richer perspective. She no longer internalized powerful grief in 'self-blaming' terms, but 'allowed' it as appropriate, proportionate and inevitable. At the same time, she was aware that frustration and grief had not wholly overwhelmed her life. I had no need to 'raise the dilemma' by exploring whether she wished her life to remain as it was because her decision to take legal action on behalf of her husband was energizing and therapeutic, giving her a sense of taking control rather than being a passive victim.

Use of therapeutic documents

The therapist may introduce written documents, sometimes creating them herself and sometimes encouraging the person to write them. These documents summarize the person's discoveries and describe the person's own perceived progress. The person may keep them for future reference, or use them in any other way she may decide. Formats include letters, memos, statements, lists, essays, contracts and certificates. Sometimes they may be private to the person, sometimes they may be shared with the therapist, and sometimes they may be shared with other people. Their use as a device for consolidation is based on recognition that the written word is more permanent than the spoken word and, in Western society, carries more 'authority' – here, the authority of the person.

During the period of her therapy I wrote several letters to Louise, sum-marizing our discussions and referring to unique outcomes and the mean-ings she had found in them. Louise decided to write a personal book, an account of her 'love story', and to illustrate it with drawings, photographs and other mementoes.

Continuing therapy: 'telling and re-telling' towards enrichment of the self-story

Sometimes no further sessions are needed. When therapy continues it aims to facilitate the person's building on and expanding the 'richer story' she has begun to 'write' about her life as it was, as it is and as it might become.

Louise attended for several further sessions in which she consolidated her decision to act, discussing details of legal steps she was taking and of a newspaper campaign she hoped to initiate. In several sessions she simply talked quietly and movingly about her husband and her memories of their life together, especially the 'golden year' of their marriage before his illness began.

Using 'outsider witnesses'

White has increasingly emphasized the importance of an 'audience' for the person's telling and re-telling. In earlier papers he describes encouraging persons to identify people whom they would like to tell, outside the session, the 'revised stories' of their lives and especially their discoveries of success against the problem. Audi-ences might consist of friends, relatives, peers and so on. From this idea he developed the practice of providing an audience in the therapy room at an appropriate stage, consisting of other therapists, people chosen by the person, or both. White defines the audience as 'outsider witnesses' and organizes the session into several differ-ent tellings and re-tellings. Sessions may be video-recorded and the recording given to the person for private re-hearing. Members of the 'outsider witness' team may share experiences from their own lives with the person, not to diminish or take from her account but to reinforce it by resonances from their own lives. Members of the wider community may also be recruited as an audience for the person's re-tellings – in the therapy room or by receiving the person as a visitor to their home or workplace.

Louise completed her 'personal book' several months after counselling ended, then made an appointment to show it to me and to discuss what writing it had meant to her. She also wanted to bring me up to date on her campaign about safety at her husband's workplace. At this session she agreed to my tentative request for her to discuss her whole experience of loss, grief, retribution and healing with two of my colleagues, who were exploring narrative ways of working. This session took place three weeks later, and Louise said at the end of it that sharing her experiences, and hearing others relate these experiences to their own lives, had been moving and helpful.

Re-membering

As an extension of outsider witnessing, persons can find comfort and support by drawing on memories of significant people who have been lost to their life – relatives and friends who have died, or lost touch; strangers who made an important positive contribution to the person's life on only one occasion; famous people who have indirectly contributed to the person's life by examples of courage and integrity. Assisted by the therapist, the person metaphorically invites these people to re-join the 'club of her life'. White calls this process *re-membering*. The person may, on the other hand, wish to *exclude* from her 'life club' people who have behaved abusively, neglectfully, coercively or in other detrimental ways.

Louise's personal book, and the reminiscences of her time with her husband which she shared with me, assisted her at this time to keep his 'presence' in her life rather than to follow the advice of others to try to exclude him from her life and 'move on'.

Ending therapy

Therapy ends when the person decides that her self-story is rich enough to sustain her future. The final session may be organized as a joyful occasion. People significant to the person may be invited for re-tellings and there may be a ceremony to mark the occasion, such as the presentation of a therapeutic certificate.

A final session with Louise, my colleagues and myself, where she re-told her story and heard further re-tellings and personal meanings from the three of us in response to her story, took on an atmosphere of ceremony and affirmation which ended counselling on a confirmatory note.

2 *Ideas Informing Narrative Therapy*

A synthesis of ideas

My background in person-centred counselling had not prepared me for ideas and practices familiar to family therapists, and I soon began to realize that White and Epston were saying things that were not orthodox even in this field. For me, this presented more than a struggle to grasp new ideas. These ideas were set in an utterly unfamiliar conceptual framework, with few apparent connections to the assumptions underlying my own training. I hope that this chapter will provide a 'map' by means of which readers new to narrative ideas may gain some sense of conceptual location and direction when exploring the territory of this therapy.

Some readers may prefer to omit this chapter now, returning to it after reading subsequent chapters about practice, when the ideas it outlines may fall more clearly into place. Others may prefer to read it now and bear in mind the ideas it outlines when reading later chapters. Chapter 9 discusses the implications of post-structuralism, a central issue only touched on at this point.

Michael White seems to me to have exceptional skills for synthesis; he draws on ideas from diverse sources where he sees their relevance to therapy, sometimes conceptualizing and integrating them in ways which might not wholly meet the approval of 'specialists' in those fields. This is an evolving process. I have noticed that some ideas which were emphasized in White and Epston's earlier writings, such as strategic and systemic approaches to family therapy, Gregory Bateson's concepts of negative explanation and restraint, and 'cybernetic' metaphors for describing interactions between persons and events, are less prominent in White's more recent publications and teaching. I give these less emphasis, identifying them only where they illuminate White's recent thinking.

In offering a version of the principal ideas which I understand to inform narrative therapy I am conscious of my limitations. My training is in literature, teaching and counselling; I am not a family therapist, linguist, philosopher, psychologist, anthropologist or historian of ideas. But the discovery and exploration of some recent thinking in these fields has been immensely exciting, and of great value in reaching a more complete understanding of the mode of therapy I now attempt to practise. In a few pages I cannot do justice to themes which have engaged some of the most original minds of our time, have an extensive literature and have played a major part in recent Western thought over a very wide range of disciplines. I hope readers will remember that the phrase 'According to my understanding . . .' is implicit before every statement. I have not interrupted the text of this chapter with sources unless direct quotations are given.

Two related meanings of 'narrative'

A dictionary definition

> *Narrative*: narrating: giving an account of any occurrence: inclined to narration: story-telling. – *n* that which is narrated: a continuing account of any series of occurrences: story. (*Chambers Concise Dictionary*, 1985)

This is a helpful starting-point. 'Narrative' can mean an account of an event or events – 'story-telling'. Poems such as *Sir Gawain and the Green Knight* and Tennyson's *The Lady of Shalott* tell stories; they describe events in a sequence. They are narrative poems. Gray's *Elegy Written in a Country Churchyard* is meditative. It does not tell a story; it is *not* a 'narrative' poem. 'Accounts', 'stories' and 'narratives' are terms used interchangeably in this therapy. They refer, in the sense given by the dictionary definition, to *selected sequences of life* which come into existence as an entity through the very act of being 'told'.

A person's *self*-story is a first-person narrative through which he defines his identity, based on his memories and perceptions of his history, his present life, his roles in various social and personal settings, and his relationships. These self-stories, these accounts of life, are often told to others, and are frequently told to himself, in fragmented 'inner' monologue, changing in precise detail at each telling but with recurring dominant themes and concepts. A person will often project this narrative, this existing story, into an *assumed* future: 'So I've always been depressed and I suppose I always will be'; 'Our marriage has dragged on till now and I can't see there'll ever be any way out.' And sometimes a person will narrate his story into a *preferred* future: 'I've always been depressed but I expect I'll be able to sort it'; 'Our marriage has dragged on till now but no way can it carry on like this.' The process of a person's telling such narratives is often called 'storying' in narrative therapy.

'Narrative' as a 'postmodern' concept

The dictionary definition is only one sense in which the term 'narrative' is used in this therapy. If that were all, then it would have very little specific meaning compared with its use in the many other therapies where persons are invited to tell their story to the counsellor. A significant, wider meaning relates to a relatively recent way of thinking about the nature of human life and human knowledge, which has become known as 'postmodernism', where two ways of describing the world and human life are recognized and given equal status: the 'scientific' and the 'narrative'. Since scientific descriptions have traditionally enjoyed a higher truth status in Western culture, postmodern expositions tend to give more attention to the previously undervalued narrative mode.

Many traditional therapies are based on 'psychological' ideas defined by those who have developed them as scientific: derived from observation, formed into theories which offer explanations for those observations, and confirmed by what is believed to be objective research (for example, Rogers, 1961: pt v). Creators of therapies often assume that with much reading, thinking and training the trainee therapist can share the assumed 'objective' knowledge enshrined in their theories, learning, for example, to locate and assess the sources of motivation, the roots of distress, the mechanisms of relationships, the causes and cures of issues brought to therapy. But in a postmodern perspective it is assumed that, rather than anything described by the many diverse and often mutually contradictory psychological theories behind the various schools of therapy, it is our immediate, day-to-day, concrete, personal apprehension of our lives – expressed through the 'stories' we tell ourselves and others about our lives – that is primarily knowable. The stories are also *influential*. In a postmodern perspective, these stories or narratives form the matrix of concepts and beliefs by which we understand our lives, and the world in which our lives take place; and there is a continuing interaction between the stories we tell ourselves about our lives, the ways we live our lives, and the further stories we then tell.

During an interview, White was asked what he meant by 'a story or narrative of life, as being the basis of your work'. He replied:

This is to propose that human beings are interpreting beings – that we are active in the interpretation of our experiences as we live our lives. It's to propose that it's not possible for us to interpret our experience without access to some frame of intelligibility, one that provides a context for our experience, one that makes the attribution of meaning possible. It's to propose that stories constitute this frame of intelligibility. It's to propose that the meanings derived in this process of interpretation are not neutral in their effects on our lives, but have real effects on what we do, on the steps that we take in life. It's to propose that it is the story or self-narrative that determines which aspects of our lived experience get expressed, and it is to propose that it is the story [or] self narrative that determines the shape of our lived experience. *It's to propose that we live by the stories that we have about our lives, that these stories actually shape our lives, constitute our lives, and that they 'embrace' our lives* . . . (White, 1995a: 13–14, emphasis added)

'Interpretation' is used in this passage, and elsewhere in post-modern therapies, in a 'hermeneutic' sense which may not be evident on a first reading. In this context 'interpretation' does *not* refer to an activity where one person, perhaps a professional, tells another person what their experience 'really' means; equally, it does not mean a person's gaining 'insight' into their experience by applying a social, psychological or philosophical theory to it. Such practices are not used in narrative therapy, although they are of course in some other therapies, and the distinction is important. 'Interpretation' here refers to the way in which, according to relatively recent ideas in sociology, social psychology and anthropology, people understand the world not 'as it is' (since this is impossible) but always through the lens of their *preconceptions*. These preconceptions are formed out of their past subjective experience and its resulting mind-set, and these are powerfully influenced by the norms and assumptions of the micro- and macro-societies in which people happen to live.

White's use of 'interpretative' expresses the assumption that *cultural* and *social* factors (interpersonal, local and global) are the principal influences on the stories through which we make sense of our experience. We are seldom aware of these factors, although we can choose to stand back, identify them and consider how they work on us. Social and cultural influences include the taken-for-granted assumptions and values of the groups we belong to and the wider society in which we live, which we have to a greater or lesser extent incorporated into our perceptual 'lens'. Language, with its capacity both to clarify and yet to distort and oversimplify, plays a mediating and influencing role in these interpretative processes, as it is through language, including our inner unspoken monologues, that we define and organize our thoughts and feelings. Language, because it is the product of our culture and embodies its assumptions, influences in its turn our interpretations of what happens to us by providing 'ready made thinking.'

> In describing to someone the situation in which I find myself placed, in giving them an account of what it is like to be me . . . I scan over my situation this way and that distinguishing in it certain crucial features . . . while my description works to give it structure, what allowably I can say is grounded in what might be described as my 'preunderstanding' of my situation . . . (Shotter, 1985: 182–3)

Postmodernism and 'narrative ways of knowing'

Postmodernism, with its principal starting-point in the 1970s, despite some historical antecedents, questions the modernist assumptions that have underpinned Western thinking about the observable and subjective worlds for about three hundred years: 'Modernity is held together . . . by stories of progressive rational scientific discovery of the nature of the exterior world and the interior of individual people's minds' (Parker et al., 1995: 14). From the Renaissance onwards, there was a belief among the educated minority that reason and logic could and would unravel the mysteries of the world, the universe and humankind. By the seventeenth century, with its discoveries in astronomy, the exploration and mapping of many of the previously unknown territories of the world, and the scientific discoveries of Newton and others, it appeared as if this process was fully under way. Later discoveries and theories confirmed this assumption: theories such as Darwin's on evolution and Einstein's on relativity met opposition at first, but in simplified versions took on the status of 'known facts'. Much the same happened to Freud's theories: today, interviewers almost automatically ask people about their childhood as an assumed means of throwing light on their subsequent personalities and actions. Certain core beliefs arising from the tradition of 'progress through knowledge' became so taken for granted that they were invisible as *beliefs* – they took on the status of 'assumed', or 'dominant', truths.

'Dominant truths'

Postmodern perspectives have not permeated Western culture beyond certain limited circles, and modernism is still a dominant way of thinking in contexts untouched by controversial new ideas. Perhaps most Western people's picture of the world still incorporates modernist 'dominant truths' such as the following:

- Cause and effect are universal and knowable.
- There is a real world of fixed and knowable phenomena independent of human observation.
- Facts about the nature of physical reality exist, but are hidden from everyday view.
- Humans can understand this reality as objective observers.
- Language refers to and reflects reality.
- In order to become known these realities need the attention of 'experts' with rare, highly developed skills.
- The history of the growth of knowledge consists of exceptional persons applying their skills, and through such people humanity appears to have a limitless potential for 'uncovering' the actual nature of physical and biological reality.
- These modern knowledges are often 'deep', rather mysterious and out of reach of the understanding of ordinary people.
- Such strides in scientific methods and so many discoveries have taken place that, given time, it will be possible to reach a state of near-complete knowledge, and to apply this to the betterment of human life.
- Just as methods have been developed for discovering the hidden truths of the physical and biological world, so truths have been discovered about the hidden world of human motivation and social dynamics.
- In the 'social sciences', distinct disciplines are based on real distinctions between various areas of human life. At the same time, a common 'human nature' can be identified across cultures.
- In the arts, new forms of expression often baffle the ordinary person by their apparent strangeness and obscurity, and it takes experts to understand them.

*Post*modernism incorporates a spirit of dissatisfaction, disbelief and challenge to such thinking. This reaction arose partly out of the failure of many of the venerated activities grouped as 'science' to fulfil their optimistic promises. Even before the term 'postmodern' began to be used, there was a widespread revulsion against the idea that science was intrinsically objective, truth-based and benevolent. Its claims to represent objective knowledge became suspect. Scientists began to lose their self-assigned status as objective investigators of a reality assumed to exist behind appearances, and began to be recognized as people whose work was influenced by social, political and personal issues, just like anyone else's. Scientists in 1930s Germany had published research which, they claimed, demonstrated scientifically that certain groupings of people were sub-human. Millions of these people were then murdered 'scientifically' in gas chambers. The Second World War ended in 1945 with the Allies dropping atomic bombs, and soon after this the development of hydrogen bombs faced mankind with the possibility of extinction. The gas chambers and the hydrogen bomb entered the consciousness of humanity and, for some, that consciousness changed.

In other areas the optimistic promises of 'the modern' also began to crumble – or, at least, to be severely modified. Medical advances have failed to cure cancer or to prevent the growth of AIDS, and today antibiotics are vulnerable to increasingly resistant bacteria. Pollution, global warming and the population explosion pose new threats to the world. Despite the application of 'scientific' economics, poverty, unemployment and recession continue. Stress and mental ill health are widespread. The early idealism of communism resulted in the horrors of Stalin's totalitarianism, but when Eastern Europe finally broke from that totalitarianism it was replaced by violent nationalism and criminal dominance. The meltdown of the nuclear reactor at Chernobyl threatened the world with radiation poisoning, and the existence of hundreds of unstable and deteriorating nuclear reactors in Eastern Europe has created the fear of more such disasters. Wars, civil strife and famine continue to kill millions.

This partial, selective, pessimistic and superficial 'story' of recent history suggests some of the background against which the assumptions of modernism were and are being called into question. The apparent march of technical and scientific progress has produced much of great value, but has also resulted in disasters and dangers. Not only are the procedures and results of the 'rational' and the 'scientific' suspect, but also the very idea that 'rationality' and 'scientific objectivity' are possible independent of cultural and social influences. The postmodern intellectual climate represents a move towards relativity, flexibility, reconsideration of the past and the identification and re-thinking of assumed norms. It assumes that all 'knowledge' is provisional, socially and politically influenced, and linked with social power. Science is redefined as just one particular way of knowing.

Physical and social 'sciences': a misleading analogy

In a postmodern perspective it is legitimate to state 'This has been my experience' or 'I believe this, and this is why I believe it.' Postmodernism does not crush belief or conviction or moral position, but it does take the stance – *Why?* In the answer may recur some of the beliefs of modernism, but re-examined, thought through, taken apart, checked out, re-assembled in new ways. *Deconstruction* is the term for this detailed, scrutinizing, nothing-taken-for-granted, fresh look at assumptions and beliefs. The touchstone for this deconstructive examination has increasingly been identified as our own, personal, immediate, lived experience. That is all we can truly *know*.

Western society has venerated 'science' and its methods, treating them as opening the doors to 'truth' rather than as just *one* way of thinking and acting about experience with all the inherent fallibility of any human pursuit. Through this veneration, people have assumed parallels between physical and biological 'knowledge' and areas of human life and behaviour. The same concepts and language have been used for both; 'social *sciences*', 'research findings', 'mechanisms', 'symptoms', 'dynamics', 'maladjustment', 'functioning', 'dysfunctional', 'pathology', 'trauma', 'healthy', 'breakdown' and so on. The use of such metaphors invites and confirms an assumption that human life functions in much the same way as the biological or mechanical worlds. In a postmodern perspective, human life, whether studied through the lenses of economics, psychology, sociology, anthropology or any other self-defining 'discipline', is too changing, variable, unique, multi-faceted, uncertain and complex for 'certain' definitions and conclusions reached through 'expert knowledges'. Human reality cannot be tied down to generalizations. No 'expert knowledge' can generalize with accuracy about human life – only hypotheses can be formed, and these are impossible to 'prove' because no test methods will include all the moment-by-moment changing kaleidoscope of factors needing to be taken into account. Postmodern thinkers do not deny that carefully worked out and controlled research can provide useful suggestions as to what *might* be, on the evidence available. But they do bring a sceptical caution to universal claims. 'Expert knowledge' is seen as partial, provisional, biased and often remote from the specific concrete knowledges of people living their unique lives from day to day. The Postmodern thinkers have recognized that such 'local knowledge' expressed in narrative – people's know-ledge derived from their immediate concrete experience – is as worthy of respect, and as genuine a form of knowledge, as 'expert' knowledge.

A complementary 'knowing'
Postmodern writers do not venerate experiental/local knowledge or sentimentalize it as folk wisdom. The 'modernist' mistake had been to elevate 'scientism' and 'recent thinking' above other forms of knowledge, and postmodernism attempts to avoid making the same error in reverse. '*Opposing* postmodern to modern involves a dichotomy which is contrary to a postmodern move to go beyond binary oppositions and to descriptions of differences and nuances . . . *the term is not "antimodern"* . . . The approach to history is rather that of re-use and collage, of taking up elements of tradition and recycling them in new contexts' (Kvale, 1992: 7, emphasis added). Michel Foucault, whom White acknowledges as an important influence in his thinking, made the point when asked his views on postmodernism:

> I think that there is a widespread and facile tendency, which one should combat, to designate that which has just occurred as the primary enemy, as if this were always the principal form of oppression from which one had to liberate oneself. Now this simple attitude entails a number of dangerous consequences: first, an inclination to seek out some cheap form of archaism or some imaginary past forms of happiness that people did not, in fact, have at all . . . a good study of peasant architecture in Europe, for example, would show the utter vanity of wanting to return to the little individual house with its thatched roof. (Foucault, 1984: 248)

Foucault's target is sentimentalism about the past which attempts to justify itself in the name of postmodernism, and he refers to architecture because postmodernism found its first expres-sion in new thinking about architecture. 'Modern' architecture for large buildings was characterized by the increasing use of pre-fabricated units held in place by a steel framework, and at least since the 1930s, avoiding rounded shapes. These gleaming glass and concrete structures often began to crack, weep dark stains and eventually be hated by people whose traditional housing com-munities had been destroyed to make way for this modern way of living, where stairways became dangerous, lifts did not work and there was no garden of one's own. Postmodern architects began to ask people what *they* wanted and, responding to their answers, to design a different kind of building. Stark geometrical styles gave way to softer-textured materials and echoes of traditional shapes and proportions: a supermarket in a small, early Victorian market town where I used to live had brick walls which would mellow in time, a high, steeply sloping roof of crinkly tiles and, overall, something of the appearance of the old barns characteristic of the area. It did not pretend to be a barn but it echoed a barn's proportions and materials. Postmodern architects sometimes included elements of fun, humour and vividness, even brashness, which people enjoyed – the architecture of Disneyland is a supreme example (Ghirardo, 1996: 45–62). Tower blocks gave way to smaller-scale buildings incorporating local traditional shapes, materials and textures, allowing both privacy and access to neighbours and relatives. This was a trend rather than universal practice; many tower blocks are still built, and many new houses are designed with, at best, lip-service to postmodern design – a wall textured in natural stone, or stained wood rather than metal for window frames.

Postmodern attitudes soon spread beyond architecture. In anthropology, there was a movement away from assumptions of 'expert knowledge' towards respect for what people themselves could contribute from their knowledge of their lives. Instead of anthropologists assuming they could understand, for example, the significance of a community's artefacts, they asked the members of the community what the artefacts signified to *them*. People's knowledges were valued and taken seriously, no longer subsumed to culturally biased theories which attempted to generalize common elements out of diverse examples from different cultures. Connections and universals had been presumed, and it had been the task of 'scientific method' to discover them. But the more they were sought, the more they vanished in the light of the differences and diversities of the uniquely actual: 'The only thing that links Freud, Piaget, Von Neumann and Chomsky (to say nothing of Jung and B.F. Skinner) is the conviction that the mechanics of human thinking is invariable across time, space, culture and circumstance, *and that they know what it is*' (Geertz, 1983: 150, emphasis added).

Postmodernism, then, does not represent an attitude of 'What we now know, think and do is better than the "knowledge" of the past.' Postmodernism is, rather, an attitude of 'We have no "expert knowledge" of what is true *and we cannot ever have this* – we must continually start our thinking anew, always in the knowledge that our conclusions will be partial.' Jean-François Lyotard says of art and writing what could equally be said of postmodern thinking in all areas of human life:

> A postmodern artist or writer is in the position of a philosopher: the text he writes, the work he produces are not in principle governed by preestablished rules, and they cannot be judged according to a determining judgement, by applying familiar categories to the text or to the work. Those rules and categories are what the work of art itself is looking for. (Lyotard, 1979: 81)

Lyotard points out that scientists affect to despise narrative modes of thinking and yet use them and are influenced by them:

> The scientist questions the validity of narrative statements and concludes that they are never subject to argumentation or proof. He classifies them as belonging to a different mentality: savage, primitive, underdeveloped, backward, alienated, composed of opinions, customs, authority, prejudice, ignorance, ideology . . . [this attitude] is the entire history of cultural imperialism from the dawn of Western civilization . . . what do scientists do when they appear on television or are interviewed in the newspapers after making a 'discovery?' . . . They play by the rules of the narrative game; its influence remains considerable not only on the users of the media, but also on the scientist's sentiments. This fact is neither trivial nor accessory: it concerns the relationship of scientific knowledge to 'popular' knowledge, or what is left of it. (Lyotard, 1979: 27–8)

'Popular' knowledge: narrative knowledge. As postmodern thinking spread, people were in quite a new way invited to give accounts of their lives, and of the meanings they derived from aspects of those lives, and in quite a new way were having those narratives taken seriously. It was recognized that both scientific *and* 'local' knowledge were needed for the most complete pictures of human reality to be hypothesized: concrete, experiential, 'narrative' knowledge providing the precise, unique, 'experienced' subject matter, with researchers applying 'scientific' methodology in order to hypothesize theories from this multiplicity.

> We must, in short, descend into detail, past the misleading tags, past the metaphysical types, past the empty similarities to grasp firmly the essential nature of not only the various cultures but the various sorts of individuals within each culture, if we wish to encounter humanity face to face. In this area, the road to the general, to the revelatory simplicities of science, lies through a concern with the particular, the circumstantial, the

concrete, but a concern organized and directed in terms of . . . theoretical analyses . . . That is to say, the road lies, like any genuine Quest, through *a terrifying complexity*. (Geertz, 1973: 53–5, emphasis added)

Such an enterprise was more difficult than the previously fashionable attempts at 'empathy' by means of which anthropologists had sought to make sense of other cultures: 'The trick is not to get yourself into some inner correspondence of spirit with your informants. Preferring, like the rest of us, to call their souls their own, they are not going to be too keen about such an effort anyhow. The trick is to figure out what the devil *they* think they are up to' (Geertz, 1983: 58, emphasis added).

In a passage quoted by White and Epson (1990: 77), the psychologist Jerome Bruner makes a distinction between two modes of knowing:

> There are two modes of cognitive functioning, two modes of thought, each providing distinctive ways of ordering experience, of constructing reality. The two (though complementary) are irreducible one to the other. Efforts to reduce one mode to the other or to ignore one at the expense of the other inevitably fail to capture the rich diversity of thought . . . A good story and a well-formed argument are different natural kinds. Both can be used for convincing another. Yet what they convince of is fundamentally different: arguments convince one of their truth, stories of their lifelikeness. (Bruner, 1986: 11)

In whatever form or context this 'popular' knowledge emerges, whether in a discussion between friends, a three-volume biography, a documentary television programme or a problem outlined in therapy, it takes the form of *stories* – selected experience 'told' in a sequence – and it is through these self-stories that we form our sense of identity:

> for the last several years, I have been looking at another kind of thought, one that is quite different in form from reasoning: the form of thought that goes into the constructing not of logical or inductive arguments but of stories or narratives . . . just as it is worthwhile examining in minute detail how physics or history go about their world making, might we not be well advised to explore in equal detail what we do when we construct ourselves autobiographically? (Bruner, 1987: 12)

Narrative and meaning

> Narrative is a scheme by means of which human beings give meaning to their experience of temporality and personal actions.

> Narrative meaning functions to give form to the understanding
> of a purpose to life and to join everyday actions and events into
> episodic units. It provides a framework for understanding the
> past events of one's life and for planning future actions. It is the
> primary scheme by means of which human existence is rendered
> meaningful. (Polkinghorne, 1988: 11)

A crucial difference between 'expert' knowledge and 'experiential'
knowledge is that the latter incorporates *meaning* – it has no claims
to be objective. It fully embodies the significance for the person of
her first-hand experience. The term used in narrative therapy for
this knowledge-from-immediate-concrete-experience is *local knowledge*, borrowed from the title of a book by Clifford Geertz (1983).
The term applies both to communities and to individuals. All the
'unheard' members of a community of old terraced houses, corner
shops and local pubs, moved to a high-rise tower block in (say)
1965, would have possessed shared but untapped 'local knowledge' that this would be a disaster for their way of life. Equally, a
single member of that community who was affected by a depres-
sive illness, perhaps a woman physically and emotionally bullied
by her husband and with nobody to turn to for assistance, would
have possessed unheard 'local knowledge' that her husband's
actions were the primary problem, not the depression which the
marital situation produced.

Dominant cultural narratives concerning issues of power

Issues of ethnicity, disenablement, sexuality, gender, age and all
other areas where therapists may have different cultural and personal bases from others are a particular focus of concern in narrative
therapy. Taking gender as an example, feminists have deconstructed
ways in which patriarchal attitudes have permeated social institutions and popular thought and have demonstrated how these
assumptions lead to real injustices. Because of this, in many circles,
traditional Western assumptions about the 'essential' – and subordinate – nature of women, formed and promoted by men, are no
longer taken seriously, although I believe that these ideas are still
alive, often demonstrated in ways we do not recognize by those of
us men who think of ourselves as 'liberal'. A determination to maintain alertness to gender issues is characteristic of White's practices
of therapy and teaching, not only in the specifically gender-related

problems many persons bring to therapy, but also in a constant self-monitoring focus around the interactional politics of therapy itself. Gender issues are not the only factors White keeps in mind; all issues of cultural power in the therapist's unacknowledged attitudes are seen as potentially able to inhibit or distort work with persons who identify with different cultures or subcultures. Racism and patriarchy are, I assume, cultural beliefs rejected by most therapies, and taken into account in the work of most therapists (I imagine that few counsellors consciously support male chauvinist, racist or similar beliefs), but the emphasis in narrative therapy on the need for continual vigilance against the more subtle manifestations of these elements is particularly consistent and emphatic. White values feminist analysis of the patriarchal assumptions embedded in 'established' psychologies, and he acknowledges that feminists have alerted him to subtle ways in which sexism and chauvinism may be demonstrated by men, including male therapists, through vocal tone, dominance of conversation, marginalization through vocabulary choice, unverified assumed capacity for empathy, and assumed cultural and gender 'norms' (White, 1997a). White insists that these manifestations are impossible to avoid altogether because male therapists live in the culture in which those attitudes are embedded – they cannot think of themselves as standing in a morally superior position (White, 1995a: 158–9) – but he emphasizes that, by critical self-monitoring and regular checking out with persons, therapists may go some way towards minimizing these factors, and that this is a moral obligation.

Post-structuralism

Questioning metaphors of 'structure', 'symptom' and 'depth'
We exist, outside the hypotheses of astronomers and particle physicists, in a solid, three-dimensional, physical world, where naturally occurring or manufactured objects such as lakes, trees, houses, computers, cars and people incorporate structures, interrelating parts which make up the whole. These objects have surfaces, and beneath these surfaces are hidden elements essential to function and stability. When the internal parts of a structure start to malfunction, alterations in the surfaces may give clues as to what is wrong, at least to the trained and experienced eye. A rash on the skin may indicate an internally located disease; an unpleasant

message on a monitor screen may indicate an electronic 'virus' in the computer; cracks in a house wall may indicate hidden subsidence. If there is malfunction *without* any surface evidence indicating what might be wrong, it is usually necessary to look *beneath* the surface – lift the car bonnet, open up the computer casing, perform exploratory surgery, strip away the soil round the house walls. An expert, someone with special knowledge and training, has to get to the source of the problem, assess it, work out a solution, and put that solution into operation. The perfectly appropriate language we use for these factors in the physical world is frequently transferred to descriptions of human experience and to concepts of mental and social functioning. Post-structuralism, a strand of postmodernism, invites us to re-examine this use of language and its results.

It is all too easy not to notice that the language of structures, when applied to human experience, is not literal – it is *metaphorical* – and it is easy not to realize that the images and concepts embodied in such language can be deceptive or misleading. Comparisons implicit in the metaphor can appear to indicate actualities about the human world that the metaphors refer to. 'Structural' and 'depth' metaphors used to describe human life have often become absorbed into the language of everyday life – and into the language of psychology and therapy. Some metaphors characterize the mind as a structure with interacting parts. Freud's explanations can be understood as metaphors from hydraulics, for example, with 'repression' and 'resistance' echoing concepts of steam pressure needing to be released (Freud, 1917: ch. 19). White and Epston's early writing used metaphors from mechanical control systems, such as self-correcting mechanisms, before the narrative metaphor became predominant in their language.

This way of using language is 'structuralist', and the thinking which underpins it has its origins in modern linguistic philosophy. Structuralist thinking asserts that both in psychological and social terms 'man [*sic*] is what he is made by structures beyond his conscious will or individual control' (Kearney, 1991: 256). Structuralists hold that there are permanent 'deep structures' – 'human nature', for example, the 'workings of the unconscious', systemic interactions between individuals or the quintessential content of all mythologies – which apply over a range of human life despite 'superficial' cultural differences. White now firmly rejects structuralist positions: narrative therapy is a *post-structuralist* therapy (1997a, 1997b: pt iv; and see Chapter 9 below). In examining and questioning the 'surface as opposed to depth' metaphors of structuralism, and the language of mechanical interactions, White has proposed alternative metaphors. These can help us to break away from the limitations of language embodying concepts of 'difficult to uproot' and 'needing experts to understand and put right'. He suggests that, in the language of therapy, the continuum between 'surface and depth' might be replaced by a continuum between 'thin and thick' or 'thin and rich'.

Thin and thick (rich) descriptions of life

The thin/thick or thin/rich metaphor for the description of experience, originated by Gilbert Ryle, is explored by Clifford Geertz in *The Interpretation of Cultures* (1973: 6–10). Ryle pointed out that the same action can have different meanings according to the intentions and circumstances of the actor, and that external observers may misinterpret the action because of their own preconceptions. Geertz distinguishes between 'thin' descriptions, defined as interpretations of events which embody an observer's unexamined and socially influenced preconceptions, and 'thick' (or 'rich') descriptions of those events, which embody the meaning of those events to the persons actually involved in them. Geertz illustrates this by describing a complicated series of sheep-stealing incidents between Moroccan and Jewish tribesmen, completely misunderstood by a French colonial official who interpreted their warfare in terms of his own cultural assumptions, unaware of the specific meaning of these incidents for the tribes.

White's distinction is between 'thin' descriptions of life, which derive from a person's unexamined socially and culturally influenced beliefs, and 'rich' or 'thick' descriptions, which more nearly correspond to the actuality and complexity of life as experienced by that person. A 'thin' description may arise from the person's having been subject to 'expert' diagnoses and commentaries, where the power status of the 'expert' can obscure his own immediate, or local, knowledge. Thin descriptions can originate from the influence of many kinds of power figures and power institutions. A domineering man may make a woman doubt her worth, a teacher's sarcasm or slashing red-ink commentaries on a child's written work may affect his confidence, an adult who was treated without tenderness in her family of origin may still believe she is unlovable, a man abused in childhood who reads an 'authoritative' article saying that abused children grow up to be abusers may believe he is likely to abuse his own children. These examples are instances of 'thin' descriptions that I have come across in my work. Appropriate practices in narrative therapy can assist persons to re-examine their lives and to focus on their own local, experiential knowledges, and this can have a counter-balancing effect, producing 'richer' or 'thicker' descriptions of their lives and relationships, which assist them to escape from the effects of power-based influences. Their self-stories become more 'experience-near', to use another term from Geertz (who borrowed it from Heinz Kohut). The woman may recognize that her worth does not depend on her husband's opinion of her, the boy may regain confidence, the adult may recognize that she has been loved, and the abused man may be able to dismiss the article for perpetuating a crude myth. The 'thin' metaphor of truths accessible only to the 'expert' or to the power figures in the person's life have been replaced by the convincing 'rich' or 'thick' actuality of the person's lived experience.

Social constructionism

Interpersonal and cultural influences on persons' dominant self-stories

The branch of social psychology called social constructionism has influenced White and Epston's thinking. Social constructionism emphasizes the interaction between persons, and the *social and cultural* influences and norms which permeate and activate those interactions, rather than theoretical individual dynamics conceived as within the person. The focus of many traditional approaches to therapy has been on individual rather than social psychology, and the individual or couple as a discrete unit has been put at the centre of therapy. According to these traditional perspectives, individuals or couples may be affected, influenced, even 'conditioned' by inter-actions with others, or by the impact of unfortunate experiences, but then they 'contain' and perpetuate the 'damage' or 'pathology' as an inner essence or dynamic. It is this 'damage' which has been perceived as needing to be put right by the expert attention of therapists. The range of 'treatments' in the (modernist) counselling culture includes such diverse practices as 'rooting out' assumed unconscious influences in early life; and supplying a context for the facilitation of the person's assumed innate capacity to overcome his problems, such as regular meetings where the person is listened to with acceptance and respect. In these individualistic, pathologizing, counsellor-as-expert ways of seeing therapy, the 'social location' of the person and the issues she brings to counselling are missing. Social constructionist psychologists, in contrast, focus not on theories of assumed 'inner' damage or pathology, but on the social and cultural processes through which we gain our views of the world, and the nature of those views, which in turn influence our actions. Social constructionists propose that this range of unexamined and invisible socio-cultural norms take on 'truth status' for individuals, subgroups and communities. They propose that we continually 'construct' our view of reality via these norms, through the influences of our culture and of other people. As Jerome Bruner puts it, implicitly also referring to individual self-stories, . . . 'the very shape of our lives – the rough and perpetually changing draft of our autobiography that we carry in our minds – is understandable to ourselves and others only by virtue of . . . cultural systems of interpretation' (1990: 33). The French colonial official in Geertz's account, baffled by the apparently illogical feuding of two tribes over sheep ownership, was interpreting his observations in his own cultural terms – and the tribespeople were interpreting the situation in theirs. In England recently, a young man followed, terrorized and eventually brought about the deaths of a young couple in a small car who failed to give way and let him overtake. Social constructionist psychologists would consider this behaviour not in terms of 'inner dynamics', but in terms of his choosing to act, or 'perform', a view of the world derived from his social subgroup, where certain road behaviours are interpreted as affronts and violent and dangerous responses are seen as valid and appropriately 'masculine'.

The perspectives of social constructionism are postmodern in that, although paradoxically the whole approach is itself a theory, it questions the possibility of actually 'knowing' through psychological theory, especially when applied to individuals as distinct entities. It is postmodern in its emphasis on the multiple, changing, complex, interactive nature of human life. In a forthright and witty essay, Peter Ossario asserts:

> Psychological theories portray persons in ways which are not merely limited, but highly distortive as well . . . is there any observation whatever that would tell us that in fact behaviour is *not* a way of discharging instinctive energy, or that in fact behaviour is *not* the inevitable outcome of a learning history and present circumstances or that in fact a person is *not* a being-in-the-world? Of course there is not. (Ossario, 1985: ch. 2)

Ossario suggests that traditional psychological theories are inadequate to provide a rationale for 'clinical practice', and that the assumption of 'clinical judgement' as genuinely inferential from evidence is 'rank superstition' and 'nonsense'. He suggests that two thousand years of history have shown 'truth' to be 'an intractable myth', and that what is needed is a psychology with the perspective that 'truth is always relative'. The enterprise of this psychology would be to formulate a systematic range of concepts deriving from people's direct experience. Ossario believes that, through social constructionism, such a 'fresh start' has been made.

The philosopher Alisdair Macintyre emphasizes the intertwined nature of our construction of our own identity: 'The narrative of any one life is part of an interlocking set of narratives' (1981: 218). In less trenchant mode than Ossario, John Shotter (1985: 175–7) also suggests that narrative can be the basis of a social constructionist psychology:

> Everyone's social life is . . . a whole mosaic of interlocking activities with the function of mutually supporting and reciprocally defining one another, each known in terms of the part it plays in relation to the rest . . . what we need is an account of personhood and selfhood in the ordinary sense of the term 'account' as simply a narration of a circumstance or state of affairs . . . that allows us to see all the different aspects of a person as if arrayed within a landscape, all in relation to one another, from all of the standpoints within it . . . we have concentrated far too much attention on the isolated individual studied from the point of view of an uninvolved observer. . . .

An alternative view of 'the self'
Social constructionist psychologists have questioned the concept of a single definable core 'self', arguing that this concept is itself merely a Western 'humanist' social construct. They propose that identity is socially constructed – 'negotiated' – from moment to moment, varying according to circumstance, its apparent continuity an illusion based on the generally consistent and repeated social circumstances within which most people operate (Gergen and Davis, 1985; Gergen, 1992; Anderson, 1997). These ideas are disturbing. They appear to contradict our actual experience, rather in the way in which it is disorienting to realize that colours are not inherent in objects but are formed subjectively by physical reactions in our optical apparatus. But there is room for a more 'middle-road' viewpoint, where the concept of moment-by-moment social re-creation of identity exists together with a recognition of subjective continuity:

> To have a sense of self is to have a sense of one's location, as a person, in each of several arrays of other beings, relevant to personhood. It is to

have a sense of one's point of view, at any moment a location in space from which one perceives and acts upon the world, including that part which lies within one's own skin. But the phrase 'a sense of self' is also used for the sense one has of oneself as possessing a unique set of attributes which, though they change, nevertheless remain as a whole distinctive of just the one person. These attributes include one's beliefs about one's attributes. 'The self', in this sense, is not an entity . . . It is the collected attributes of a person. The word 'self' has also been used for the impression of his or her personal characteristics that one person makes on another . . . We seem to have three aspects of personhood in focus at the same time. Though none of these are really entities, that is thing-like in the manner of existence and behaviour, we have forged a way of speaking about them using nouns, the very grammatical form that entity talk takes, in our several uses of the expression 'the self'. (Harré, 1998: 4–5)

Social constructionism is a postmodern psychology and postmodernism can create feelings of insecurity by its refusal to accept the psychological world at face value. However, there are compensations: postmodern psychology can be a stimulus and a breath of fresh air. It forces us to re-examine the bases by which we live, and to link theory with real life.

Postmodern consciousness does not . . . invite skepticism regarding the potentials for psychological enquiry. Rather, by demystifying the great narrative of modernism, it attempts to bring psychologists and society more closely together. Not only is technology placed more directly and openly in the service of values; more important, the psychologist is encouraged to join in forms of valuational advocacy, and to develop new intelligibilities that present new options to the culture . . . the possibility for escaping the pretences of the past, and more fully integrating academic and cultural pursuits, is one to which I, among others, feel greatly drawn. (Gergen, 1992: 28)

Power and knowledge

Michel Foucault's writings from the 1970s onwards 'deconstruct' (re-examine in detail) the history of the relationship between ideas, political power and social institutions in the West. Foucault's explorations of the development of beliefs, practices and institutions around themes such as mental health and madness, discipline and punishment, and sexuality, took place within a postmodern framework; his concern was always to define what these institutions and concepts meant to the persons at the historical time he discusses, not to interpret them according to some absolute, modern perspective. 'For Foucault, there is no external position of certainty, no universal understanding that is beyond history and society. His strategy is to proceed as far as possible in his analyses without recourse to universals. His main tactic is to historicise such supposedly universal categories as human nature each time he encounters them' (Rabinow, in Foucault, 1984: 4).

Foucault proposed that in Western society there has been a steady development of people's capacity to maintain positions of power through their actual or assumed expert knowledge, and that this power is perpetuated in interrelated social institutions such as medicine, psychiatry, class divisions, sexual morality and the law. This social power has not primarily been established by force and threat, though that has of course occurred, but by jealously guarding the specialist knowledges which established power in the first place, and then by subtly persuading people to 'interiorize' their subordinate positions and maintain these in their attitudes and actions as a matter of course – to 'become' persons who continually create their own subordinate identities. In the early nineteenth century, new prisons were built where inmates could be seen by gaolers but where they could not be sure that they were being observed, and Foucault's discussion of one of the most famous of these, the Panopticon, assigns significance to it as representing a particularly modern *attitude*: 'The prison, the place where the penalty is carried out, is also the place of observation of punished individuals. This takes two forms: surveillance, of course, but also knowledge of each inmate, his behaviour, his deeper states of mind, his gradual improvement; the prisons must be conceived as places for the formation of clinical knowledge about the convicts' (Foucault, 1984: 216).

The prison authorities' knowledge is psychological knowledge, *clinical* knowledge, and is a factor in their power over the prisoner, just as important as the bars and the cells. This knowledge is gained by 'surveillance' – the prisoner is watched, and knows he is or might be watched, and since his behaviour is not private, it is subject to (or at least influenced by) the wishes of the watchers. To survive in the institution he has to perform the role of a good prisoner, and in performing this role he is likely to interiorize the role, *become* the subordinate person demanded by the institution. 'Big Brother' in Orwell's futuristic novel *1984* projects a benevolent image to hide the power of the state, and Foucault's analyses of power/knowledge/control situations examine many institutions which are, or believe themselves to be, benevolent. He quotes an early nineteenth-century doctor who, after suggestions for observation of symptoms and choice of treatment, stresses taking account of the patient's feelings ('affections'). The doctor uses the language of benevolence but actually urges the maintenance of power:

> 'make yourself master of your patients and their affections; assuage their pains; calm their anxieties; anticipate their needs; bear with their whims; make the most of their characters and command their will, not as a cruel tyrant reigns over his slaves, but as a kind father who watches over the destiny of his children' . . . So many powers, from the slow illumination of obscurities . . . to the majestic confiscation of paternal authority, are just so many forms in which the sovereignty of the gaze gradually establishes itself – the eye that knows and decides, the eye that governs. (Foucault, 1963: 88)

Foucault's analyses of the ways in which people in positions of power establish and maintain that power through 'techniques of subordination' involving 'expert knowledge', apparent benevolence, surveillance and the subtle promotion of interiorized subordination, are echoed in Erving Goffman's (1961) study of the institutional power of mental hospitals.

Foucault's influence on White and Epston's work relates to the 'political' dimension of narrative therapy, their proposal of therapy as a means of assisting persons to counteract the effects of overt or invisible power relations on their lives. Many of the problems brought to therapy are seen as socially constructed issues arising from 'practices of power' which lead persons to define their identities and their lives in circumscribed ways, and these 'political' dimensions are directly addressed in narrative work. Here are some examples from my own practice where I was aware of addressing a powerful 'power/political' dimension:

- A woman's husband occasionally attacked her physically, perhaps once a year, so she was permanently terrorized by the fear that an attack might come at any time.
- A woman's partner accompanied her everywhere, chose her clothes and hairstyle, selected what books she should read and what television programmes she should watch, and visited her unannounced at her sports club to make sure she was not talking too intimately with the male members, all in the name of 'caring'.
- A teacher was brought to the point of breakdown by the uncontrolled increase in administrative paperwork arising from

government policies of pupil assessment and recording, which his headteacher was always pressuring him to complete.

- A grieving widow felt guilty at not being able to 'let him go' in the way demanded by her friends.
- Parents were at their wits' end because of the emotional and physical domination of the household by their teenagers.
- A woman caring for her very elderly mother found it hard to have any life of her own and her brothers, living nearby, refused to take part in their mother's care on the grounds that is was 'a woman's responsibility'.
- A man whose wife was seriously ill had been told by her consultant that he had an 'open door' policy, but always found his attempts to communicate with the consultant barred by administrative staff. When he finally managed to corner the consultant in the corridor of the hospital he was threatened with the police.
- A woman whose husband insisted that he must continue to maintain a sexual relationship with another woman because he 'loved them both in different ways' was racked with guilt because she found it hard to accept this arrangement.

I see many instances of persons 'controlled' by their partners; bullied in their employment; afraid to speak out against malpractice because of fear of losing their jobs; humiliated by arrogant and domineering attitudes of some people in the 'helping' professions. *Self*-surveillance is also common, often in terms of an inability to live up to the norms and expectations of partners, family, subgroups or wider society. Quite frequently, persons suffer from a belief that they can never achieve the standards expected by their parents, and this can be particularly powerful when the parents are no longer alive.

Summary

'Narrative' in this therapy refers both to the accounts or stories that persons tell themselves and others about their lives, and to persons' and communities' first-hand, experiential knowledges, which postmodern thinkers validate as of equal legitimacy to 'scientific' ways of knowing. This experiential or 'local' knowledge comes about, and is expressed and reinforced, through first-hand interaction with others. Postmodern perspectives emphasize the socially influenced nature of all knowledge, and question the claims of many 'dominant truths' widespread in Western society. Many of these dominant truths arising from 'expert knowledges' are seen as the self-justifying assumptions of persons in positions of power, disguised as benevolence and/or scientific truth. The originators of narrative therapy locate it within post-structuralist thought which challenges the description of human life in terms of physical mechanism or biological functioning. Metaphors of 'depth', 'structure' and 'symptom' for aspects of human life are considered less helpful than metaphors which contrast 'thin' descriptions of life against 'rich' (or 'thick') descriptions, where the distinction refers to unexamined culturally and politically influenced beliefs and assumptions, on the one hand, and, on the other, beliefs and assumptions derived from a full apprehension of first-hand, lived experience. The originators of narrative therapy identify it with the social constructionist proposal that the stories we continually tell each other and ourselves, which represent our view of ourselves in the world and our history of relation to events and people, are the most powerful influence on the ways in which we live our lives. The actuality of these stories is often undermined in the memory by the unrecognized power of unexamined social norms and assumptions, and by 'expert knowledges' imputed to others, through which concrete experience is filtered and interpreted. *It is not just that memory distorts, but that it distorts in ways which are socially and culturally influenced.* Because of this, self-stories can often be 'thin'; so a re-examination of the bases of these stories can lead to richer, more 'experience-near' narratives, incorporating previously sidelined 'local knowledge'. Awareness of these recovered knowledges, told through more experience-near narratives, can give persons an enlarged sense of the possibilities of life, facilitate their overcoming problems, allow them to redefine their identities in more positive terms, and promote their movement towards effecting the changes they discover they wish to make.

3 Assisting the Person to Describe the Problem

This chapter describes some of the ways in which I encourage persons to tell, extend and enrich their self-stories. Where White and Epston are not quoted the descriptions represent my own views and practices.

Self-stories

We tell improvised 'stories' of our lives in many social situations, describing our experience. We populate our stories with ourselves and others, creating the stories from our memories and interpretations of events in the very process of recounting them. We use gestures; we imitate others' speech; we use dramatic pauses and inflections, and body movements. When alone we may deliver an *interior* story-telling monologue, ungrammatically and with abbreviated syntax, weaving the event into the episodic, fragmented, yet colourful soap-opera of our own life.

Jerome Bruner quotes Dewey's conclusion that children have an innate capacity for grasping the structures of language, and Chomsky's theory that we use language not merely to communicate, but to 'make sense of the world' (Bruner, 1990: 88, 69). Bruner also suggests that studies of childhood language development show that children possess 'a "protolinguistic" readiness for *narrative* organisation and discourse' (1990: 80, emphasis added). More recent research by Gary Marcus appears to confirm this hypothesis (Radford, 1999). Creating narratives through our need to get a grip on experience, and then getting a grip on experience by using narratives, starts young. Bruner describes a delightful experiment (the subject of a book by Nelson, 1989) where a little girl was sound-recorded, talking to herself in her cot over a period of 18 months with only her toys as audience, and the results analysed. As she developed language skills her spontaneous utterances became more and more organized into *narrative* forms. They became accounts which incorporated events and reactions to events *in sequence*, which allowed the development and expression of cause-and-effect concepts, awareness of and hypotheses about motivations, awareness of events departing from their normal form, and attempts to resolve uncertainties by 'talking them through' (Bruner, 1990: 87–94).

> Emily by her third year masters the forms for putting sequence, canonicality, and perspective at the service of *her push to narrativize her experience*. The genre serves to organize her experience of human interactions in a life-like, story-like way. Her narrative environment is, in its own way, as distinctive as the environments of the Black ghetto children in Baltimore. In her case, we learn from her pre-soliloquy exchanges with her parents, there is enormous stress on 'getting things right,' on being able to give 'reasons,' and on understanding the options open to her. Her parents, after all, are academics. (Bruner, 1990: 93–4, emphasis added)

Anthropologists have described how, in a wide variety of cultures, telling stories both informally and ceremonially has central importance (for example, Turner and Bruner, 1986). It seems that both everyday experience and academic studies confirm the importance and ubiquity of peoples' narrativizing – and, not unexpectedly perhaps, that the forms and content of such story-telling are influenced by the social context in which the persons live, with the language, concepts and assumptions of their culture permeating their stories.

As persons move through life their experience, and the stories they tell themselves and others about their experience, become multiple and complex – or rather, *the complexity of experience produces multiple stories* in the 'rough and perpetually changing draft of our autobiography', to borrow Jerome Bruner's marvellous phrasing (1990: 33). Even little Emily, soliloquizing in her cot over 18 months while the turning tape-recorder reels silently accompanied her, had the events of over 500 days as her subject matter;

> For all her tender years, she was in the midst of life. A brother, Stephen, was born and displaced her not only from her solo role in the family but from her very room and crib . . . And shortly after the arrival of her brother, she was introduced to the boisterous life of nursery school. With both parents working, there were baby-sitters as well – all against the background of an ill-planned city where even the carpool pickups could become tense and erratic . . . her soliloquies were rich. (Bruner, 1990: 87–8)

By the time we reach later life, the multiplicity, complexity, variety and sheer quantity of our experience are huge. And so is the number of self-created stories which have accompanied us in our thoughts and interactions and become woven into the remembered texture of our lives. But we cannot actually hold firm to images of more than a tiny fraction of our experiences since the content of stories we tell ourselves about our lives, even the experiences of an hour ago, are immediately subject to selective memory. Even important memories – the sparkling or dulled moments and events punctuating our overall self-story which serve as its markers and definers – are subject to distortion. An episode in Kingsley Amis's novel *The Old Devils* (1986) illustrates this movingly and with comic irony. For 40 years Malcolm has treasured the memory of a day he spent with Rhiannon whom he loved. After a long separation they meet again and he takes her back to the scene. He recalls the day emotionally, detail by detail – the appearance of the scene after a storm, the weather, the car he borrowed, an incident at a garage – with Rhiannon uneasily agreeing with his description. Then Malcolm falters:

> When she looked at Malcolm again he was still staring, but at her now.
> 'Doug Johnson was away in France the whole of that summer,' he said, 'doing his teaching prac. He certainly wasn't around to lend his car to me or anyone else. So that must have been a different day altogether.'
> 'M'm' she forced herself to go on looking at him.
> 'We must have taken the bus down. You couldn't have remembered it like that, the way you said you did.'
> 'No.'
> 'You don't remember any of it, do you? Not having lunch or walking up to St Mary's or what I said or anything.'
> It was not to be got out of the way or away from. Coming on top of the little tensions of the day the unashamed intensity of his disappointment was too much for her. She hid her face, turned around and started to cry.
> He forgot his own feelings at once . . . 'I didn't remember it very well myself, did I, confusing those two times? Anyway you remember coming down here? To Pwll Glan?'
> 'M'm.'
> 'And perhaps me bringing you? You know, sort of vaguely?'
> 'M'm' perhaps she did.
> 'Even this bit? Just . . .'
> Suddenly it went impossible to say yes, even to this bit. 'No . . .' She shook her head wretchedly. 'It's gone. Sorry.' (Amis, 1986: 166–8)

For 40 years Malcolm has been telling himself the story of that day, but at some point his memory has become subtly distorted. In narrating the story of that day to another person, Rhiannon, with the images of past events recalled and ordered into sequence, he re-experiences it more concretely and his memory appears to clear – to his dismay and disappointment. What's more, his previously comforting narrative had included the idea that Rhiannon, many miles away and living another life, would very occasionally recall that day with pleasure. Malcolm's own self-narrative had incorporated assumptions about *her* self-narrative. Suddenly he has lost treasured images and associations which have been a comforting counterpoint to his impoverished emotional existence described in other parts of the novel. He desperately tries to salvage what he can – but there is nothing.

I have occasionally, in workshops for counsellors, invited people to write their autobiographies in ten minutes. They attempt this, but of course they need more time. How much longer? Half an hour? A day? Ten years? Even if exact recall were possible, a full account would take longer to complete than the life so far – and then it would be incomplete, having omitted the time after starting to write the account! We can only, even in telling the most detailed stories of our lives or parts of our lives, create partial representations, 'maps' of our experiences, not fully accurate all-inclusive representations. Partial maps are all we have. Which is not to say that some of these maps, or parts of them, may not be accurate – nevertheless they do not represent the entirety of the experience.

When persons come for therapy they have a story to tell, a map to show. They are often upset. Confused, worried and feeling defeated, their story is 'problem-saturated' (White, 1989: 39) and real to them, representing accurately what they remember and what they are going through. The problem-saturated story deserves both respect and belief. But there are other stories.

> people come with *stories*. They have stories to tell you, because they want to make up a *new story* with you. Somehow they can't. They are the authors of their stories and they need a co-author . . . People organise their meaning, their existence in conversation. They cope with each other by inventing a story about themselves. Every human being is basically a story teller. All human beings have a story to say. If they have no story they don't exist as humans. Their story is what makes them human, but it is also their prison . . . they become extremely loyal to their terrible stories and that's where therapy comes in. Slowly you engage in co-authoring a new story. They construct a new reality. (Ceccin, 1988, emphasis in original)

Ceccin does not describe himself as a narrative therapist in the sense defined in this book; he is a pioneer of systemic therapy. But as this quotation shows, and as McLeod (1997) argues, persons' narratives are central to more therapies than give themselves that name. It is interesting to compare Ceccin's words with this extract from White and Epston (1990: 14–15) written at about the same time:

> we make the assumption that persons experience problems, for which they frequently seek therapy, when the narratives in which they are 'storying' their experience, and/or in which they are having their ex- perience 'storied' by others, do not sufficiently represent their lived experience, and that, in these circumstances, there will be significant aspects of their experience that contradict these dominant narratives . . . we could also assume that, when persons seek therapy, an acceptable outcome would be the identification or generation of alternative stories that enable them to perform new meanings, bringing with them desired possibilities – new meanings that persons will experience as more helpful, satisfying and open-ended.

In encouraging persons to tell stories of what brings them to therapy, narrative therapists attempt from the start to be alert to aspects of the story which are not quite consonant with the general tenor of the person's account and which may prove to be gateways to alternative stories at a later stage of therapy. But I am a little ahead of this chapter's topic – I return to the theme in Chapter 4.

Familiar ground

As a narrative therapist, how do I respond to the person who has just sat down – perhaps meeting a counsellor for the first time ever – expecting to talk with an unknown man in an unfamiliar room about issues that are painful, frustrating, probably very personal and possibly embarrassing, and which up to now he may not have shared fully with anyone else? Since narrative therapy has been developed by family therapists, accounts of their work often refer to therapy settings with aspects unfamiliar to many counsellors, such as one-way screens, video cameras or sound recorders, and more than one therapist taking part. I do not think these elements are essential for narrative therapy, although adaptations of them can be very helpful, but when I do wish to use such elements their purpose is explained to the person before the session gets under way. His agreement to their use is sought and, if he does agree, I check from time to time that he is comfortable with them, aban- doning them if he is not.

I invite the person to talk about what brings him to therapy. If the person is hesitant I wait, suggest that he takes his time and attempt, by body stance and eye contact, to convey a relaxed yet alert readiness to listen. This will be familiar ground to readers: initial narrative therapy sessions open very much like those of most other therapies. Most persons settle to telling their story and soon start to feel a little better by doing so. The strangeness of the context quite swiftly becomes less influential than the *familiarity of the process of story-telling.* In outlining his problem or problems to the counsellor, the person may, of course, need to cope with a more powerful emotional impact than when telling less central and upsetting stories, but he is nevertheless being invited to do something he has done countless times. He is used to scanning his experience, selecting significant aspects, then conveying them verbally according to their approximate time sequence.

Encouraging a more complete account

Once the person has come to a natural pause and indicates that his initial account of his problem or problems is complete, I encourage him to stay with the problem description and to extend it. I use detailed, low-key questions to demonstrate an interest in and concern for the whole range of the problem's effects: the 'influence of the problem in . . . lives and relationships . . . the problem's sphere of influence in the behavioural, emotional, physical, interactional, and attitudinal domains . . . [to] identify the effect of the problem across various interfaces – between the problem and various persons, and between the problem and various relationships' (White, 1989: 8). I *ask questions* like the following: not as a series or list, not as an interrogation, but aiming for a natural and conversational mode in response to the person's responses:

- Is anxiety about your exam results having any effect on your sleep or your ability to relax?
- Are you experiencing any health problems which might be related to anxiety's attempts to invade your life?
- What do you find yourself doing /saying/thinking which seems to be a result of anxiety?
- Is anxiety affecting how you feel about anything else in your life, which you haven't mentioned? Would you like to say more about that?
- You say your lack of confidence goes beyond the exam anxiety

you're suffering from. I'd be interested to hear more details, if that's OK with you.

- So depression sometimes makes an appearance too. Does this affect how you get on with people or how they seem to treat you? Would you like to tell me a bit more about that?
- Has worry attacked your work routines at all?

Further questions are asked from the person's responses: for example, if he is sleeping badly I may ask more detailed exploratory questions on the pattern and frequency of sleeplessness, whereas if there is no sleep issue I will move to another area. I elicit in detail topics of particular significance to the person if he feels comfortable with this; reluctance is noted but questions are not pursued. The aim is not for the person to be, or to feel, 'diagnosed' or 'assessed', but for him to take part in a conversation with someone who is interested, who really wants to know what life is like for him at this difficult time.

No initial questioning can elicit *all* aspects of the person's experience of the problem. But drawing out a more complete description clears the air; the person finds that his story is taken seriously and not dismissed or minimized. At the same time, drawing out the effects of the problem in such detail helps the person to begin to recognize that there are *limits* to the problem's influence. He finds that there are aspects of his life, now noticed and identified, which the problem has *not* affected, or has only affected in part – so the issues may be seen as less crushing than at the initial, unprompted telling. These discoveries of the problem's limits arise from the person's *own* perceptions as he is engaged in a description, then a more detailed description, of the problem and its effects on his life. They are not suggested by me as 'reassurance' or 'optimism' or 'looking on the bright side' – they emerge in conversation, as discoveries.

Richard, a 27-year-old accountant, came to counselling because of worry about outbreaks of extreme anger with his wife Rose. Richard had smashed objects in the house, but had not hit Rose, although he feared that sooner or later he might. His reactions frightened him, and he did not understand them. They were getting more frequent and he thought there must be 'something wrong with him'. However, in answering my detailed questions he confirmed that he did not experience anger outbursts at work despite being 'put on' and undervalued – he had decided to look for another job which, with his qualifications, would not be too difficult to get. This

meant that work was less of a worry. His physical health had not deterio-
rated. When asked whether the problem affected or was affected by relation-
ships in the wider family, he began to talk of his mother's attitude to Rose,
Rose's attitude to his mother, and his sense of being caught between them.
He thought his wife exaggerated his mother's hostility towards her, but
Rose told him he turned a blind eye to subtle but perfectly visible hostile
behaviour towards her by his mother. He thought that if Rose would only
make more effort with his mother then things would improve. However,
sometimes he realized he was feeling angry with his mother too, which
immediately let guilt in. This made him all the more angry with Rose
because she was, in his opinion, perpetuating the situation. He had lost all
ability to assess appropriate filial loyalty and obligation compared with
appropriate marital loyalty and obligation. He just wanted everyone to get
on and be happy together – but all his attempts to encourage the two
women to meet and relate made the situation worse. By the end of the
session his conception of the problem was moving from 'something wrong
with me' to 'something difficult in my situation – and not only in mine'.
His recognition that the problem was inherent to a context, a process,
rather than 'internal' to him and his wife, led to his agreeing to my sug-
gestion that he might invite Rose to our next session.

My detailed questioning certainly revealed that problems were
affecting many aspects of Richard's life, but also that there were
limits to the problems' influence. In the short time since deciding
to come to counselling he had begun to feel better about work
issues. His responses about the effects of the problem on relationships led to further questions from me, especially in the area of the
relationship 'triangle', leading to further responses, leading to
further questions encouraging Richard to tell an even more detailed
story. I said that the story seemed to suggest that he felt he must
choose between his wife and his mother. My implicit further
question was: is this really how it is? Are there other possibilities?
This question did not call for a swift answer – it was a seed sown
to grow in its own time.

Inviting the person to 'name the problem'

Persons often feel disempowered by problems: they have tried to
overcome them but feel they have failed. Failure to sort out problems
can lead to a sense of 'being' a failure, and the decision to see a
counsellor can be seen as confirming that they have failed, that they

have been forced to choose a last resort. Sometimes persons have read some psychology, or self-help books, but this has often had little positive effect – they may have decided what they 'ought' to do, but found they couldn't do it, and this makes them feel even worse.

One aim of narrative therapy, from the earliest possible moment, is to assist the person to regain her sense of control over her life, or at least to assist her to begin to chip away at her sense that she has no possibility of control. This is one of the reasons for systematically and persistently inviting her to 'name' the problem. To name is to regain a little control; naming is taking the initiative, it is imposing a chosen identification on something, or someone, threatening. Children are particularly aware of the 'magic' empowerment of naming (Opie and Opie, 1967) and are often reluctant to reveal their own name to unknown children. Few schoolteachers escape 'naming': from my own childhood I remember many, particularly 'Dracula', the beak-nosed headmaster who swept imposingly through the school, hands behind back, gown streaming. Examples of deflating naming are found in most institutions where people have positions of power over others.

In the case of persons who come to therapy, problems have gained power over them, and so 'naming the problem' can be morale boosting. But it is more than a symbolic step towards regaining some sense of control, helpful though this can be. It is a means of clarifying problems and normalizing them – both of which contribute to a person's sense that he can position himself differently in relation to the problem. Persons who are experiencing a bewildering and distressing combination of intense pessimism, self-doubt, irritability, forgetfulness, apathy, sorrow and early waking can gain much lightening of anxiety, and a sense of some empowerment, by referring to their problem as 'depression'. If they also read articles or books which help to normalize depression as a common reaction to significant loss or continual frustration or, if these factors do not apply, as a physiological imbalance which may be responsive to medication, persons' reactions are often of relief and re-energizing, which in itself increases their capacity to see problems in a different way. Persons sometimes name their problem unprompted – 'depression' as 'the black cloud', anger as 'the monster' and so on – which gives them a sense of being separated from the problem, able to consider it objectively and make plans for it. One person gained much satisfaction from naming panic attacks by a term I can't possibly quote in a publication such as this!

Questions I may ask at this point may be something like:

- I wonder what we can call this problem?
- Do you have a particular name for what you're going through at the moment?
- There are lots of things happening to you – shall we try to pin them down? What are they, what name shall we put to them?
- I've been calling what they did to you 'constructive dismissal'. Does that seem the right term to use?
- Judging by what you say, you've been subject to emotional abuse. How would it feel if that's what we called it from now on? Or perhaps there's a better name?

For a couple, naming the problem can diminish the tendency for each to blame the other – 'blaming language' becomes 'process language'. They may have started with accusatory definitions such as 'John's bad temper' and 'Felicity's nagging' but may agree on a definition of their problem as 'stress in the relationship'. Definitions like 'habits of hiding feelings from each other' or 'difficulties in being honest with each other' or 'worry about sexual satisfaction' are helpfully impersonal, as they locate problems in the interactions of the relationship rather than in imputed characteristics of either individual. Clearly there may be problems which are *not* appropriately defined as part of a mutual process but are primarily located in one partner's actions – womanizing, violence and abuse are instances. But for many couples, trapped in a vicious circle of mutual recrimination and defensiveness, naming the problem promotes a view of it as a mutual 'enemy' and opens up possibilities for cooperative efforts.

If persons cannot come up with a name, I tentatively suggest some possibilities, and use the one the person prefers. If all my suggestions are rejected then I do not press the point – but often persons are stimulated, by rejecting my ideas, to define a name themselves: 'No, it's not quite any of those – more like . . .'. I invited Richard to name his problem, and his difficulty in doing this was perhaps related to the complexity of the situation and the amount of pain he was feeling, but when we started to refer to 'in-law stresses' and 'marital disagreements' the issues began to take on a potentially manageable aspect. In his first, spontaneous account he defined the problem as within himself and within Rose – 'my temper', 'my anger', 'her suspicions'. Moving to talk of 'in-law stresses' and 'marital disagreements' not only conceptually neutralized the problems, rendering them to a degree potentially manageable, but typified them as problems of process and context – not as personal characteristics or faults. As his account proceeded, becoming more detailed in response to my questions, he began to define problem elements in changed ways – his mother became central to our conversation, as well as Rose, which led to our discussing the complex *interactions* between the three of them. Naming such complexities was hard, and in the event only partial, but even this demonstrated that naming *and re-naming* can become a means of clarifying *fullness*, of paying tribute to and holding in mind the multiple facets of issues, of preventing oversimplification, of encouraging persons to formulate focused, increasingly 'rich' descriptions. Naming is progressive, and its progress reflects and re-structures the person's widening story. Richard's inclusion of his mother was a richer description than his initial focusing on himself and his wife, and his description of the interaction 'triangle' was a richer description than his naming the personal characteristics of each person as separate individuals.

Another function of 'naming the problem' is to encourage 'calling a spade a spade'. Referring to acts of domination by unadorned wording such as 'He abused you time and time again over three years' rather than 'It happened over three years', 'He attacked you and kept on attacking you' instead of 'It kept happening,' and so forth, can be of assistance to persons who have previously used evasive words or phrasing like 'interference' or 'It went on for years'. Further specificity – 'He touched your penis even though you said you didn't want him to', 'He punched you in the eye and on the nose', 'He terrorized you for years by a permanent unspoken threat of violence' – encourages a recognition of the actuality and seriousness of abusive actions. Obviously, this naming takes place as part of a sensitive exploration of issues and when the person is thought to be receptive to such directness. Naming is a signal to both abuser and victim that I will not go along with the abuser's attempts to step out of responsibility for his acts, and it encourages the victim not to understate and thus underestimate what she really experienced. It allows for the exploration and discussion of widely held attitudes and beliefs which make it difficult for victims to be heard and which make it possible for abusers to construct self-justifications (White, 1995a: 89–90).

'Externalizing' the problem

'Externalizing the problem' means maintaining an attitude, reflected in particular verbal forms when referring to problems, where the difficulties brought to therapy are implicitly characterized as something *affecting* the person, rather than as characteristics or qualities *intrinsic* to him. Metaphors introduced and maintained by the therapist refer to problems as attacking the person, invading his life, speaking to him, trapping him or in some other way attempting to hurt or damage him. Externalizing embodies, through use of this syntactical device, a centrally important assumption underpinning narrative therapy: that persons are responding to problematic situations, not 'embodying problems'; and therefore that the problem is something that a person can work towards excluding from her life, or in some other way stand up to. It is a language of implicit hope and encouragement.

David Epston has expressed his debt to Michael White, describing the development of their personal and professional relationship since their meeting in 1980, and how their work increasingly started to 'merge':

> If I were to restrict myself to only one aspect of White's work that I have taken over, it would be that of 'externalising of the problem', which is summarised in his maxim: 'The person isn't the problem: the problem is the problem.' This provided a rationale and a practice to position myself in therapy, to be neutral, that is, to be on everyone's side at the same time and to act with commitment and (com) passion against the problem, whatever the problem might be. (Epston, 1989: 26)

In one of his most engaging papers, White (1989: 5) calls externalizing 'an approach to therapy that encourages persons to objectify and, at times, to personify the problems that they experience as oppressive'. He describes how he discovered this idea when working with children, finding that they and their families found it appealing, and later extended it to 'a wider range of presenting problems' (1989: 6). White stresses that he does not always introduce externalizing language, and I find myself that when I do it needs a de-emphasizing lightness of touch to be effective. But it is particularly appropriate when working with persons who give 'problem-saturated' self-descriptions. These are descriptions in which the negative stories persons tell themselves about their lives are so powerful that any contradicting evidence, any counter-stories which might call into question their entrapment, have become invisible to them (White, 1995a: 25). Some persons *are* trapped in circumstances where they can bring about little or no change, such as being unemployed in an area where jobs are impossible to find and without the resources to move elsewhere, in debt without any hope of repayment, or terminally ill. Narrative therapy's emphasis is always on the real effects on peoples' lives of the problems they are grappling with – it is not a 'feel-good' therapy. It would be an abuse of externalization to use it to soften or deny the reality of the person's experience. However, externalization can sometimes, through characterizing a problem as an inescapable situation *extrinsic to the person enmeshed in it,* assist him to recognize and honour his survival and coping skills. In the case of a person with a terminal illness it would be inappropriate and cruel to externalize 'death' as if it were something he might defeat. However, it might be helpful to talk to the person in terms of 'despair affecting you' rather than to speak of 'your despair'.

Externalization is simultaneous with, or rather another facet of, inviting persons to name the problem. Its use embodies an awareness of, and a positive calling on, the power of language to counter the effects of persons' seeing their problems as intrinsic to themselves, as part of their identity. Persons often come to see me believing that there is 'something wrong with them' producing and perpetuating their predicament: for example, that they possess or incorporate certain faults or inadequacies which mean that they are not capable of living their lives satisfactorily. These 'deficiencies' are often characterized by them as personal moral or intellectual faults or as 'psychological mechanisms'. Influenced by ideas about psychology current in Western culture which are widely taken as 'true' and 'established', even when satirized, in articles, films, novels, jokes and cartoons, the person may believe that unknown factors in childhood have formed him, are present in him still, and need my assumed specialist expertise to be identified, neutralized or expunged. He may see himself as acting out behaviours attributable to mental states defined in terms of illness or pathology. Persons experiencing difficulty in a relationship sometimes send their partner to therapy with an instruction to get 'sorted out'. Persons often *excuse* their own or their partner's abusive or inconsiderate behaviour by suggesting psychological explanations to me: for example, that the behaviour stems from 'damage' caused by unhappy childhood experience, that they are helplessly following patterns established in the family of origin, or that they are 'mental'.

When I use externalizing language with persons who make such claims I am not trying to deny that we are powerfully affected and influenced by many experiences, including in particular those of our early life, or to deny the possible long-term effects of unhappy or traumatic events. However, I see these ideas as particularly powerful, but not always the most important, examples of the unknowable multiplicity of factors that shape the accounts we tell ourselves and others of our lives, which, once the events have passed, are all that we *have* of our past. But if the person holds a different view, reflected in her language, I try to bear in mind Jerome Bruner's argument that 'popular psychology' is at least as deserving of respect as academic psychology (Bruner, 1990: ch. 2). I try to avoid engaging in discussions of psychological theory with persons – not always successfully! But I do wish to convey and encourage a perspective that is possible to *separate* from whatever psychological factors may have contributed to problems, to see them as *influences* not as *determinants,* to recognize that habits of thought and action are not fixed *within* us but, on the contrary, are learned or habitual behaviours which can (often with great effort and painful thought) be recognized, reviewed, dismissed, changed or abandoned. Externalizing the problem assists me in this. A person's pessimistic 'essentialist' viewpoint brought to counselling – 'This is what I am' – can move to the more hopeful and helpful social constructionist or post-structuralist viewpoint of 'This is what has influenced me.' So I avoid metaphors which characterize difficult or painful behaviours as 'symptoms of underlying causes' and do not characterize persons as 'being', 'containing' or 'having' problems.

White's (1989: 6) description of the effects of externalization is worth quoting in full:

I . . . have concluded that, among other things, this practice:

1 Decreases unproductive conflict between persons, including those disputes over who is responsible for the problem;
2 Undermines the sense of failure that has developed for many persons in response to the continuing existence of the problem despite their attempts to resolve it;
3 Paves the way for persons to co-operate with each other; to unite in a struggle against the problem and to escape its influence in their lives and relationships;
4 Opens up new possibilities for persons to take action to retrieve their lives and relationships from the problem and its influence;
5 Frees persons to take a lighter, more effective and less stressed approach to 'deadly serious' problems; and

6 Presents options for dialogue, rather than monologue, about the problem.

Metaphorical language

Externalizing may take the form of direct personification, as when White called a child's encopresis 'Sneaky Poo's tricks' rather than something like 'your habit of soiling' (White, 1989: 8–12) or when a therapist says 'The voice of self-doubt speaks to you powerfully' rather than 'You are very self-doubting.' It is a deliberate choice of a way of speaking, using words or phrases carrying an externalizing implication in the low-key, 'natural' atmosphere of ordinary conversation:

- When did these nightmares start to attack you? (rather than 'When did you start to have nightmares?')
- Loneliness seems to have been with you for most of your life (rather than 'You have been a lonely person most of your life')
- So you've always used comforting rituals to give yourself confidence? (rather than 'So you're a compulsive-obsessive?')
- Alcohol has had a lot of success in its attempts to take over your life (rather than 'You're an alcoholic')
- You and Joan have found that jealousy invades your relationship (rather than 'You and Joan have been jealous of each other')

All language is metaphorical – written or spoken units symbolize their referents; they are not the referents themselves – and, in the case of ideas, the images which words evoke in the imagination are all too easy to mistake for 'reality'. It seems to me that some of the metaphors most commonly used in therapy have become reified: the Core Self, Transference, Repression, Denial and so on. They have subtly become conceived as 'real' and known entities, rather than remaining as mere words symbolizing hypotheses.

Metaphors which locate problems 'within' people are just that: compressed comparative images in language. *Alternative metaphors are available.* Externalization is not chosen in narrative therapy because the therapist has some idea that Sneaky Poo or Anxiety, or Depression, or the Voice of Doubt (White, 1997a) actually exist as malign entities independent of the person experiencing them. They are chosen because externalizing language can result in beneficial effects such as those outlined in White (1989, quoted above).

Externalizing the problem is potentially helpful by its gently and unobtrusively introducing 'a different atmosphere round the problem' (White, 1995a: 21). Different, that is, from the 'atmosphere' generated by assumptions, likely to be brought to the session by the person, that there is something wrong 'with him' which needs to be put right, and that the therapist is the person to do this 'fixing'. Such assumptions are doubly unhelpful: they attribute the problem to internal, character-based, faulty or missing aspects of the person; and they also imply that the therapist as 'expert' is going to sort these characteristics out. An underlying 'medical' analogy is at work in the person's anticipation of therapy, which can be reinforced by a consultation-room-like physical setting and by therapists using terms such as 'referrals', 'case notes', 'clinical work' and so forth. Powerful and ubiquitous pop culture images of counsellors, therapists, psychologists and psychiatrists suggest extraordinary, near-magical insight, wisdom and penetration into human life and motivation, out of reach of the uninstructed. Such mythical, culturally induced views of counsellors are reinforced by the style and tone of some therapists' written or spoken presentations in the media. In my experience these are seldom tentative and exploratory but are usually presented as firm assertions implying certain knowledge, wisdom and insight born out of expertise. Naming and externalization counteract such assumptions by encouraging persons to define their problems according to their own knowledge, and to begin to disentangle their problems from their identity.

Examining cultural pressures to see problems as 'internal'

Since 1990, White has further developed the concept of externalization in ways congruent with the post-structuralist and social constructionist perspectives which inform his work (see Chapters 2 and 9). 'Problems' are conceived by White as *constructions created through the stories persons tell themselves and others*, and these stories are seen as shot through with ideas, assumptions and 'given truths' which have cultural and social origins. This is not at all to imply that persons are deluded, exaggerating or imagining things. The proposition is that the representations of experience we make to ourselves and others, through self-narratives which define and influence our lives, are *maps*, not accurate and exact accounts of every nuance of every experience and relationship. This does not deny the actuality of these constructs for the person, or deny the actuality of the events and issues which are troubling him. But persons' accounts of their problems inevitably *leave out* much of their experience, and in so doing, contain contradictions.

> There isn't a single story of life that is free of ambiguity and contra-diction, and that can handle all the contingencies in life. These ambi-guities, contradictions and contingencies stretch our meaning-making resources. We really work hard to resolve or make sense out of these contradictions and ambiguities, and of our experience of these con-tingencies – to make sense out of significant experiences that cannot be so readily interpreted through the dominant stories that we have about our lives . . . (White, 1995a: 15)

In my own work I take it as a starting-point that the experiences persons describe have occurred, but that once these began to be 'representations', woven into persons' self-stories, they began to lose the fullness of actual experience. They have become 'thin descriptions' – and these thin descriptions are all we have as the initial material of therapy.

Externalizing internalizing discourses

Culturally and 'politically' derived assumptions which encourage persons to attribute their problems to identity, personality or inescapable conditioning can themselves be closely and critically examined in therapeutic conversations. White has called this process 'externalizing internalizing discourses' (White, 1995a: 41). Here, 'discourse' does not mean a conversation or a speech but is a philosophical term meaning the habitual ways of thinking and assuming, with resultant language habits, which are common currency within a particular social grouping. Social and cultural groupings which possess their own discourses, their own shared values and vocabularies, range from small to very large. Let me invent a couple, Jill and Elaine. Lovers and flatmates, they share intimate 'in-jokes' and relationship games, private to them and a part of their unique way of loving and relating; a 'Jill–Elaine' dis-course. The jazz club to which Elaine belongs and the brass band in which Jill plays the trombone have different discourses from each other: the very words 'concert', 'music', 'band' and 'brass' carry quite different connotations in these two discourses. The couple shares the discourse of the local lesbian community, which in turn largely shares the discourse of lesbian feminism world-wide, but they have many painful experiences of ways in which homophobic persons try to situate them within 'sexual norm' discourses of society as a whole. As Jill and Elaine are both psychiatric nurses, they share a vocational medical-model discourse, also largely present in wider society, which includes a degree of 'labelling' of 'patients' and assumptions concerning the nature of 'mental illness' and the expert status of psychiatrists. The 'stories' each tells herself in internal monologue, the stories they tell each other, and the stories they tell others in wider social contexts derive from and express these diverse discourses. The two women are multi-discourse-skilled.

Where the language in which persons express their problems appears to indicate that the discourses of their local or wider cultural and social groups are having a restricting, limiting or harmful effect on their lives, narrative therapists encourage persons to examine these discourses. The most common type of story told by the person at this early point of therapy incorporates elements of self-blame, self-doubt, self-accusation and attribution of the problem to her own character, faults, personality, sin or other forms of assumed 'inner essence'. Such interiorization has been influenced and encouraged by many 'taken-for-granted-as-true' assumptions propagated in the discourses of local and wider social contexts. 'Externalizing internalizing discourses' goes beyond the use of verbal formats which invite an 'influence' perspective rather than an 'essence' perspective. It comprises explicit examination of the nature of the ideas which inform beliefs and narratives, thus directly bringing issues of 'politics' into the therapy room. The results of such examination may offer the person more local-knowledge-based ways of conceptualizing her problems, allowing her the choice of further escape from her dominant self-blaming.

In the following example from my own practice I was not concerned to 'point out to the person that she was thinking distortedly'. I wanted to assist her to tell a 'different story' if she discovered that habitual, significantly limiting discourses, deriving from her history and from 'assumed truths' in contemporary society, no longer made sense to her.

Gina, aged 50 at the time she came to therapy, had been brought up as a girl and young woman in her native Italy. Her father had been an enthusiastic fascist during the Mussolini years, and this former political allegiance was congruent with the way in which he later treated his family, especially the female members. His wife and daughters had been subject to a domestic regime of extreme male dominance where their subservience to perceived male needs and characteristics was rigidly enforced, and the assumption that women existed to serve men never questioned or allowed to be questioned. Gina had to leave school as early as possible despite the ability to go on to higher education, and she and her sisters had been denied almost all forms of social life outside the immediate family. Despite these restrictions she fell in love with a British businessman whom she met when 20 years old and briefly staying with relatives, and through this relationship she escaped to England and a new life. She came to therapy because of problems in relating to her teenage daughter, whose behaviour often appeared to Gina to be very self-centred and inconsiderate. Gina said that the extreme restrictions of her own background made it hard for her to distinguish between reasonable rule enforcement, and unfair parental imposition. At the same time as being infuriated by her daughter's behaviour, she felt that she 'ought' to give in to her daughter's demands on her time, money, possessions and patience, because when she had occasionally refused these demands she had been 'selfish'. We looked in detail at ways in which women's subservience was still a major assumption even in less overtly patriarchal contexts than her family of origin, and also ways in which mothers were both blamed and idealized in Western society, often putting them into impossible 'no win' situations. I asked her if she was 'hearing her father's voice' at moments when she felt she was being selfish, and whether she herself felt there might be any difference between women's 'selfishness' as defined by her father and by much of society, and 'meeting one's own legitimate needs'. There was a long pause while Gina thought. Then she began to nod, saying with great emphasis and considerable emotion, 'Yes – so I'm not selfish!' This proved to be a turning point, allowing her to define, and then gradually and with great determination to put into operation, preferred ways of relating to her daughter which took her own legitimate needs into account.

Through 'externalizing' questioning and discussion Gina had identified the discourses which contributed to the conflict between fury at her daughter's behaviour and her inhibitions in opposing these behaviours. She had looked at the nature and possible origins of these inner 'voices'. She had recognized through 'naming', including rejecting a previous naming, that a distinction in behaviours and attitudes existed which had formerly escaped her. She had examined the location, origins and 'political' aspects of the entrapping discourses. Through this new perspective she was able to reject her former, family-of-origin-based conception of herself as 'selfish', reinforced by cultural veneration of the 'selfless mother' role, and discover a freedom, through a changed self-narrative, to refuse her daughter's unreasonable demands without feeling guilt. She was now able to tell a story to herself of looking to legitimate needs *and of always having done this*. It was not just a discovery of 'what she might do from now on' or even primarily a discovery that 'what she had not been able to do had been influenced by oppression in her family of origin' but a discovery that 'what she had always wanted to do, and had tried to do but without success, *had always been OK*'. Internalizing discourses were externalized; her self-story became 'enriched'.

Questions I might ask a person when 'externalizing internalizing discourses', inviting him to examine the things he tells himself about himself, and to examine the discourses which underpin those self-narratives, take such forms as:

- How did you come by those ideas? Have you always told yourself you are unlovable?
- Is this idea yours or someone else's? Have you ever come across ways of looking at what makes a person tick which make you wonder about your own views?
- Am I hearing you speak, or is this the voice of your abuser?
- So you tell yourself you are treating her like that because your father treated your mother like that. Are you a carbon copy of your father? Do you do the same job he did? Do you dress like him? Do you like the same music as him?
- Has the habit of self-blame ever seemed like something you might try to give up? Who has encouraged you to continue the habit? What techniques have they used to do this?
- I wonder what films, books, magazines and television programmes might have had an influence on your belief that the only way to solve a dilemma is to face it out by yourself?
- What has the management philosophy in your firm contributed to your being undervalued and pressurized? What political ideas have influenced your firm to take on a 'hard management' philosophy? In whose interests has such a philosophy become widespread in modern society? What are the effects of these policies on the lives of your colleagues and on their relationships within the organization?
- What part has been played in your life by the influence on your

husband of his mates' beliefs about how women should be treated by men?

- Have your workmates' stories about the women they've 'pulled' made you want to boast about similar 'successes'?
- Why might it be in the interests of some commercial manufacturers to promote the idea that only very slim women are attractive?

Examples in the form of summaries on the page, out of context, are truncated and abrupt. Most 'externalizations of internalizing discourses' are not single questions but *explorations,* invitations to consider ideas, invitations to follow up a statement with clarification, tentative open-ended comments, and even – if the person and the situation seem right – direct challenges.

Externalization: some cautions

(1) *Externalizing is of limited value unless it is used within a framework of post-structuralist assumptions.* The whole point of 'externalizing conversations' is to assist the person to break away from the concept of the problem being part of her, 'within' her, an aspect of 'her' assumed 'fixed character', or in any way 'pathological'. Unless the therapist has himself broken away from these ways of thinking, externalization is pointless and even potentially damaging. Stephen Madigan describes a 'case' conference where 'a colleague stated that "Anorexia may be pushing the family around, however, anorexia is also pushing forth what we have always suspected about this family – that they are manipulative and dysfunctional".' There were nods of agreement. Madigan comments wryly, 'Their comments made me think about the dangers of therapeutically mixing together apples and oranges; in this case Narrative practices together with popular psychological traditions' (Madigan, 1999: 1).

(2) *Externalizing may not always be appropriate.* White suggests that externalizing conversations are most useful when persons come with very fixed and habitual dominant stories. Therapy needs to be flexible:

> I am not proposing that recourse be made to these [externalizing] practices for all persons, in all situations, and at all times. For example, there are those who seek therapy in relation to various crises, and whose lives and relationships are not fixed by problem-dominated stories . . . it might be appropriate for the therapist to assist the person to address

various aspects of their experience of the crisis, and to review their handling of it. Then there are those seeking therapy who have accounts of their life that are not problem-saturated, but ones that they regard as rather mundane. Under these circumstances, it could be appropriate for the therapist to encourage persons to identify the 'sparkling facts' of their career in life . . . (White, 1989: 27–8)

(3) *Externalizing through 'naming' can sometimes become too simplistic or too difficult to be helpful.* When assisting a person to put a name to his problems I sometimes recognize an awkwardness and artificiality which militates against the low-key, conversational atmosphere I prefer to encourage in therapy. We struggle to encapsulate a range of complicated and distressing aspects of his story into a single word or phrase, and it doesn't work – there *is* no such word or phrase or, if there is, we can't think of it. Such struggles can be counterproductive, puzzling for the person, and at times even oppressive. It is best, in these instances, to abandon the attempt and to move on. Here is an extract from a session in which, it seems to me, the therapist becomes over-insistent in attempting to impose an externalized naming, 'losing' the person in the process:

Robert: . . . uh . . . I still think a person, um . . . who feels good about himself sometimes can overcome his problems.
Therapist: Well, it takes feeling really good about yourself to escape *immobilization. Immobilization* is a powerful thing. And as you know, for example, you haven't let *immobilization* turn you into an agoraphobic . . . how'd you manage that?
Robert: I just don't think I . . . I never had a fear of going outside.
Therapist: Yeah, but *immobilization* can reduce someone to that. You've just pointed that out. And you're quite right. So how have you been able to not let *immobilization* turn you into an agoraphobic? I'm really curious about that.
Robert: I don't know. I think I like people . . . I don't know . . . I don't have an answer. I think that when I was younger, I might. I don't know. I had a period of not going to school, maybe, maybe, a fear of not doing well. But I don't think . . .
Therapist: No, no, no.
Robert: Being successful at school.
Therapist: That's different. So what I'm curious about is . . . I think you're quite right when you said a moment ago that, um, you have to have enough self-esteem, you know, to not let immobilization turn you into an agoraphobic. So what is it about yourself that you're able to notice? Let me ask it this way . . .
Robert: Yeah, yeah, I'm not going to answer it.
Therapist: What do you think it tells me about you? When I see you haven't let immobilization turn you into an agoraphobic. What do you think that tells me about you?

Robert: I don't know . . .
(Zimmerman and Dickerson, in Stephen Gilligan and Reese Price (eds),
   Therapeutic Conversations, 1993: 210, emphasis in original. Reprinted
   by permission of W.W. Norton & Co. Inc.)

(4) *Externalization is not appropriate when defining oppressive practices.* In the interview from which the above extract is taken, Robert's partner Susan has given distressing examples of Robert making her feel guilty by his stepping out of responsibility for family organization, then blaming her for 'over-giving' when she insists on doing what has to be done. The therapist's insistence on defining Robert's behaviour as affected by 'immobilization' prevents this behaviour from being named – indeed, the therapist praises Robert for fighting immobilization by never actually becoming agoraphobic, which leads to Susan's attributing his success in resisting agoraphobic behaviour to his 'liking to be around people'. She has rescued him again, praising his 'strength' (on a specific hint from the therapist), a quality not at all evident in her account of Robert's relating to her. The therapist moves on to looking at Susan's 'taking-care-of habits', a collusion with Robert which reduces her to tears (1993: 210).

White suggests that when a situation brought to therapy involves 'persons' experience of oppression' then externalizing is best used in relation to *attitudes, beliefs and strategies which maintain the oppression.*

> it is important that therapists do not make generalizations about situations, but keep in mind the specifics of every circumstance and think ahead to the likely consequences of particular courses of action . . . lest the therapist inadvertently contribute to persons' experience of oppression, this consciousness discourages therapists from inviting the externalizing of problems such as violence and sexual abuse. When these problems are identified, the therapist would be inclined to encourage the externalizing of the attitudes and beliefs that appear to compel the violence, and those strategies that maintain persons in their subjugation. . . . (White and Epston, 1990: 49)

I do *not* take a neutral stance on oppressive practices by defining them as part of interactive processes 'driving' a person, or as reflecting some damage or pathology from the past which needs cure. I do try fully to recognize that a person's chosen oppressive practices can sometimes be rooted in unexamined beliefs and attitudes current in his local and wider social context – the discourses of his subculture. I see oppressive practices as unequivocally wrong, needing to stop, and needing acknowledgement and redress. How can I encourage this yet avoid promoting a superficial acting out of what the oppressor senses he has to say or do for the moment in order to get what he wants? And what part can externalization play here? Certainly any attempt to moralize, or to confront or accuse the oppressing person, will be both ineffectual and, perhaps more important, a power-based action in itself which by its 'top-down' stance enacts the very oppression it is criticizing.

The following illustrative examples of externalizing questions are conflated from several instances of working with heterosexual partners where the man's behaviour was verbally abusive and physically violent.

Externalizing the problem by defining it as attitudes and beliefs:

- How has the temptation to speak to Dot with contempt got a grip on you?
- What habits of forgetting have stopped you from seeing your son's distress when you insult your wife?
- Might others' everyday use of obscene language have persuaded you that it's OK to call your wife a whore?
- Has your habit of seeing the time you once gave Janet a black eye as trivial got you completely in its power?
- Have you forgotten that love usually urges people to be gentle with each other?
- Is it possible that self-justification has become a more powerful force for you than clear-sightedness?

Externalizing the internalizing discourses:

- What beliefs about how men can talk to women persuaded you to call your wife a 'fucking slag'?
- What ideas do your mates have about how women like to be treated? Where have those ideas come from?
- Do you ever feel a bit as if you're acting in a film, being a tough guy?
- When you're alone do you ever find yourself winding anger up and enjoying it?
- Where have you got the idea that resenting the past has to be permanent?
- Who has persuaded you that forgiveness is weak in a man?

These, like many questions given as examples in writing about narrative work, are illustrations where brevity has taken precedence over naturalism of presentation. The first question in 'externalizing internalizing discourses' above, woven naturally into the text of the session, was expressed more like this:

> *George*: I just told her what I thought about her.
>
> *Martin*: Do you think she found this an expression of honesty by someone who cared for her?
>
> *George*: What?
>
> *Martin*: Right – do you think Dot saw your comment as a frank and honest opinion coming out of your love for her, or might she have felt it was – well, words are hard – insulting? Contemptuous? Dismissive?
>
> *George*: She bloody well deserved it, anyway.
>
> *Martin*: So if it was something you think she deserved, it was a sort of punishment?
>
> *George*: I suppose so.
>
> *Martin*: When an adult 'punishes' another adult is that a loving act or an act of contempt?
>
> *George*: She asked for it.
>
> *Martin*: An act of contempt then?
>
> *George*: Right.
>
> *Martin*: For someone you love? You've told me lots of times that you love Dot, and you've told her that too, here in this room.
>
> *George*: I do love her. She knows that. But she winds me up. I couldn't help myself.
>
> *Martin*: You love her yet something or someone seems to have made you think that it's OK to throw contemptuous insults at her when you feel she makes you cross.
>
> *George*: What?
>
> *Martin*: From what you say, you're influenced by the idea that it's possible to love someone and yet heap degrading insults on her. This idea seems to have got a firm grip on you. How did that happen? I see quite a lot of men who are angry with their wives but who don't think that way or speak that way. I wonder how you got that idea? – who persuaded you that you can love someone yet it's OK to call her a 'fucking slag'?
>
> *George*: Her sister's a slag too . . .

In this example I am not skilful enough in choosing my time or in framing my questions to encourage George to look at the sources of his beliefs or to recognize that there are such sources. He sees his opinions as facts, and his insulting Dot as deserved by her, and that's that. No chance, yet, to encourage him to examine and separate from the influences which have contributed to the unrecognized beliefs about women, men and verbal violence which govern what he does. But at least I am framing the externalizing questions without pulling my punches when naming his actions, and offering the idea that beliefs influencing his actions are leading him to do and say things which directly call into question his statements that he loves Dot. It didn't work, but it might have, given that the possibility of losing Dot filled him with genuine terror.

Even so, it would not have worked just by itself. White suggests that violent or abusive men must be encouraged to take responsibility for the abuse, recognize its consequences, apologize, commit to change and confront patriarchal ideas so that their whole way of thinking, the discourses they have adhered to perhaps all their life, are left behind. The therapist must be painstaking, precise and detailed, both in deconstructing those discourses and in encouraging the transition to new and liberating discourses:

> It is important to establish a context in which it becomes possible for these men to separate from some of the dominant ways of being and thinking that inform the abuse. These are those ways of being and thinking that inform, support, justify, and make the abuse possible. But even this is not enough. It is crucial that we engage with these men in the exploration of alternative ways of thinking and being that bring with them new proposals for action in their relationships with their women partners and with their children, and that these proposals be accountable to these women and children . . . *To achieve this, the specifics of these alternative ways of being and thinking need to be very carefully worked through.* The particularities . . . must be carefully drawn out. (White, 1995a: 159–60, emphasis added)

Externalizing internalizing discourses can play a valuable part in therapy with violent or abusive people but equally, to risk labouring the point, misapplied externalization can encourage and reinforce the abuser's tendency to blame 'the situation' or the victim, and to see contributing factors as inescapable causes rather than as influences only.

Externalizing may help, but is it ethical?

What about situations in which the therapist introduces externalizing metaphors which by their repetition and development draw the person into their use, with the person beginning to take a different attitude to her problem, perhaps never realizing how this has been brought about? Is this not manipulation? Is it not using a position of power to brainwash the person? How does it square with White's insistence that therapists should not be secretive about the methods they use? And would externalization still 'work' if, in the name of transparency, the therapist explained it in advance?

For a long while the ethics of externalization really bothered me. I felt that I might be using a technique intended to influence the person without her knowledge, 'for her own good' as conceived by myself, not her. Perhaps I was not respecting *her* beliefs that she was the problem, but attacking her assumptions without saying so, thinking 'It would be better for her to stop attributing her problems to her personality and to start to see them as separate from herself, and externalizing should do the trick.'

My conclusion is that externalization is transparent anyway – it is not hidden, the person can hear exactly what I say. In using externalizing language, I am not in any way forcing it on the person. It is not hidden as is, for example, a person-centred therapist's assumption that the person needs to 'get in touch with his true self' or a psychodynamic therapist's assumption that a process called transference is at work in the session. Of course, such ideas *can* be explicitly conveyed to a person. No doubt many therapists working in those traditions take care to explain just what they are doing and what they believe is happening in the session, but unless the assumptions and practices *are* explained they will remain invisible, whereas the linguistic forms of externalization are overt. They will only 'catch' if they have meaning for the person. I have known persons use internalizing language throughout therapy despite my own externalizing language. I have known persons take on some externalizing language and still keep to some internalizing language. And I have known persons take up externalizing language and use it throughout. Externalization follows naming, and naming is *negotiated*. I discuss choices of names for the problem and from then onwards the externalized definition is fully in the open, agreed by both of us. I try to keep a balance between focusing on the concerns of the person and explanations of the practices and ideas I use, but too great an emphasis on the latter starts to put me too much at the centre. The person has come to therapy for assistance with difficulties in her life, not to discuss therapy theories!

Summary

Despite the stress of coming to see a counsellor, a person soon settles to giving a verbal review of his situation, being familiar with the process of 'story-telling'. The therapist encourages this, first by an open invitation to the person to talk about his concerns, and then by questioning him in detail about how the problem is affecting him, over a wide range of life areas. This full description provides the material for therapy, almost always revealing some aspects of life which the problem has not affected, or where the person has defied the problem. If the person appears to be overwhelmed by the problem, the therapist uses externalizing language in talking about it, and in any case invites the person to join him in deciding upon a name to give to the problem in order to give it an identity of its own, separate from the identity of the person. As the session progresses and more information emerges through the therapist's questioning, the therapist may suggest different, more precise naming and will check this out with the person. The therapist may 'externalize internalizing discourses' by encouraging direct discussion of relational and social 'politics' contributing to the person's attribution of the problem to his own personality or psychology. This practice is not followed when counselling concerns violent or abusive actions chosen by the person. By the end of this phase of the session the person has been listened to with respect and interest, the problem has been defined by agreement, and he has been encouraged implicitly and explicitly to consider the problem as located in factors influencing him rather than as intrinsic to him or as 'symptoms of damage'.

4 *Encouraging a Wider Perspective on the Problem*

Stories

In some therapies the counsellor literally tells stories to persons. Milton Erikson, one of the founders of hypnotherapy, based much of his work on this technique (Rosen, 1982). The power of stories is universal. We hunger for absorbing accounts of experience – from the books read in childhood to television soap-operas. In shops specializing in second-hand children's books I have seen people eagerly seize copies of story-books they owned in childhood, moved and excited. White has written delightfully about the improvised 'Mouse Stories' he told his sister when they were young, and how these took on new life when telling them to his daughter, and he describes how this link between past and present is 'with him' when he works with persons (White, 1997b: 4–10). The significance of stories in human life is certainly an undercurrent in White and Epston's thinking.

But there is a difference between 'therapeutic tales' *told by the therapist* to persons and narratives *told by person*s when encouraged by the therapist to outline the issues which they bring to therapy. I find the 'story' metaphor confusing unless I hold this distinction in mind. Jim Sheehan suggests that since the contrived 'closures' characteristic of fiction are not true of persons' lives, narrative therapists may unwittingly and damagingly think in terms of resolution or finality if the 'story' metaphor is taken too literally (Sheehan, 1999). On the whole I prefer the term 'narrative' to 'story' in the therapy context, but since 'story', 'storying' and 're-storying' appear so frequently in White, Epston and other writers on narrative therapy the term cannot be abandoned.

Suppose I write an account of events in someone's life or my own. These events happened in the past. Historical accounts, biographies and autobiographies are all told sequences of *selected* past events because no single narrative can include everything that happened. Even if my subject matter were so brief that an almost complete account might be possible, such as 'My life in the past five minutes', the bare statement of remembered events, feelings, actions and circumstances will be incomplete. I simply cannot include everything: the exact times when I blinked, my shifts in the chair, the precise moments I looked out of the window and for how long, the sequences of subtle changes to the rhythms of my heart-beat, the nature and timing of birdsong from the garden, all the complex movements of the computer mouse, and so on – and I have not yet considered my thoughts and feelings over this five minutes, how they relate to my past life and my hopes for the future, as well as to my present situation seated in a room in England early on a Monday morning towards the end of the twentieth century. What is more, a near-total account would lack point and interest: it would be just an unstructured sequence of arbitrary information. An incomplete account – inevitably so – and also boring.

Suppose I decide to write about something slightly more inter-esting than the past five minutes of my life. I might choose a uni-fying theme – say, the various motor vehicles I have owned. I can't imagine why such an account would actually be of interest to anyone, but its nature may illustrate some characteristics of 'stories'.

Between 1963 and 1999 I bought and sold 19 motor vehicles – mostly cars, but also two motor-caravans. All but three of these vehicles were second-hand. My present car is the best I have owned.

I have scanned my life, chosen a theme, selected out elements related to the theme, and threaded them into a unique narrative sequence. Before I wrote the above sentences buying and selling motor vehicles were isolated elements embedded in my life as a whole; now they have been distilled into the bare bones of a story. If I decided to write on my previous career, in education, I doubt whether my vehicles would feature in that narrative at all. The events and circumstances selected out of my life would be differ-ent, and the 'story' around my vehicles would never emerge. Yet another possibility for a story coming out of my life might be an account of all my significant relationships – and this story might feature some of the vehicles incidentally, and aspects of my past career, but *only incidentally*. The focus would be elsewhere; the elements selected out for description and elaboration would be different. The shifts of emphasis would produce a different focus-ing and a different elaboration, ignoring elements which would have emerged had I written the other accounts. In writing any one of these narratives I would look over my remembered experience and choose to identify and elaborate certain particular aspects rather than others, from the enormous range of possibilities which exist; then link them. The story formed from these connections would be a *construct* linking selected aspects – none of which were, *as an identified sequence,* a recognized history until I created the narrative. Narrating is a little like drawing connecting lines in the matrix of dots used for the paper-and-pencil game of Battleships, or linking points on a blank graph paper to produce a represented sequence of body temperatures, population growth and so on. By choosing these points, then linking them, I create a new entity, making visible the previously invisible. Perhaps, like the statue 'hidden' in a block of marble worked by Michelangelo, the structure was potentially there, but only by my choice of presentation have I produced an artefact, a new structure which can be recognized, contemplated and experienced by other people and by myself.

Of course, talking of Michelangelo's statue as 'in the marble awaiting liberation' is deceptive. The block of marble was just a block of marble, and only his choice of chisel movements, his following one stroke by another according to his vision and genius, produced the statue. It was not previously 'there' to be 'liberated' at all. And the narratives I imagine above, my stories linking previously disparate elements of my life, are also 'creations from raw material' – *not* pre-existing in the astronomically huge number of events comprising my life from moment to moment over many years. The story does not mirror or represent my life, or even those parts of my life it claims to portray. It does have a tangential relationship with my life, but in the telling it emerges as *itself* – an independent artefact. This representation of selected events, which took place in sequence even if I choose not to *portray* them in actual sequence, remembered subject to the distortions of time, joined in a linkage which gives them coherence by isolating them from the rest of my remembered experience, becomes a 'sub-plot' of my life.

Sub-plots of life

There is an enormous number of stories, an enormous number of sub-plots, ready to be written from the various elements of a life. They are all potentially there, they have been experienced; all that remains is for the person to choose which to isolate out and link. In this sense, *'all lives are "multi-storied" '* (White, 1995a: 32, emphasis added). These stories, once created through narration, are not just passive: they *influence me*; they form the structures within which I ascribe significance and meaning to my life, including the picture I have of myself and others, what has been and is now meaningful to me. 'Stories provide the frames that make it possible to interpret our experience, and these acts of interpretation are achievements that we take an active part in' (White, 1995a: 15). Once created, that narrative will take on meaning; it will be part of my mental furniture. It will influence how I construct the memory of my life from now on, having an influence on the life I lead in the future by its very existence in my awareness. It may even become my dominant story.

Elements of 'stories'

In narrative therapy, a relatively simple conceptualizing of story elements is perhaps all that is needed, as we are dealing with a metaphor: nobody suggests that human life is literally the same as life as portrayed in fiction or biography. In explaining how he draws on the idea of 'plot' in his work, White refers to Jerome Bruner's summary of elements in stories (White, 1995a: 30–2). Bruner suggests two simultaneous 'landscapes' which a story must construct: 'One is the landscape of action, where the constituents are the arguments of action: agent, intention or goal, situation, instrument . . . The other landscape is the landscape of consciousness: what those involved in the action know, think or feel, or do not know, think or feel. The landscapes are essential and distinct' (Bruner, 1986: 14). Bruner refers to the source of this idea: 'A. Griemas's view . . . that a primitive or irreducible feature of story (whatever else it may include) is that it occurs jointly on the plane of action and in the subjectivity of the protagonists . . . The matching of "inner" vision and "outer" reality is, moreover, a classic human plight' (Bruner, 1986: 20–1). Summarizing other writers, Bruner suggests that the 'timeless underlying theme' of a story's 'fabula', or plot, comprises 'a plight into which characters have fallen as a result of intentions that have gone awry . . . And it requires an uneven distribution of underlying consciousness among the characters with respect to the plight . . . what one seeks in story structure is precisely how plight, character and consciousness are integrated' (1986: 21). The way in which 'story' can be a metaphor for the accounts given by persons who come to therapy is well brought out here. They are 'living' or 'performing' their own stories in a day-to-day drama where the interactions of 'action' (events) and 'consciousness' (feelings, thoughts, beliefs) have produced a sense of life going awry – a 'plight' (the problem).

I originally felt that the visual or painterly metaphor 'landscape' for a definition of literary/life constituents was rather inappropriate. But, like most metaphorical uses of language, it soon began to feel 'natural' in context. More recently, White has referred to the 'landscape of identity' rather than the 'landscape of consciousness' (White, 1997a), but this does not detract from the idea of stories comprising four main elements: (a) 'outer' events and (b) 'inner' experience, both (c) set in a time sequence and (d) producing confusion. This simplified, pared-down definition of the essence of stories, and how the interaction of these elements produces meaning for the person, is the template which White appears to have in mind when listening to persons and assisting them:

> When persons come into therapy and talk about what they've come to see you about, they usually give an account of the landscape of action of the dominant story. At this time, persons will also provide an account of the landscape of consciousness or the landscape of meaning of that dominant story ... The landscape of consciousness or meaning is derived through reflection on events in the landscape of action to determine what those events might say about the desires, preferences, qualities, characteristics, motives, purposes, wants, goals, values, beliefs, commitments of various persons ... In re-authoring work, we invite persons to traffic in both of these landscapes ... *so that alternative landscapes of action and of consciousness are brought forth.* (White, 1995a: 31, emphasis added)

I now return to therapy, at the point where we left the process at the end of Chapter 3. I offer my understanding of how the idea that persons' lives incorporate many potential stories, not yet told but ready to be identified and 'written', usually through speech rather than literal writing, is at the centre of narrative therapy.

A change of direction in the session

What I try to do when the person has told her full problem-saturated story, and what I have observed White doing with enviable skill, is 'both very simple and extremely complicated ... what is complicated and difficult is the delicate means by which it can be achieved' (Tomm, 1989). Tomm is referring to externalizing, but his words are just as applicable to the practices of encouraging the person's 're-storying' which comprise the whole of the rest of narrative therapy, and which begin at this point. I encourage the person to tell and re-tell new sub-plots from her life, previously uncreated because the 'points to be joined in the continuing graph' have not been identified, noticed, remembered or recognized by her as significant, as having meaning for her. Unlike my past person-centred practice, I do not continue to 'stay with the problem' throughout therapy. I invite persons to move their descriptions away from 'the effect of the problem on the life of the person' to its opposite – 'their own influence in the life of the problem' (White, 1989: 10). I invite persons to confirm, identify, describe and expand descriptions of occasions on which the problem was not fully present – when it was to an extent absent or diminished or defeated or contradicted. I encourage the person to tell sub-plots. These new sub-plots are created by the very act of telling. The means of facilitating this, the techniques used, their pacing, their sequence or lack of sequence, the language used, the atmosphere of the counselling session, elements similar to different therapies and elements quite different from them, the number and frequency of sessions, the organization of sessions and so forth, are the subject of the rest of this book.

From 'clues' to 'unique outcomes'

Throughout the early, expository, problem-describing phase of therapy, I maintain alertness to any aspects of the 'problem description' which appear to be at odds with its dominant themes: which contradict them, suggest that a different perspective is possible, sit uneasily with them, appear not to match them. When I think I have noticed such instances I attempt to keep them in mind, to 'log' them. Using the word in a different sense from de Shazer (1988), I think of these instances as *clues* which may indicate a potential alternative 'storyline' running alongside the story being told, one which when told may become significant for further exploration of the person's experience.

I see such 'clues' as possible 'points on a graph which has not been drawn' or, more literally, as possible starting and linking points for a parallel story to the problem-saturated story the person has already told. I think of these elements, *before they are checked out with the person*, as 'clues' since at first they are merely hypotheses of my own. I may easily be mistaken; I may have misunderstood what the person said; I may be imputing significance to occasions or thoughts in ways that the person would not confirm; I may be over-influenced by my own experience of similar instances; I may be under the influence of cultural or gender-based assumptions not shared by the person; I may be worrying about how the session is going and only too pleased to seize on something which may take it forward. Conceptualizing these aspects of the person's story as 'clues' helps me to avoid over-eager imputations of significance, and reminds me to check their meaning with the person before offering invitations to explore them.

When a person clearly identifies a 'clue' as *significant* to him, I then think of these significant story points no longer as clues, but as *unique outcomes*. 'Unique outcome' is a term borrowed by White from Erving Goffmann, who uses it for the thoughts and behaviours of institutional mental patients which are unique to themselves as individuals, as persons with unique histories and unique experience. Goffman suggests that these uniquenesses, and the outcomes in behaviour and thought they produce, are usually 'invisible' to the staff of the institutions, who tend to perceive patients through the distorted lens of stereotyped expectations about how mental patients think and behave (White, 1989: 49, quoting Goffman, 1961).

'Unique outcome' as a term

I have sometimes realized that colleagues taking an interest in narrative therapy find the term 'unique outcome' off-putting and puzzling. Writers about narrative therapy sometimes attempt to compensate for the rather abstract and jargon-like nature of the term by describing the process of selecting out contradictions to the dominant story in quite poetic and evocative language. Mary Sykes Wylie (1994) writes of 'panning for gold' and Ian Parker of finding unique outcomes 'sparkling in the undergrowth' (Parker, 1999: 3). White himself suggests that words or phrases other than 'unique outcome' might also be used:

> I do not have an investment in 'unique outcome' as a name for a contradiction of the sort to which I have referred, and thus I am not prepared to defend the term ... there are many other candidate descriptions, including 'distinction' that could be appropriate – and perhaps it would be better to refer to actual 'sites,' using descriptions like 'tension,' 'breach', 'disjunction', and so on. (Gilligan and Price, 1993: 131)

Despite this qualification, White has continued to refer to 'unique outcomes' in his writing and teaching, and my experience is that, like other specialist vocabulary in counselling, it soon loses its odd quality with familiarity.

Unique outcomes in historical context

White stresses the importance of unique outcomes becoming situated in the person's *overall* self-story:

> I'm vitally interested in history. I think that the opportunity to identify the real effects of certain ways of being on persons' lives and relationships is very important. To do this we need critical reflection, and for critical reflection we need history . . . it is largely through history that *unique outcomes* or *exceptions* render alternative stories . . . rarely is it difficult to achieve this storying of the unique outcome by a process of historicising. Even the fact that persons will judge these unique outcomes to be positive developments suggests that they must fit, in some way, with some prior conception that the person has of a better life. So, once articulated, it makes a lot of sense to show a sense of interest in the history of such conceptions, and the experiences of life that relate to this. Through this exploration, exceptions or unique outcomes become deeply rooted. (White, 1995a: 26, emphasis added)

This bringing out of significance for the person occurs through his gradually formulating and thus telling an unfamiliar and 'new' story in response to my questions about unique outcomes, and then, also in response to my questions, considering what this richer story means for him. Once elicited, once told and considered, the 'new' story may become woven into his overall self-story. By the sometimes lengthy and difficult process of his telling this alternative story, and others, in addition to his original problem story, I hope he will gain a new perspective. The overall self-story will be 'enriched'. It is not that the original narrative was 'wrong', to be abandoned, dismissed or rejected – it remains a valid expression of the person's experience – but it is *added to*. As these additional strands, these storylines, become more and more visible and held in mind through being told and re-told, examined and re-examined, they take on further meaning: they affect the person's view of himself and his situation, relationships and social context; they reveal new possibilities for thought, action and feeling.

Here are some condensed summaries of dominant stories, with 'clues' within them suggesting that the person might be able to 'author' *richer* stories. All are examples from my practice. In most of these simplified examples I have made the 'clue' fairly obvious;

in others it is less so. The reader may like to consider these examples as if they appeared in a detective story: what is the clue? What might be the nature of an unrecognized, as yet untold story indicated by this clue?

- A person's account of her childhood is bleak, as she is certain her parents did not love her, although in passing she mentions enjoying her tenth birthday party.
- A woman outlining her marital situation gives many examples demonstrating how lucky she is, with a husband who is a good provider and basically loving and caring – in fact, he hardly ever hits her.
- A woman expresses deep shame and regret about her son's homosexuality, and attributes his sexual preferences to her failure as a mother. She hates and distrusts the man with whom he has been living for many years and dismisses her son's assurances that this is a permanent, loving relationship.
- A person describes how he is affected by panic attacks, which are nearly always present when he goes to work, and often occur at weekends too.
- A person who has been unemployed for a year, with only one near-successful interview in that time, is affected by intense depression and anxiety.
- A woman who presents her life as dominated by her husband's aggressive and financially irresponsible ways of behaving briefly mentions that she occasionally 'escapes' by imagining a different life for herself.
- A person sexually abused over several years in childhood by her uncle blames herself for what she remembers as initially encouraging and enjoying his attentions, and also blames herself for not telling her parents what was happening once she found the abuse frightening and 'dirty'.
- A person unhappy in his third marriage attributes what he believes to be a permanent inability to form loving relationships to a cold and stern upbringing when, apart from occasional solitary visits to his grandparents, he never felt loved.
- A woman in her thirties diagnosed by her doctor as long-term agoraphobic, claustrophobic and subject to panic attacks describes how, despite gaining some help from group therapy many years ago, she has become reliant upon evasive ways of coping with her problems. She never faces up to her fears but instead organizes indirect solutions such as asking friends and

relatives to accompany her when she goes to work or the shops.

- A woman powerfully affected by the recent death of her partner after a long and painful illness occasionally feels a surge of impatience with her, as she finds she cannot 'move on in her life', despite this being her partner's express wish a week or so before she died.

- A teacher who has never sought promotion because she enjoys teaching and has never wanted to lose classroom contact for administration feels an increasing sense of failure as she sees her contemporaries appointed to senior positions.

- An accountant whose firm expects him to put in many hours' work a week over and above his contract has become so exhausted and stressed that he occasionally pretends illness and guiltily stays at home to work in his garden.

- A heterosexual couple whose relationship appears to them to have deteriorated beyond all hope of renewal experience a moment in the counselling room when their eyes meet and they grin at a humorous memory before plunging back into recriminations and accusations.

There is an infinite number of ways in which a 'clue' might emerge, and an infinite number of possible 'stories contrasting with the dominant story' which clues might suggest. One very important type of clue – often the easiest to identify – is the kind of swiftly passed-over aspect of the person's story which might indicate that he has demonstrated strengths, resourcefulness, tenacity, courage or other qualities which he himself is not acknowledging in the overwhelming tenor of his account. Sometimes this may be through modesty, or a wish to emphasize the seriousness of problems rather than understate them, and sometimes because he is feeling bad about himself and has not noticed or remembered these occasions. They have not had meaning for him, as they have become swamped by the dominant story. But *they are there,* and the evidence for their existence is in clues supplied by the very story which otherwise ignores them. I shall illustrate this process by elaborating one of the abbreviated stories above.

Diane's story

Diane had a long history of being affected by fear. She was afraid of large, open spaces, of small, enclosed spaces, of driving, and of going out alone.

She hated walking in the town or shopping in supermarkets. Occasionally she experienced panic attacks, especially in new social situations. For many years, she said, she had been coping with these problems in unsatisfactory and cowardly ways, by avoiding facing up to them, and finding ways round them.

At the age of four she had been trapped in a lift for several hours. She had vivid memories of this incident and of her terror. She attributed her life-long difficulties to that trauma – and she wondered whether being very protected by her parents, as the youngest of three children, had also contributed to her inability to face up to her fears. Her doctor always referred to her 'phobias' and she used the terms 'subject to panic attacks', 'agoraphobic' and 'claustrophobic', when describing herself, with familiarity and ease. Many years ago she had attended group therapy with persons facing similar problems and had found these sessions quite helpful – mainly in being encouraged to take small one-by-one practical steps towards overcoming her fears, with support and encouragement from the group. However, during this time her first marriage ended, and circumstances following the divorce prevented her from continuing in the group. Paradoxically, she had found her husband's dismissive and unsympathetic attitude towards her problems a stimulus to 'pushing through' them – she had been forced to 'get on with it' and had to an extent succeeded, although she had experienced great stress in doing so. When this marriage ended she began to develop what she described as habitual 'weak' behaviours around the problems, 'evasive' compromises or 'false solutions'. She organized other people, at first her friends and later her second husband or her daughter, to accompany her when she went out, and she took taxis when there was nobody to accompany her on public transport or as a passenger in her car. Recently, she had not been driving even with a passenger. By 'running away from the problem' she had managed to get out of the house for shopping and social events and to hold down a job in a supermarket close to her home. Now she had been offered a more interesting and better-paid job as a receptionist and general assistant in a dental practice some distance from her home, but this would involve a more difficult travel pattern, at times of the day when there would be nobody to accompany her – taking taxis to and from work every day would certainly be too expensive. To her dismay, she had been told at the interview that the job would include, from time to time, walking alone in the town to areas some distance from the dental surgery, to the bank and to various suppliers. She was, with much regret, thinking of refusing the job, but wondered without much hope whether counselling might offer some ideas on a way forward – but even walking alone to the counselling appointment had been frightening and she had arrived in a very nervous state.

Much of the first session was taken up by encouraging a full account of how the problems affected Diane's life. As she was at ease with psychiatric definitions of her problem, I also used these 'names' at first, in externalizing language such as 'agoraphobia's attempts to control your life' or 'claustrophobia's invasion of your leisure time'. Externalizing continued throughout the therapy, including some 'externalizing of internalizing discourses' when I discussed with her, and encouraged her to question, ways in which 'facing up to' issues rather than 'moving away from' issues is valued in Western society.

I kept alert for clues to possible alternative or contrasting self-story elements, which might be made explicit and mutually investigated if they turned out to be unique outcomes, i.e. resonant for her. Of course, I had the advantage of hearing Diane's account in full, but the reader might still find it interesting to look over the above summary to identify such 'clues' before continuing to read this account, perhaps jotting some notes before returning to the text. *The aim is to identify 'clues' which it might be possible to bring to Diane's attention for her consideration – clues which might indicate the possibility of a different story around the same events.* If the clues did turn out to be significant for her, Diane might be invited to expand her account of these occasions, and link them to similar story elements. The ultimate aim is for these re-tellings, building up in this and later sessions, to comprise a parallel story calling into question or modifying Diane's original, dominant story. The dominant story embodies events, feelings and beliefs which influence her belief that she is evasive, weak and compromising in her inability to address her problems directly. For years she has 'run away from' these problems, she says, and she can't see how she can possibly overcome them and do the new job she has been offered.

Here are the clues to unique outcomes which I noted and which led to a dialogue with Diane exploring whether they had resonance for her. These clues led me to hypothesize that her history might include significant examples of when she had outwitted or defeated agoraphobia and claustrophobia's attempts to dominate her life:

- She held a driving licence and owned a car – she must have decided to learn to drive, risked failure, faced her physical vulnerability as a learner driver, taken the test and passed it.
- She was not housebound, as until recently she could drive her car when accompanied.

- She had held down a job in a supermarket – and supermarkets frightened her.
- She did not have panic attacks in taxis despite the fact that they are confined spaces.
- She had sought help in the past from group therapy, which even people without these particular problems often feel nervous about.
- She accepted that the group therapy had been helpful, and remembered the ways in which she had started to use it successfully.
- When motivated she could make progress against the problems, even under stress.
- She had been able to think of, organize and maintain creative solutions to her problem situations and reactions which had allowed her to drive, to travel to work and in general to live a full life.
- She had applied for a more demanding job, attended the interview, performed well, been offered the job and accepted it.
- When (through the interview) she had become aware of aspects of the job which felt threatening to her, she had not refused the job but had given herself time to think things through and seek a solution.
- She had not tried to 'tough it out' alone but had recognized that therapy might help.
- She had come to counselling walking alone, despite her fear.

The conversation which I began to hold with Diane towards the end of the session, and which continued into the next, invited her to consider these clues. I asked what they might indicate about her history of resistance to attempts by agoraphobia, claustrophobia and panic to wreck her life through inducing fears. The clues did indicate unique outcomes; Diane swiftly recognized them as significant. In re-examining her life and in re-telling it, Diane began to change her story from one of ' weakness and evasion' to one of 'resistance and creative solution-finding'. The events described were sometimes the same as those included in the initial description, but their *meaning* began to change for her. Other events where she had opposed the results of her fears were recalled, and threaded into the sequence of the story. This was not a process of my 'positively reframing' or 'suggesting positives' or telling her she was strong and resourceful, and I certainly wished to avoid implying that there were no real problems still to face. The self-story discoveries were Diane's, encouraged by questions, not offered by myself as opinions. The new story gave solidity and conviction to Diane's work in carrying these past successes forward into the present and the future, in building on them, in enhancing and varying them as she undertook her self-generated task of seeing off agoraphobia, claustrophobia and panic. Calling on her knowledges from past experience of what had helped (gradual, step-by-step experiments, none taken further until the present stage felt comfortable), together with regular conversations in counselling when she examined her past and present successes in detail, she was, among other achievements, able to gain enough confidence to walk in the town alone, which led to her accepting her new job and succeeding in it.

As well as discussing the practicalities of her experiments with stage-by-stage challenging of her problems, Diane talked about the overall changes she was experiencing in the way she thought of herself, and the differences others might be seeing in her. Sometimes I would just 'let it run' but more often I encouraged the 'telling of the developing new story' by encouraging her to 'track' developments in her feelings and beliefs about herself in a sequence from past to present – and also to the possible future. I encouraged her to talk in *considerable detail* about the actions she was taking and the achievements they were producing. In these discussions I encouraged her to trace connections between 'landscapes of action' and 'landscapes of identity/consciousness' – what did her feelings tell her about the appropriateness of her actions, what did her actions tell her about herself?

By the time counselling ended, after ten further, quite widely spaced sessions, Diane had been admitted to hospital for a minor operation. She knew that when being taken on a trolley to the operating theatre she would be transported, helpless and drugged, *in a lift* – and she had avoided lifts for over 30 years. We discussed how she might cope with this situation and she developed a number of strategies. She decided not to prepare for the situation in advance by travelling in the lift, as she judged that the additional stress this produced would be counterproductive. By this decision she chose to depart from the 'stage-by-stage' policy which had led to many other achievements. She would make sure to wear her wedding ring in the lift as an 'object associated with safety' (cf. another context in Dolan, 1991: 92–4). She would write to the medical staff in advance of her admission to make clear her fears and she would reinforce this verbally once admitted. The hospital took her seriously, made sure she was given the maximum safe dosage of calming medication before going to the operating theatre, and ensured that a familiar nurse went with her, talking to her and holding her hand. She did not feel panic in the lift.

Following is an extract from a summarizing letter at the end of therapy. I wrote:

> [. . .] For many years, fears of closed spaces and of venturing from home had invaded your life and attempted to limit it. You were very skilled in overcoming these situations – but you were increasingly impatient about the influence of the fears and were feeling that you had had enough of what you saw as avoiding the problems rather than facing them. By the end of counselling, during which you concentrated on recognizing, learning from, building on and enhancing small successes, without feeling internal pressure to 'push' yourself, you had learned that you are not at the mercy of the fears but can face and challenge them. You developed the confidence (among other successes) to drive your husband to work (with your daughter in the car), to go shopping in the supermarket and the mall, regularly to walk into the town from your place of work, to walk through a local path which had formerly felt frightening, to go with your family for a day out in a completely strange town, to walk to the counselling service regularly for appointments, and in general to balance two things: a continuing strategy of avoiding stressful situations (without guilt), and recognizing when you were ready to take the next small step towards defeating the fears. As counselling ended you dealt with a difficult situation at the hospital, echoing the origins of your 'closed space' fears, and you are able to conceive that you will, at some time in the future, be able to take the major step of driving your car alone. [. . .]

What if the clues I had identified in Diane's account had not had resonance for her? Suppose that in answering my questions, Diane had not confirmed the clues' possible significance? There is always a danger of the therapist 'falling in love with his hypothesis' and attempting to impose it. I hope that I would have been able to recognize and respect Diane's lack of response, and I hope that I would then have abandoned the clues. I hope that I would have been able to continue to encourage her to tell her story and that I would have been able to identify other clues for her consideration, until one or more 'spoke to her' and were revealed as unique outcomes.

Using unique outcomes

When I first grasped the idea that persons often unknowingly incorporate clues to counter-plots alongside their predominantly negative dominant story, I went to town on this with a relish, in ways I now look back on with considerable embarrassment. White clearly suggests that this aspect of narrative therapy does *not* comprise 'pointing out positives' (1989: 38). Despite the very full expositions in his and Epston's writings of unique outcomes either emerging naturally from the story or being discovered by simple invitations to identify occasions when the problem was not present or had been overcome to some extent, it was an oversimplified idea that 'persons have unrecognized strengths' which took hold and became my own dominant 'therapy story'. I sometimes forgot or shortened the process of encouraging a complete problem description and, once the person had finished his account, either seized on any apparent evidence of strength, courage, resourcefulness or success or immediately asked for an example. I then congratulated him on this example, or asked what was becoming my standard question: 'What does that tell you about yourself?' I then usually destroyed any saving remnants of genuine curiosity or open-endedness by conveying the sort of answer I was hoping for, by my tone of voice or by a follow-up comment suggesting what the clue meant to *me*: 'That shows you are not completely dominated by depression, then!' I only began to be alert to the power position I was taking, the potentially toxic effect of this condescending and congratulatory behaviour, when, to my shame, one or two persons started later sessions by apologizing for 'not having anything positive to report this time'.

Rather more careful reading of White, Epston and other narrative therapists followed, but it still took me some time to grasp that, although 'clues to different strands in the story' *may* often indicate 'hidden strengths', 'underestimated capacities' and so on, that is not the point. The point is not that the clues should always indicate 'hidden strengths' or other 'positive' factors but that they may contradict or call in question the dominant story *in any way that is potentially helpful for the person*. The helpfulness may be painful rather than pleasant or initially heartening. Alan Jenkins, in describing work with men who have victimized their women partners or children with violence and abuse, asks at an appropriate stage questions such as 'Do you think that Jill has lost some trust and respect for you as a result of your abuse?' and 'Have you lost some respect for yourself also?' (Jenkins, 1990: 135). I imagine that answering in the affirmative, and *meaning it*, must be extremely painful for the man, but such an answer is nevertheless an in-session unique outcome. It contradicts what may up to then have been a dominant story of self-justification: 'I've got a short fuse'; 'I knew it was wrong but I couldn't help myself' (Jenkins, 1990: 19). If the remorse signals a recognition of the pain he has caused, together with a wish to make amends, it may be possible to discover other instances in the man's history when a similar recognition, or even a momentary doubt of his dominant story, may have occurred. Such unique outcomes might then be plotted into a parallel story of *potential* to empathize with victims, to escape from self-justification, to make amends. The emerging alternative story must not, of course, itself become a 'softening' dominant story justifying or excusing the abuse, but it may contribute towards the man's finally and genuinely choosing to break with his habits of violence and abuse, and contribute to his maintaining permanent change.

A unique outcome that was not a 'strength' in a direct and literal sense occurred in my conversation with a young woman who was holding her family together despite enormous social, financial and relationship difficulties. She said 'I *know* I'm strong – everybody keeps telling me that – but I just want someone to look after *me* for a change.' The unique outcome was her recognition that she had a legitimate wish to be cared for, which her husband was not recognizing, and we had a re-storying conversation where she traced other times when she had been able to stand back from taking sole responsibility for the family and find time for herself. This and similar conversations played a part in her decision to take a satis-fying job that she had been hesitating to apply for, and no longer to take everything on herself. She faced her husband with the responsibilities he was neglecting, and his habits of withdrawal were to an extent reversed.

Sometimes the person will only recognize that a clue has sig-nificance for them at a later stage of therapy, when other unique outcomes give it resonance; and sometimes I find that a little per-sistence is needed around a particularly powerful clue (powerful for me only, at this stage) to allow time for a person's mind-set to clear and a significance for her to emerge. The choices between leaving well alone, pursuing the clue for a while before abandon-ing it, and deciding that I am on the wrong track altogether, is often difficult, and I am sure I often misjudge. Clues, then, suggest that a different simultaneous story of some sort may be there to unfold because certain potentially significant 'plot elements' in the given story are understated, have been near-invisible or are contradictory to it. Once it is confirmed that the clue has a meaning for the person, that it is a unique outcome, this alternative parallel story may be made more visible through therapy, by being drawn forth and told.

Taking a position on the problem

Inviting a person to narrate a richer, more experience-near account of her life results in her developing a different relationship with the problem – being differently 'positioned' in relation to it. She has been encouraged to move from the problem-saturated account, where the problem was seen as dominating her life, and to begin to 'map [her] own influence in the "life" of the problem' (White, 1989: 8). Questions asked in sensitive response to her story, inviting her to join in negotiating a name for the problem and to explore her thoughts and feelings about it, have further objectified the problem and assisted her to position herself differently in relation to it. She begins to think of the problems differently, she begins to define her identity differently, and above all she begins to think of herself differently in relation to many previously unrecognized aspects of her history concerning these and similar issues. She has recognized that the problem has not in fact fully taken over her life in the past or the present and she can conceive that it is not going to dominate her life from now onwards.

White prefers to define where the person is at this stage of therapy as 'taking a position' rather than to use the concept of her recognizing she has been 'fighting' problems or 'battling with problems successfully' or 'defeating problems'. He has two misgivings about such descriptions (White, 1999).

In the first place these descriptions presuppose an attitude as a means of solution. 'Fighting back' is not always the answer. Persons may simply discover that the problem 'dissolves' on a richer telling, when limitations in the influence of the problem become clearer to her, and re-storying through responses to the therapist's questions has 'precipitated significant changes that are empowering' (White, 1989: 38; and see also Anderson, 1997: 91–2). There are also many situations where 'fighting back' language can oppress the person further when she is already oppressed by overwhelming difficulties, with her capacity to 'fight back' severely limited by the actuality of her circumstances.

In the second place, and more importantly, White identifies 'fighting back' language as an example of a modernist Western discourse which over-values individualistic reactive 'battling' as a means of addressing problems. Unthinking use of such discourse may reinforce the problems it appears to address, by ignoring the political, social and cultural components of the problems brought to therapy. It implies that, primarily and as a matter of course, the person should recognize then draw on and enhance her 'strengths' and 'inner resources' – themselves structuralist and essentialist concepts at odds with the post-structuralist assumptions of narrative therapy (see Chapter 9 of this volume).

Therapy's assisting persons to 'take a position on the problem' is a particularly helpful concept to bear in mind when working with persons who have been 'positioned' by others, including self-defined 'experts'. Narrative therapy assists persons to step out of such impositions and to take up chosen positions of their own.

> What happens to people who are pushed to the edges of what is considered normal, or to the ends of a psychiatric dimension, is that they are *positioned*, a place is set out for them and a set of behaviours and experiences is defined for them . . . what the cultural representations of women and mental disorder [for example] may point to is not so much the function of internalized stereotypes but the existence of different historically constructed discourses which carry with them certain positions for individuals to adopt and play out. (Parker et al., 1995: 39, 41, emphasis in original)

Identifying unique outcomes in working with a couple

In working with couples I try to remain alert, during their initial description of problems, to clues which might suggest that their dominant story as a couple, or their individual dominant stories, reveal elements of contradiction, possible points which might be threaded into an alternative story. As in working with individuals, my assumption is that the initial story is only one of many possible stories which might be told out of the multiple experiences of the persons, and that this dominant story is (a) the one which the couple have increasingly selected out as most present for them at this time, and (b) the one which in its turn has become most powerful in self-reinforcement. In working with two persons, there is usually the complication that each person has a different dominant story, and that the clash between these dominant stories exacerbates the problem. A's story will usually include the belief 'It's B's fault' and B's story will usually include the belief 'It's A's fault', leading A to the conclusion 'We'd be OK if B would change!' and B to the conclusion 'We'd be OK if A would change!' To add to this, since both A and B see the other partner as not grasping the 'obvious' fact of being to blame and needing to change, the partner is seen as wilfully stubborn. Many couples' attempts to overcome their problems consist of increasingly heated attempts by each to assert their point of view, and ever greater exasperation that instead of accepting blame and putting their behaviour right, the partner refuses to hear 'the truth' and goes on accusing the 'innocent' party. So as well as hypothesizing unique outcomes which might modify the couples' *agreed* problem-story, I have the task of locating clues in each indi-vidual's separate account which might lead to different and more hopeful re-tellings of their individual stories – more hopeful in that their re-told story may contribute to a new understanding of the other's perspective, and a withdrawal from a self-righteous point of view.

One way through which I attempt to encourage the withdrawal of 'self-righteousness-saturated' stories is to negotiate appropriate, agreed, externalized definitions of the couple's problems. The couple then has a chance to cooperate in fighting a 'mutual enemy', such as 'suspicion' or 'mistrustfulness' or 'wedges between us' or 'habits of not being frank' or 'defensiveness', and to escape the habit of locating the problem 'in' their partner, or attributing their conflict to the other partner's behaviour and 'blindness'. I only encourage this 'mutual enemy' metaphor when there is no history of violence, abuse or one-sided selfishness. I do not believe that stress between partners is always caused equally, or that abusive behaviour by one partner is appropriately seen as part of a recip-rocal and neutral process.

When holding conversations with couples I attempt four things, not always equally or in the same session:

1   To encourage a full description of that person's own experience of the situation as it stands, and of how he/she sees it affecting their lives.
2   To encourage the person to discuss his/her perception of how his/her partner might be experiencing the situation or, if his/her partner has already spoken, to discuss whether what

he/she heard the partner say matched his/her previous conception of his/her experience.

3   To encourage each person in turn to identify aspects of their
    account and/or of their partner's account which they find
    surprising or which helped them to see things in a different
    way. (Sometimes these different perspectives are given spon-
    taneously; at other times they result from my questioning.)

4   To encourage the couple to embed these new perceptions or
    memories in a 'historical' or 'autobiographical' context, linking
    with past, present and possible future themes of the relation-
    ship which contrast with, and can be set against, the dominant
    story or stories.

The following extracts are from the second joint session held with
Rose and Richard, the married couple introduced in Chapter 3. My
account left them at the point where Richard remembered occasions
in the past when he had felt anger at his mother's attitudes. This
unique outcome, contradicting Richard's dominant story that Rose
was being unfair to his mother, had been a turning point in his
beginning to re-story his version of his mother's behaviour.
However, the groundwork for that turning point had been laid in
preceding sessions, where the couple's individual dominant stories
about their relationship were on the point of change – the dominant
stories asserting themselves as 'habit' but a modified parallel story
beginning to emerge as unique outcomes came into focus.

Adapting a technique developed by Jim Sheehan (1997), I
encouraged each person in turn to hold quite a lengthy conversation with me (about 20 minutes) while the other sat out of vision,
listening without interrupting, taking written notes if they wished.
After the second person had taken his/her turn to speak the other
partner was given a few minutes to comment, so as not to be left
feeling 'pent up' and un-heard. However, no discussion between
the pair or between the pair and myself took place in the session. It
consisted entirely of one-to-one interviews, with the other partner
listening. So, instead of addressing issues with each other, with
myself as mediator, each person *told their story* then *listened to the
other's story* – and in doing so, listening attentively without having
to gather their thoughts for a reply, each person discovered how the
other's story was *changing* as unique outcomes were identified and
explored for meaning. The couple took the tape to hear at home,
either individually or together. The individual changing stories
were thus re-heard, and the effects of fading memory and its

selectivity overcome. I gave no suggestions as to what the couple might do then – I left this up to them.

I do not offer the extracts as an error-free or perfect example of narrative therapy – they do not neatly form a demonstration text. Nevertheless, the reader may like to consider the extracts in the light of the four aims stated above. I have tidied up some of the more hesitant, awkwardly expressed and repetitive parts of the conversation. Richard was interviewed first, with Rose listening.

1 *Richard:* We haven't actually seen my mother since the last session with you.

2 *Martin:* That must have been about five weeks ago.

3 *Richard:* Yes – that was my birthday.

4 *Martin:* So it's a long time since, five weeks ago. What about any changes in you – not necessarily huge changes but new thoughts, new perceptions, new ideas, new insights into this whole triangle of events of you, your mother and Rose and the stresses that sets off?

5 *Richard:* No, I don't think there really has, I still play by the old rules. If I think it's easier, I'll go round [to my mother's house] by myself. Obviously nothing major must have happened when we [both] went round last time but I really can't remember that occasion.

6 *Martin:* So things have sort of been held, you've either not seen your mother or you've hardly seen her. So at least we can say things haven't deteriorated. How would you define the problem at the moment, if this was our first session . . .? Can you just redefine the problems again?

7 *Richard:* The problem initially was partly due to the way my mother, myself and Rose don't get on as a nice happy bunch, and more, the way I react from that – from the anger and the actual 'throwing things about' side of me. I didn't like it, and I wanted it out of the way. I think to some extent I could manage the bit that all three of us don't get on, as long as it was something that didn't raise arguments all the time. Almost as I've said before, I like to sweep things under the covers and say 'All right, it happened, now let's forget about it and start afresh.' If I could just have some way where I could just get on with life and not get angry with Rose and things, it would be a lot better. I don't think anger has gone away a lot – I may raise my voice, but it's no way as bad as it's been, there's no storming off or throwing things about or anything, so I think that's improved that side. But I'm not sure if that's because we possibly tend to pussyfoot around the problem or if we are getting better with it.

8 *Martin:* It may be that you have made a step forward in that you are holding back on the severe anger and got that under more control, and that's creating a better atmosphere at home, and that's a real step forward? But I really respect what you say, when you say it feels incomplete. If I've got it right, it isn't quite so much the fact that there is tension between the three of you but your reaction to that tension, which again feeds into it . . . if you could take the element of your tension out, it wouldn't solve the problems but it wouldn't make them worse, and you would be able to accept that reasonably OK?

9 *Richard:* I think that my major concern is upsetting Rose. If the three of us don't get on that's not the end of the world. When we were younger Rose would have friends that she got on with and I suppose to some extent I would feel jealous about how good that friendship was, so I would have a dislike towards those friends – and so I can understand that you just can't have everybody all happy and seeing each other all the time, but there should be something in between which me and Rose could cope with that.

10 *Martin:* Interesting about that word 'jealousy'. I've been struggling a bit to try and define what the problem is. There is a complicated problem, so it may not be possible to use just one word for it, but if in the past you have been affected by jealousy when thinking about Rose, in the way you have described, about friendships, and your mother is affected by jealousy in her relations with Rose, then there may be something about jealousy at the centre of this. Is this right?

11 *Richard:* I don't know. I guess from what we have said before – I guess it could be that my mother is jealous of Rose, basically me spending all of my time with Rose and some of my time with my mother now. But the reaction – as Rose says – that she feels my mother says things that are almost nasty towards her that I just can't see – that side of it, I don't think I have ever done in retaliation with Rose's friends. I've never given that side of it, I don't feel – plus I've never really seen it, which is probably the main problem here. Rose will see something that I don't manage to see, and probably if I did see it then it would be a lot better, because I do feel I am 'on the line' a lot of the time. Rose will say, 'Your mother is really getting on my nerves because of so and so.' *I* never saw that – whereas if I saw that, I could say she was right – 'My mother shouldn't have said that.' Or hopefully I would have got to the stage eventually where I could actually say something when we were there, which I'm sure would have made Rose a lot happier – that I'm showing I'm standing up for her and not just sitting on the fence all the time.

12 *Martin:* So it sounds as if for you there is a mystery here. There is a puzzle, because either Rose is wrong and your Mum isn't being nasty, and she is over-reacting or imagining it and therefore that is the problem; or your Mum *is* saying these things and you are not aware of them. And you don't know which the problem is.

13 *Richard:* I think there was a time earlier in our relationship where I just thought Rose was being stupid, or 'Why should Mum ever want to be nasty to you?' In some ways I could see it is, as well – 'She is being nasty to you – she is hurting [you] – because what's the point of [Rose's] up-setting me?' whereas now I think I understand there *must* be something more there, because it's not something you would make a mistake over time and time again, that 'Your Mum's been upsetting me' – it would be something you would get to understand – 'That was just her approach', or whatever it was, that 'She just talks nastily to people and you just had to accept it', or 'That is the way she always is.'

14 *Martin:* So what you are saying is that on balance you are inclined to think that Rose is seeing something there even if she might exaggerate it or sometimes imagine it – but it is there. That you are not able to see it.

15 *Richard:* That's right.

The interview continues with Richard explaining in more detail how his being torn between loyalties to his mother and to his wife makes him feel he can't win with either of them, and how the situation has resulted in Rose and himself becoming hypersensitive to sometimes innocent remarks from the other. I attempt to invite him to focus on behaviours which he would like to be in place in his and Rose's relating to a hypothetical daughter-in-law, implicitly inviting him to contrast these with the behaviour of his mother towards Rose. If in the future he and Rose had a daughter-in-law, he would just like them all to get on well together, he says. My question is not carefully worded enough to help him to be specific in his reply, and he simply re-states his generalized wish that everything in families could be 'Everybody getting on – I don't like to see rifts between people.' The transcript shows that Richard then tactfully cuts through a rather bumbling attempt on my part to get the conversation back on track, with a clear statement moving the discussion into a recent and very significant development in the couple's relationship:

16 *Richard:* I think in the last few weeks I've definitely seen almost more 'glow' between myself and Rose. We seem happier there, especially recently where there has been a bit of a work issue, where my work seems to think that I should work 24 hours whereas Rose thinks I should work nine to five – and again, with my attitude that I want to keep both sides happy, which is totally impossible. I decided to side with Rose, which I think was the right decision, because at the end of the day I have to have two sides, I've got to have a work side which I do to bring in the money and to keep the family side of us going, but at the same time I need some life away from work so that we can spend some time together and be happy. And I think that side has improved a lot, we used to have a lot of time where I would see very little of Rose because of whatever else was going on, and I feel we are now a lot happier [now] we spend a lot more time together.

17 *Martin:* If we had a whole afternoon for this session I would really want to go into more detail with you about that. I would be really interested to tease out in considerable detail what those differences are and how you find them – what has been changing, what processes have been going on in you that produced the change. When you hear this tape you might like to give yourself a chance to think about 'what is happening within me, what is happening within the relationship, what are the shifts that are occurring that produce change?' There are two changes here – you are less likely to 'flip', although it's early days yet, and you have made decisions about time together and putting work a bit more in the background. All right, thank you . . .

Richard and Rose change seats, and it Rose's turn to have a conversation with me while Richard listens and takes notes.

18 *Martin:* If you were a friend listening to that, if you were not involved, what do you think might have struck you about that? What was the most striking thing that came over, in your perception?

19 *Rose:* That Richard is desperately trying to make an effort to calm down and that he appreciated that nothing will be resolved by just flipping and walking away, because it makes the situation more difficult to come back to. And I think that's one of the most important things because if you can stop that happening and then not necessarily talk about it then, but talk about it at some point, that's got to be the way forward to actually try and resolve anything.

20 *Martin:* Did you mean that he was desperate, that he was so anxious he was almost falling apart, or did you simply mean that as an emphasis – that he was really trying hard?

21 *Rose:* Yes, he was really trying, he was making a conscious effort not to, and I think he has realized how important it is.

22 *Martin:* Have you had experience of that in the past with Richard in any other situation? Has he faced situations at work, for example, or with friends, or in his life in other ways, where he has made a real and concerted effort to overcome problems?

23 *Rose:* I think every day at work, he comes home, or he used to come home a lot and be really fed up, he is basically too nice a person and people take advantage of his good nature and I think just recently especially he has turned around and said 'No – this is too much to do.' That's the whole work issue. I think that's why he's realized he'll end up having a nervous breakdown or something if the work pressure continues, so that's why he's suddenly decided 'No, this can't go on, it's got to stop', and he has stood up and said, 'No, I'll leave it, work isn't the be all and end all.'

24 *Martin:* So compared with some people Richard goes rather longer before he thinks 'OK, this is far enough' – but when he does come to that point then he reacts, and part of how he reacts is maybe to move away from the problem? . . . in this complex and difficult emotional tangle you've come to talk about, that's a much more complex situation and perhaps even more painful than being treated badly at work, but the fact that he is able to stand up and make changes and say, 'No more!' may be helpful to you in this respect as well? I was also quite moved by what Richard said. It's hard to say 'no' and if you are as Richard is, a very sensitive person, then you are inclined to give people the benefit of the doubt. That's a nice characteristic.

25 *Rose:* Yes – that's one of the things that attracted me to him.

26 *Martin:* Is there anything else in your notes or that you have thought about or that you really want to share with me about what you heard, or what . . .

27 *Rose:* I'm just trying to think . . . I think it's on BBC2 at the moment, is actually televised counselling sessions between couples and I saw one the other week, and an idea that they have there that I thought we might try is silly, but it seemed to work for them so we might as well give it a go. The counsellor gave them a stone to take home with them and said that whenever you want to talk one of you has to hold the stone and whoever has the stone can talk for as long as they are holding the stone

and the other person can't interrupt and then you pass the stone and the other person can't interrupt and then you pass it over. I thought that would be a physical sign. So I thought I would go and pick something off our drive and try that because it's then something physical rather than thinking 'Ah – but no – I can't.' That would be a suggestion.

28 *Martin:* I'm really impressed by that. It sounds a very good idea, but I'm also impressed by the fact that you took it on board and brought it to this session as something which might help you both. What I've discovered in this job is that it's what people discover for themselves and do for themselves that's most effective, and I should have learned it by now, but it still surprises me that people do discover what brings about changes. They notice things they wouldn't have done before – for example this happens to be noticing a technique for giving yourselves space to talk . . . Richard may want to talk about it with you. I'm really interested in that idea – I might use it with my next couple this afternoon.

After more discussion with Rose about ways in which each might give the other space to talk, and Rose's describing how listening to the recording of the last session has been helpful in preparing for this, I invite Richard to join us for the last few minutes of the session.

29 *Richard:* I feel that Rose understands me a lot more than I ever thought before. I'd always felt that there was almost this brick wall between us, we were always trying to shout over it, and the person on the other side couldn't really understand what was going on, whereas what Rose was saying seems to have opened up a lot more, when she says things I can understand that are true – that is what I felt – she has it correctly. I think there was a stage when I wasn't entirely sure, the counselling seemed a good idea but I wasn't entirely sure whether Rose wanted to get involved in it. It was, 'Well, I can't do that, I haven't enough holiday – you'll have to go by yourself.' I felt I was trying to make an effort but I felt it was a one-person thing – what's the point, when it's supposed to be for both of us? – and obviously from Rose's attendance that's disproved that. The thing with the stone where she said she saw that on the telly and thought 'We could use that' makes it seem like it is a two-person thing rather than me just battling to try to get rid of my problem. It's *our* problem and *we* are going to look at it and try to resolve it.

30 *Martin:* Can you pinpoint another example of how you now see Rose understanding you more?

31 *Richard:* I think if we take the situation of last Thursday night. Basically, one week in four I have to be available to the Company for 24 hours, and they obviously pay me for that, but this Thursday it was my week off. I had a bad week last week so it was quite nice to have a few nights just sitting round watching telly and spending time with Rose. The phone rang twice and I dealt with it because it was somebody who didn't know what to do. The third time it rang, Rose answered it and basically said 'No, I'm sorry, he isn't here' – even though I obviously was – and I think there was a side of me that wanted just to get on and deal with the

problem, because I knew there would be problems later with it, whereas there was the other side of me that thought 'Why should I? – I should be spending time with Rose.' Previously, I think there would have been a stage where Rose would think I shouldn't do it, and I would think I should do it. It helped a lot that Rose said – this was a couple of hours later, about eleven o'clock – 'Well, it's up to you. You can go and do the work if you want, or obviously you can choose not to. I personally don't think you should, because you're tired and you can really do without all this, but if you want to, then do it.' I think that was one of the first times we had actually had that. I feel there is a lot of 'I want' in the relationship and there is 'Rose wants' in the relationship, and trying to get that overlap nicely is usually very difficult. Whereas I think because Rose made that effort to say, 'If you want to, do it', I had actually sat there and thought about it, and decided 'I don't really want to do it. Why should I do it?' As opposed to – 'Well, you are telling me I shouldn't do it, therefore I *will* do it' – which I suppose is almost the stubborn side of me, which would always object. Whereas because she had come to try and meet me somewhere in the middle where we could both be happy, it felt 'Well, right – you are entirely right – I shouldn't be doing this.'

32 *Martin:* My impression from you is that even if you had then decided that you *would* do it, the point isn't whether you did it or not – the point is the difference in the way you negotiated it, whatever the final decision.

33 *Richard:* In the past I would know that if I'd made the decision to do the work, then basically we wouldn't talk for a while, but then I would have said 'I don't see why she should make the decisions for me.' Whereas on this occasion I did feel that I could do the work and she would almost respect that I had made that decision, because there was obviously a reason why I had done it, and hopefully the situation wouldn't have been as bad as previously, because we would both have come to an understanding that it was what needed to be done. I think, in a similar way – yesterday was a very bad day. Because they hadn't been able to contact me, all the problems were left until yesterday. But I haven't blamed Rose for the horrible day I had, because I understood that it was a decision we had both made, rather than a decision I had made on my own – or that she had made on her own. Which I think is a lot better.

34 *Martin:* There is a great sense of growing mutuality here that I'm picking up. These things might to an outsider sound like very small things, but it's what they *mean*, that's the difference, isn't it?

Narrative therapy elements

In these extracts, my background in person-centred therapy and my interest in solution-focused therapy reveal themselves. But White is insistent that there is more than one way to conduct narrative therapy. What is happening in my session with Richard and Rose that might be identified as narrative therapy? In the following comments, I identify these elements by italic type. They include some practices outlined in later chapters.

At 4, I invite Richard to identify any perceived changes since the previous session, *seeking clues to unique outcomes* on the issue of his attitude to Rose's perceptions of his mother's behaviour. This is clumsy, a too-direct approach at this stage of the session: he is not prepared for it and at once reverts to the *dominant story*, in 5. I fail to recognize a *clue* – they have visited his mother and 'nothing major must have happened'. To prevent the dominant story's reinforcement I offer a positive re-frame – 'at least things have not got worse' – but do not pursue this. Instead *I simply invite him to re-tell his story*, from a perspective of the present. He does so at 7, and *his narrative reveals two unique outcomes: two changes of perception which contradict the previous dominant story*. First, he no longer identifies the main issue as the 'three-way conflict'. He could live with that, if only it did not lead to arguments with Rose. Secondly, he has noticed that his anger is more under control. He uses *externalizing language*: 'I don't think anger has gone away a lot.' At 9 he states the first discovery even more firmly: 'my major concern is upsetting Rose.' Without any questioning on my part *he identifies a unique outcome from the past*: the slight jealousy he once felt towards Rose's friends, which he recalls now as something helping him to be reconciled with aspects of the present. Past experience (newly recalled) indicates both 'I can be subject to jealousy' and 'It's natural for people sometimes to find they don't get on with each other.' These perceptions contradict the dominant story of its being Rose's fault that the three persons don't all get on together happily as they should: 'I can understand that you just can't have everybody all happy and seeing each other all the time.'

At 10 I follow up the theme of 'jealousy' and tentatively suggest this as *an externalized naming of the problem*. Richard then considers the idea of jealousy's part in the conflict and this appears to throw light for him on the processes underlying the issues. He agrees that it does apply; he used to feel jealousy towards Rose's friends – perhaps his mother feels jealous of Rose? – he can see how jealousy might be at work. *'Naming' has focused his thinking*. This opens the way for him even more firmly to recognize that Rose may not be imagining things – that the problem may lie in his own mistakenly optimistic view of this mother's behaviour. If he could share Rose's perceptions, the stress between them might be alleviated. In 13 he states this even more firmly: 'I just thought Rose was being stupid . . . whereas now I think I understand there must be something more there, because it's not . . . a mistake you would make over time and time again.' He confirms this in 15 in response to my checking out.

My attempt to introduce a *hypothetical future unique outcome* (how he hopes Rose would behave towards a future daughter-in-law) is premature: it was not carefully enough worded and it puzzles Richard, who reverts to the dominant story of wanting everyone to be happy together. However, he immediately goes on to describe the new and more 'glowing' atmosphere between the couple since they have spent more time together following his decision to spend less time working (16). *The dominant story of conflict is becoming replaced by a richer story*: the sources of conflict have not been eliminated, but new meanings are emerging concerning the couple's capacity to rediscover pleasure in their relationship. As it is now time for Rose to be interviewed I do not follow this up but suggest (17) that listening to the tape (and so hearing *tellings and re-tellings*) might help him to embed these differences more firmly in his awareness.

I ask Rose, now it is her turn to be 'interviewed', to try to be objective in saying what most struck her about Richard's 'inter-view' (18). She is, of course, personally involved in the issues Richard has talked about, but by inviting her to try to stand back a moment, to consider Richard's conversation with me as a 'friend' rather than as a 'wife', I am attempting momentarily to place her in an *outsider witness* role in relation to Richard (see Chapter 7). I had prepared her for this in introductory remarks to the session not included in the above quotations. At 22 I revert to addressing her in her role as wife and ask a question designed to elicit *unique outcomes from the past* – not in this case concerning Rose's own thoughts or behaviours, but concerning her perception of Richard's thoughts or behaviours. As Richard listens to her reply he is discovering Rose's perceptions of unique outcomes in his life, which are also 'signposts towards hope' for her – *unique outcomes which they might both integrate into a more hopeful story of their relationship.* Her identification of Richard's changed attitude towards his work is not quite along the lines of my question – this is a recent change, not a unique outcome from the past. But, of course, Rose is responding to my question in a way which carries meaning for her, so I do not try to pursue the 'past unique outcome' idea but instead follow her line of thought, checking this out with a summary at 24. Here I also tentatively offer a per-spective which opens up challenge to the *culturally influenced assumption* which identifies 'escaping' from situations (rather than immediately standing up to them) as weak or cowardly, and I pay tribute to Richard's pleasure at his decision to withdraw from excessive work in order to spend more time with Rose. At 27, in response to my open invitation to share her reactions to the session, Rose follows up Richard's wondering about how they might improve their discussions at home, and suggests a counselling technique she saw on television. My response to this, at 28, includes a brief sharing of what I often find happens in therapy: I am attempting a degree of *transparency* here, demystifying counselling, and also *decentring* my counsellor role.

Richard, in the closing moments of the session, confirms that Rose's noticing a way that they might improve their discussions at home, and indeed her attending the sessions with him, has enhanced his sense of their having a *mutual* problem which she is joining with him to overcome (29). He is *externalizing* the problem. I ask him for further examples of Rose's increased understanding of him, and this leads to a marvellous sequence (31 and 33). Richard gives a long, detailed, 'fully-thought-out-as-he-talks' description of an important event for himself and Rose, not only describing what happened but fully 'discovering' its significance for him through the very process of formulating his account – through *narrating*, *'storying'*. The transcript only partly conveys the slow, exploratory, thoughtful, slightly inarticulate and yet increasingly firm manner of Richard's narration. This focused, extended account of 'discovered' experience – discovered through being articulated in the session – is an example of *deconstructing a unique outcome*. Usually, a unique outcome is explored through the therapist's questions: I 'pull it down as it moves across the screen' (White, 1997a) and invite its detailed scrutiny and evaluation by the person. In this session at this point, responding to a generalized question, *the person himself deconstructs the unique outcome*. As well as addressing me, Richard is, of course, aware of Rose listening, and his narrative is also (perhaps principally?) addressed to her. His narrative is a tribute to the changes occurring in the relationship – a 'witnessing'. In itself it then becomes a potential factor for the relationship's further development – it has been told, Rose has heard it, the couple will hear it again when they listen to the tape, they may talk in the next session about their experience of listening to it again on the tape; and these 're-tellings' may weave it more firmly into the texture of memories and awarenesses which comprise their knowledge of each other. It contrasts movingly with Richard's earlier statement that nothing much has changed in the couple's capacity to resolve the 'triangle' situation (5). Richard has moved his narrative away from that source of conflict to an affirmation of 'discovered-as-he-talks' positive change between the couple. In so doing, his narrative appears to reflect a growing awareness that, for him, the central issue is Rose's happiness. It confirms, expands and concretizes that 'The problem *initially* was partly due to the way my mother, myself and Rose don't get on as a nice happy bunch' (7) (my emphasis), and that Richard has come to realize that his 'major concern is upsetting Rose' (9). Changes have been clarified and redefined; Richard is 'choosing' Rose, 'choosing' his marriage.

I am sure that therapists working in different modes and with different assumptions from those of narrative therapy also experience similar moments when persons discover and create their own priorities and preferences through talking, and the meaning of their experience comes sharply into focus, often surprising them. I certainly experienced this when working with person-centred approaches, and also in solution-focused counselling. In narrative work, I have found that such moments often emerge very swiftly (this was only the third session of joint work and the fifth session overall) and that they appear swiftly to become firmly rooted.

The persons' storying, narrating, is not, of course, random. Once the initial story is told, once it falters into silence, I do not remain silent – I do not conceive myself as an observer of processes leading to decision and change. I have a part to play, in judging the appropriateness of narrative therapy procedures at various points and in maintaining the assumption framework of the session. Encouraging a full description of the problem; negotiating naming of the problem; eliciting clues to unique outcomes; encouraging the detailed description of unique outcomes; eliciting the meaning of unique outcomes for the person; encouraging the person to weave unique outcomes into a richer narrative tapestry; and other aspects not yet described in this book – in all these I am *active*. If they had not come to therapy, Richard and Rose might have found answers to their problems and re-vitalized their relationship – of course they might – and if they had not achieved this alone, therapists working in other ways might well have been of assistance to them – of course they might. But Richard and Rose certainly felt, for example, that the organized structure of the sessions, intended to promote maximum telling and listening rather than to encourage in-session discussion and negotiation, was successful:

35 *Martin:* . . . what I'd like to talk about is . . . how you found this session . . . I don't want to do it [this way] unless you find it comfortable or find it useful . . .

36 *Richard:* I think [in the first joint session] all we were doing was having our discussions with you here to almost be the referee. Whereas this feels more beneficial. As I said earlier, on the tape, we listened to the tape and I thought 'Yes – well – we can discuss things while we are in this room but as soon as we go away from it I'm not so sure about the discussions we had.' Whereas this, I feel, has shown me that we are starting to think about how we can progress – rather than purely having discussions, and trying to get rid of today's problems, then coming back and there is another week's worth of problems . . . We can go home at night and sit there and discuss any qualms that we have got. Although obviously I realize that this is a process we have to move towards – we are not going to suddenly just walk out of here today and it's all going to be wonderful.

37 *Martin:* So are you saying . . . that it's moving to a point of resolving the problems out of the counselling room and into the home where it belongs? That it hasn't happened yet . . . but there is a sense of being free to gradually find your own way through it? I don't want to put words into your mouth, so if I've got it wrong, then say so!

38 *Richard:* No, that's right. . . [In the past] I would never come out of that little box to say, 'Help – I need some assistance' . . . I've always felt that there is *us*, and it's all private what our problems are, we need to sort them out for ourselves. We shouldn't need to get anyone else involved. And in some ways I feel it's probably more comfortable if I can move back into that situation . . . now I am hoping we can always go back into our little box and discuss things and resolve them ourselves, which would be much nicer. And also it means we can resolve the problem as it occurs, rather than in this situation.

39 *Martin:* What about for you, Rose?

40 *Rose:* I think it's been very helpful because naturally I've got responses – if Richard says something I'll scribble down bits and think, 'Oh yes – I'd like to say that about it' – but actually to step back from my responses and think, no matter what they are . . . it concentrates . . . I have to listen, because it's easy to listen with half an ear and then think, 'Well, no, I didn't think of it like this, I thought x, y and z', and just concentrate on almost the negative side of it, and say, 'He's got a poor memory – it didn't happen like this.' But [in these sessions] you have to *not* do that so much – [you] just listen to what he said, and think. I mean, it's such a huge improvement for Richard to say absolutely anything, and that's what we said when we listened to the tape . . . he was, as he said, an awfully lot more open, listening to the tape . . .

Summary

The 'story' metaphor in narrative therapy draws an analogy between (a) the inevitably selective and partial nature of accounts of fictional or non-fictional experience, and (b) the selective memory of their own lives which persons bring to therapy. As in fiction, elements of this self-story include actions, and feelings and thoughts, and the relationship between these elements – all occurring in a perceived sequence or plot which is experienced as problematic by the persons. Initial tellings by the person reflect many tellings to self and others before therapy began, and are influenced by unexamined cultural and 'political' assumptions. They embody 'dominant stories' where certain aspects and themes have come to represent the person's experience. These dominant stories have become a powerful factor in reinforcing and embedding persons' views of themselves, of their dilemmas and conflicts, and of their own identities and capacities to overcome problems. The therapist keeps alert to elements in the person's account offering clues to aspects of the person's experience which do not fit or match the dominant story. These elements are brought into focus by questions and discussion, to discover whether they comprise 'unique outcomes'. Unique outcomes are contradictions in the dominant story which the persons themselves come to recognize as significant and meaningful once they are located and explored. The therapist encourages persons to thread these unique outcomes into a new, parallel story, and this process ultimately changes the dominant story by being integrated with it into a more complete description of life. The process of telling and re-telling in response to the therapist's questions, and also in contexts outside therapy, frees persons to re-position themselves in relation to their problems and to identify and take up preferred ways of living and relating.

5 Asking Questions

Questioning: intrusive or creative?

In a sample of books bought when I was studying for my diploma in counselling there is a general unease about asking questions – even hostility. Brammer (1973: 55) suggests that asking questions in the first session is 'a tactical error' as 'Helpees often feel interrogated, and, as a result, threatened.' He concedes that open-ended questions may be helpful, and gives examples, but unease predominates: 'As a general rule, questions should be used purposefully and *sparingly*, otherwise they tend to become substitutes for making statements' (1973: 75–6, emphasis added). Benjamin (1974) devotes a whole chapter to questioning, but he warns against possible evils rather than discussing any positive aspects: 'my greatest objection to the use of questions [is that] . . . If we begin the helping interview by asking questions and getting answers, asking more questions and getting more answers, we are setting up a pattern . . . [the interviewee] will see himself as an object, an object who answers when asked and otherwise keeps his mouth closed' (Benjamin, 1974: 72). Nelson-Jones (1983) confirms that 'Questions tend to receive much criticism in the counselling literature', and devotes several emphatic pages to warnings against their misuse, although he does suggest that it is legitimate to ask questions which obtain specific information, invite elaboration, focus on feelings and 'help the client to focus on alternative ways of viewing themselves, others and situations in their lives' (1983: 74–8). Hobson (1985: 166) simply assumes that questions imply interrogation: 'I do not ask a question. In a conversation I am not an interrogator. I make a statement.'

> Questions which imply interrogation can inhibit mutual exploration. Statements, if approximately made, are less likely to put the client on the spot, are more open to correction, and provide a starting point from which diverging themes can be developed . . . By repeating crude questions, especially as a means of probing into a particular theory, a therapist can be experienced as if he were a prosecuting counsel . . . To a beginner I say: 'Make tentative statements, hoping that you will be corrected. (Hobson, 1985: 196–7, 200–1)

Since most of narrative therapy consists of conversations carried forward by therapist questions, counsellors working in traditions which see questioning as suspect may be rather dismissive of this technique, and wonder whether White and Epston are alone in using it extensively. But in family therapy, the context from which narrative therapy developed, questions are central. Far from being suspect, they are conceived as a means of demonstrating a committed interest in a person's situation, a wish to know the issues she faces, a manifestation of 'curiosity' in the best sense. An example is 'circular questioning', developed by a group of therapists working in Milan in the 1970s (Palazzoli et al., 1980), which assists therapists and family members to recognize, discover, explore and widen their perceptions of ways in which other family members perceive their situation:

> family members are asked, in turn, to comment on the thoughts, behaviour, and dyadic relationships of the other members of the family. For example, the therapist might say to the father, 'Since your mother-in-law came to live with your family has the relationship between your son and his mother been better or worse?' . . . The range of questions is inexhaustible . . . The novelty of this mode of enquiry seems to make people stop and think rather than give stereotypical answers. It is common to observe the quizzical and eager anticipation of family members as they wait to hear how another person perceives their relationship. (Burnham, 1986: 110)

Circular questioning can promote empathy – not primarily the empathy of the therapist in relation to the person, but empathy between family members:

> Rogers, working mainly with individuals, was most interested in the communication to the client of the therapist's empathic understanding, and the effect of this on the client. I suggest that the systemic therapist would see the creation of empathic understanding between members of a system as equally important, and would engage them through circular questioning . . . in a process whereby they would become involved in reaching understandings of others, as well as of themselves. (Wilkinson, 1992: 203)

White and Epston ask persons questions, and then more questions, about their lives. This has led to some suspicion that they are cold and distanced in their work. But White fully engages with persons:

> I cry with the people who consult me, and I also laugh with them. I join them in outrage, and also in joy. As I walk for a while with these people,

I experience all of the emotions that one experiences in bearing witness to testimony. As well, there are contexts in which I find myself celebrating with people – contexts in which the alternative stories of their lives are being honoured, when the other accounts of their identity are being fully authenticated. So, let me put to rest these concerns about 'intellectual ways' and about 'discomfort with emotion'. I do not regard my position to be an academic or an intellectual one. But this doesn't mean that I feel compelled to join in the dominant 'feeling discourse' of the culture of psychotherapy . . . (White, 1995a: 86–7)

I very much try to avoid putting questions 'in a barrage-like fashion' (Epston and White, 1992: 132). I try to ask questions conversationally, and then to ask further questions 'naturally' as responses to the person's reply. I have a framework of kinds of questions in mind, but this is simply a flexible resource on which to draw, to help me to facilitate the person's emerging story with, I hope, relevance and sensitivity. As with all aspects of narrative therapy, I am not engaging in a set process or applying a formula.

Since my original training taught me to avoid asking questions I still find doing this difficult at times. My questions sometimes sound awkward and clumsy to me, and sometimes I suspect I am floundering. But when my questions are expressions of a genuine wish to hear about and empathize with the person's experience, and when I am able to move outwards from this point to engage persons in examining their lives in more experience-near perspectives, questions sometimes almost ask themselves, surprising me as I hear myself putting them. And sometimes, on such occasions, my questions produce a response which appears to make a difference, to contribute in a real way to the person's evolving story. Sometimes the question I then ask in response to this response also seems to be meaningful to the person. I hope that with increasing experience I am getting a little nearer to the kind of low-key, exploratory, connection-making and imaginative questioning which I have observed in White's sessions. Although I take White's point that he does not wish to be imitated, or seen as an 'ideal' practitioner (White, 1997a), I have watched him working with persons at the Dulwich Centre and on video recordings with a profound sense of '*this* is how to do it'.

White sits directly opposite the person he is interviewing, leaning forward, making eye contact. He begins by asking the person what she would like to talk about. The atmosphere is conversational, friendly, informal and unforced. He asks permission to take notes and, if this is given, does so throughout, using a pad on his knee, swiftly returning to eye contact. From time to time he checks out how the person is finding the conversation – 'Is this conversation going OK for you? Shall we carry on with this topic?' Before his questions take a new direction, he asks permission: 'I'd like to ask you some questions around what you just said about your fears. Is that OK with you?' His tone is low key, patient and exploratory. There is no hint of 'dynamism' or intensity. He uses non-verbal encouragement: nods, smiles, laughter when appropriate; above all, quiet serious attention. When persons describe painful or confusing aspects of their life he does not register an immediate reaction which might interrupt the person's flow. From time to time he verbally checks out his understanding of what the person has said, referring to his notes. He explains what he is doing at different points in the session, and why: 'I asked you who else you might tell about these successes because persons I've talked to sometimes say that doing this has made the successes feel more real.' 'I didn't follow up your point about feeling unusually isolated in your present job because I thought it might be helpful to look at the history of loneliness in your life. Perhaps we could get back to it now?' Towards the end of the session he is appreciative: 'I really enjoyed this conversation'; 'I found your story about family pressures helpful in trying to understand what all this has meant for you.' He shares his feelings: 'I was really moved when you talked about your relationship with Jimmy – there were tears in my eyes, I think.' He reminds the person of possibilities beyond those which took place in the session: 'There are lots of other conversations we might have had – I'd have liked to hear more about how you coped with that first crisis, and I was interested in what you said about the support you got from your memory of your father's struggle against similar problems. But in the time we had, not all those topics could be followed up.'

When my own questioning appears to be at one with my belief that the person's own experience is the key to her discovering directions which are more hopeful, and when my questions appear to succeed in encouraging the person to tell more 'experience-near' stories as she examines her life, I have a sense that even though I am not imitating White I am perhaps working in the spirit which informs his sessions.

Wording

Many of White's accounts of his work contain examples of questions. Unfortunately, unlike David Epston, he rarely quotes verbatim passages in context, and very few professionally produced video recordings are available of him working. When first reading papers where White quotes actual questions he has asked, I was rather perplexed and disappointed – they often appeared over-complex, with convoluted syntax and unnatural phrasing. Other questions were more direct and simple, but with a deceptive simplicity, often reverberating with subtle possibilities for the person's self-discovery:

- If you oppose these ideas about men's supremacy, this could set you apart from other men. How would you cope with this? (1989: 104)
- I now have two pictures of you as a person, the old one and the new one, and I find the difference between them arresting. If you could hold these two pictures steady in your mind and compare them, what do you think you would discover about yourself? (1989: 54)
- Can you recall an occasion when you could have given in to the problem but didn't? (1989: 41)
- Just prior to taking this step, did you nearly turn back? If so, how did you stop yourself from doing so? (Epston and White, 1992: 128)
- What do these discoveries tell you about what you want for your life? (Epston and White, 1992: 131)
- How do you think your parents managed to keep their act together, in the face of this crisis? (Epston and White, 1992: 129)

I prefer to think of White's more elaborate quoted questions as distillations rather than models, and to work in the spirit of the questions rather than try to imitate their phrasing. I am encouraged in this by White's statement that 'Many of these [questions] are complex in structure and can be partialized to facilitate comprehension' (White, 1989: 40), and by Epston and White's point that questions which appear in their work ' "in complex form" can be easily modified according to the background and age of the persons seeking therapy' (1992: 19). White is careful to indicate that his questions are asked as part of a 'natural' dialogue: 'Of course, these questions are not asked in a barrage-like fashion. Instead, they are raised within the context of dialogue, and each is sensitively attuned to the responses triggered by the previous question' (Epston and

White, 1992: 132). When I watched White working there was no occasion where the syntax of his questions was convoluted or distorted. I heard him pose subtle questions but always within the person's comprehension, although occasionally they needed repetition or paraphrasing before the unfamiliar direction of thought became clear to the person. Put with unforced naturalness, such questions nevertheless invited persons to think hard, and to re-tell in radical ways the stories by which they described their lives and identities.

Encouraging the telling of 'sub-plots'

In my experience, stories told by the person at the start of therapy are not usually neatly linear, but form a 'web' of described elements which gains increasing coherence and meaning as these elements are told instance by instance. Persons jump from the present to the recent past, to the more recent past, to the distant past, back to the present, move to imagined futures, those futures then evoke memories of the past – and so forth. Sometimes persons unnecessarily but understandably apologize for the fact that their accounts appear incoherent or muddled, but a clear overall story accumulates. The process of questioning, as it encourages sub-plots to be told, matches this recursive sequence.

White has offered two clarifying images of this questioning process. One is a comparison with two proximate and interacting arches (1995a: 136). I personally find White's other image, given in workshops, more helpful: questions around unique outcomes in the person's past, present and possible future veer from thoughts/feelings to actions and events, and back again:

> I've been trying to emphasize what might be referred to as a 'zig-zagging' process. We might be somewhere in [the person's] history talking about what particular events might reflect: *Well, on reviewing these events that took place then, what do they tell you about what was really important for your life?* So, in the referencing of one landscape to another, we have jumped from landscape of action to landscape of consciousness. And we can go the other way: *Are you aware of any other developments in your life that reflect this particular belief about what is important to you?* So we are now back in the landscape of action . . . (White, 1995a: 32, emphasis in original)

Figure 5.1 represents my own elaboration of the 'zig-zag' diagram that White has presented in workshops. The overlapping zig-zag line represents a sequence of questions around unique outcomes, moving back and forth from one landscape to the other over the time sequence of events described by the person. The process replicates and enhances what happens in life itself, as persons seek to make sense of their experience by linking memories into a framework:

> An appropriate configuration emerges only after a moving back and forth or tacking procedure compares proposed plot structures with the events and then revises the plot structure according to the principle of 'best fit' ... it is a dialectic process that takes place between the events themselves and a theme which discloses their significance and allows them to be grasped together as parts of one story. (Polkinghorne, 1988: 19–20)

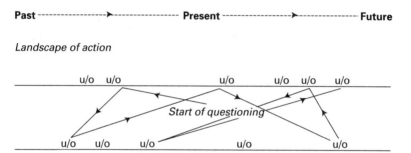

Past ----------------▶---------------- **Present** ----------------▶--------------- **Future**

Landscape of action

Landscape of consciousness/identity

Figure 5.1 *Zig-zag image of the questioning process (u/o = unique outcome)*

Metaphors for processes of questioning

Epston and White describe the process of questioning in therapy by two metaphors – from (a) literature (White, 1995a: 11–32) and (b) anthropology (Epston and White, 1992: 12–24). The *literary metaphor* is of authoring, re-authoring and storying. In response to the therapist's questions, the person tells and re-tells her self-story, increasingly incorporating additional sub-plots. In doing this she is reviewing and 're-authoring' her story of her relationship to others, to herself and her history. The *anthropological metaphor* is of moving through the process of a 'rite of passage'. In response to the therapist's questions, the person moves through a ritual of three stages. The first is of 'separation', where the person becomes detached from her previous, dominant perceptions of personal history, situation and identity. The second stage is 'liminal' or transitional, when the sense of confusion brought about by the first stage is accompanied by an awareness of new possibilities for change. The third stage is 'reincorporation', where the person's rediscoveries and new knowledges are 'authenticated' and reinforced by being communicated to significant others and by hearing their responses.

These metaphors are two figurative, mutually reinforcing ways of describing the same processes of working with persons through questioning. Either metaphor or both might be used to describe narrative therapy. Their value is in guiding the therapist through her work with the person by alternative and mutually enriching conceptualizations of the sequences she is encouraging and accompanying. In the following simplified example from my own work I illustrate this by indicating the literary and anthropological metaphors in turn.

Roger came to counselling, distressed and despairing, when he could no longer bear the knowledge that his partner Tim was having a series of affairs. Roger blamed himself for this situation, through not giving Tim all that he needed in a relationship.
(*Literary*: problem-saturated story/dominant story of self-blame)
(*Anthropological*: separation stage from previous 'certainties')

Answering questions led Roger to recognize times when he momentarily ceased to blame himself, and felt critical of Tim. He began to revise his predominantly self-blaming way of seeing the situation, recognizing that in his more experience-near perception, Tim was exploiting his affection and preying on his vulnerability and tolerance.
(*Literary*: identification of unique outcomes leading to re-storying)
(*Anthropological*: stage of separation from familiar role/status)

Facing up to his recognition of Tim's attitudes increased Roger's pain but enabled him to accept the meaning for him of Tim's behaviour, to decide to end the relationship, and to realize that he would be able to tell Tim this decision, and the reasons for it, despite the nervousness this induced.
(*Literary*: 'future' unique outcomes threaded into the new re-storying)
(*Anthropological*: liminal stage between two 'worlds')

When Roger put this plan into action he gained moral and practical support from many friends to whom he was able fully to reveal what had been happening, with firm emphasis on Tim's responsibility for the failure of the relationship. This helped him to begin his new way of life without feeling isolated, or prey to 'second thoughts' despite the grief of his loss.
(*Literary*: performing future unique outcomes and telling the new story)
(*Anthropological*: reincorporation/authentication phase)

Types of question

In his paper 'The process of questioning – a therapy of literary merit?' (1989: 37–46), White reproduces questions taken from recordings of his sessions, with the aim of providing 'a working tool with which to experiment' (1989: 39). The paper is densely written, with a detailed theoretical explanation for questioning followed by about 80 illustrative questions categorized under three main headings and 12 sub-headings. The questions are quoted out of context, and many might have been included under more than one heading. I find the categories and their rationale difficult to hold in mind, even after many readings, and White himself appears rather unconvinced by the paper: 'in the very writing of these notes I have thought of some new and perhaps more helpful ways that this questioning process could be presented' (1989: 39). He has not referred back to these categories in later writings. Two years later he produced 'Deconstruction and therapy'. Perhaps this paper represents the 'new and more helpful' way of presenting questions which White mentioned because he clearly considers it important: after presentation at international conferences in 1991 it was published in three separate contexts (1991; 1995a; Epston and White, 1992), and is used as a study text in White's intensive narrative therapy training courses in Adelaide.

The paper outlines White's concept of the term 'deconstruction' as applied to therapy: scrutinizing culturally influenced assumed knowledges and ways of thinking in order to see their previously invisible implications and to separate from them if this is what we discover we wish to do.

> According to my rather loose definition, deconstruction has to do with procedures that subvert taken-for-granted realities and practices; those so-called 'truths' that are split off from the conditions and context of their production, those disembodied ways of speaking that hide their bases

and prejudices, and those familiar practices of self and relationship that are subjugating of persons' lives ... [through this process] we might become more aware of the extent to which certain 'modes of life and thought' shape our existence, and that we might then be in a position to choose to live by other 'modes of life and thought' ... we can also consider deconstruction in other senses: for example, the deconstruction of *self-narrative* and the dominant cultural knowledges that people live by; the deconstruction of practices of self and of relationship that are *dominantly cultural*; and the deconstruction of the *discursive practice* of our culture. (1995a: 122, emphasis added)

In the longest section of the paper, White covers ground which will by now be familiar to readers of this book: questions which deconstruct persons' narratives. He categorizes and gives examples of questions to encourage this process, and it is evident that, in the two years since the earlier paper, he has re-thought the headings under which therapeutic questions might most usefully be described.

Questions deconstructing narrative
Three categories are suggested:

* Landscape of action questions
* Landscape of consciousness questions
* Experience of experience questions

Here are a few of White's examples:

(a) Landscape of action questions:
* How did you get yourself ready to take this step?
* Would you describe to me the circumstances surrounding this development in your son's life? Did anyone else contribute to this, and if so, in what way?
* What have you witnessed in your life up to now that could have given you at least some hint that this was a possibility for you?

(b) Landscape of consciousness questions:
* · What do these discoveries tell you about what you want for your life?
* What do these developments inform you about what suits you as a person?
* What does this history of struggle suggest about what Jane believes to be important in her life, about what she stands for?

(c) Experience of experience questions (what the person thinks others may be thinking):

- If I had been a spectator to your life when you were a younger person, what do you think I might have witnessed you doing then that might help me to understand how you were able to achieve what you have recently achieved?
- Of all those persons who have known you, who would be least surprised that you have been able to take this step in challenging the problem's influence in your life?
- I would like to understand the foundations upon which this achievement rests. Of all those persons who have known you, who would be best placed to supply some details about these foundations?

Questions deconstructing practices of power

These questions relate to the 'political' aspect of narrative therapy. They are the therapist's means of 'externalizing internalizing discourses'. White summarizes Michel Foucault's proposal that people are maintained in subordinate positions by those with social power through 'self-censorship', and that the basis of this self-censorship is how far they match up to assumptions, beliefs and actions expected of them in relation to the given, assumed, usually unexamined norms of society:

> for Foucault, this modern system of power was decentered and 'taken up', rather than centralized and exercised from the top down . . . The workings of this power are disguised or masked because it operates in relation to certain norms that are assigned a 'truth' status . . . and is designed to bring about particular and 'correct' outcomes, like a life considered to be 'fulfilled', 'liberated', 'rational', 'differentiated', 'individuated', 'self-possessed', 'self-contained', and so on . . . the practices of power, as detailed by Foucault, are particularly insidious and effective . . . the ways of being informed by these 'truths' are not seen, by these persons, as the effects of power, but instead as the effect of something like fulfilment, of liberation . . . This analysis of power is difficult for many persons to entertain, for it suggests that many of the aspects of our individual modes of behaviour that we assume to be an expression of our free will, or that we assume to be transgressive, are not what they first appear. (Epston and White, 1992: 138–9)

The post-structuralist concepts underpinning this extract, which controversially call in question some widely valued 'individualistic' assumptions of traditional therapy, are discussed in Chapter 9 below.

White does not give examples of questions under this 'political' category, although he refers back to several 'stories of therapy' outlined at the start of the paper to demonstrate the significance of these kinds of questions. Here are some examples from my own practice:

- Where does your idea come from that to be a good father you must be very strict with your children?
- Whose example are you following when you 'hold forth' to your wife and family?
- You respect your boyfriend because he holds firm opinions, yet some of these opinions appear a source of pain to you. I wonder, as a man myself, why we find it hard to distinguish between holding firm opinions and having closed minds.
- If you stopped doing all your family's shopping, washing, cleaning, ironing and cooking and insisted that they shared these tasks, what arguments do you think they would use against this request? Where might these ideas have originated?
- What world-wide changes in management philosophy might have influenced your firm's transformation from a generally benevolent employer to a 'hard management' organization? Whose interests are served by this new policy?
- You were made redundant because the firm is losing orders. What influences in society and the media may have contributed to your feeling guilty at not having a job?
- Where do you think your friends got their idea that since your husband died two years ago you should now start to 'get a life'?
- You say you've been grieving since your son has told you he is homosexual. I'd find it really interesting if we could talk about the use of that word 'grieving' in this situation – would that be OK?
- So members of your women's group say you should come to see me every week, instead of the three-weekly sessions we agreed on, and work towards discovering who you really are. Could we talk about what they mean by that, and where those ideas might have originated?

Questions deconstructing discursive (knowledge) practices
In the final section of the paper White carries the politics-of-power concept into areas of particular relevance to therapists: the 'truth knowledges' assumed by authority figures in professional disciplines, and the ways in which the languages of those disciplines both reflect and perpetuate those assumed expert positions. Therapy, he suggests, can assist persons to counter these expert positions by their own local knowledges.

These techniques [of 'experts'] encourage persons in the belief that members of these disciplines have access to an objective and unbiased account of human reality, and of human nature . . . the open, vague, temporary and changing nature of the world is rendered, by these truth discourses, closed, fixed and permanent . . . Therapists can contribute to the deconstruction of expert knowledge by considering themselves to be 'co-authors' of alternative and preferred knowledges and practices, and through a concerted effort to establish a context in which the persons who seek therapy are privileged as the primary authors of those know-ledges and practices. (White, 1995a: 142–4)

Therapists, suggests White, have more than a responsibility to encourage and assist persons to take a critical stance towards the 'assumed expert knowledges' of authority figures in general. In addition, the therapist should encourage questioning and critical examination of the therapy process itself as it is occurring (1995a: 143–5), by asking questions of how the therapy is experienced.

Therapists can undermine the idea that they have privileged access to the truth by consistently encouraging persons to assist them in the quest for understanding. This can be achieved by giving persons notice of the extent to which the therapist's participation in therapy is dependent upon feedback from the persons about their experience of the therapy . . . the therapist is able to deconstruct and thus embody her/his responses . . . by situating these in the context of his/her personal experiences, imagination, and intentional states . . . (1995a: 144)

This section of White's paper also omits examples, so I offer some 'deconstructing-of-knowledge-practices' questions and statements based on my own work.

- I'd like to suggest you think about that magazine article saying that abused people become abusers themselves. Did the writer offer any clear and undeniable evidence to support that statement? Do you think it was based on knowledge or might it be a myth? Would you like details of a book describing interviews with abused persons which contradicts that idea?
- Your letter from the hospital includes lots of abbreviations and initials, which you don't understand. I don't understand them either! Does the letter reveal anything about the attitudes of the person who wrote it and the persons who authorized it? Could its style have any link with the ways in which you felt 'dismissed' by the consultant?
- Can I just check – is this session going OK for you? Is it addressing the issues you wanted to talk about?

- I offered you some ideas to think about earlier in the session on ways in which some women writers have challenged the idea that women should put themselves second to the wishes of their families. Was that OK? Or did I push it a bit? Did it seem like yet another man trying to make you think the way he does?
- Is it all right to check out with you that I've understood what you were saying just now? – I sometimes get things wrong.
- I'm really grateful for your saying that the ideas we discussed last time didn't work out. I rely on honest feedback like that.
- As a man, I can never hope to understand women's experience. But I'm very willing to try to get hold of what you're telling me. Does it feel comfortable for us to carry on this conversation about your husband's neglectful attitudes and actions?
- Oh, no! – I got pretty near to telling you the reasons why you did that. I'm sorry – that's an old, bad habit.

The 'co-creation' of stories through therapist questioning

With questioning as the basis of therapy is the story as much the therapist's as the person's compared with accounts of experience given by persons to therapists working in less 'active' ways? I find the 'literary' metaphor in narrative therapy helpful here, in its implicit comparison between literary texts and the lives of persons. Literary theorists and critics have drawn attention to the part played by the *reader* in 'creating' a unique story 'in his head' by his response to the text. Words cannot embody a single overall 'real meaning' on the part of the author. Even if an author has a very clear and precise idea of the meaning she wishes her text to convey, she cannot control the response of a person at the point of reading. The text will trigger responses and meanings related not only to the author's conscious intentions but to the reader's own presuppositions, interests, apprehensions, values, beliefs and experience. As the literary critic F.R. Leavis argued, each reading of a text by a different person, and also each re-reading of a text by the *same* person, will create a different amalgam of the writer's intentions and meanings, and the reader's own creation of meanings: 'You cannot point to the poem; it is "there" only in the re-creative response of individual minds to the black marks on the page. But – a necessary faith – it is something in which minds can meet' (Leavis, 1972: 62).

When we discuss a novel, a play or a poem with another reader we may be astonished to find that their 'virtual text', their co-created version of the piece, is considerably different from our own. I have a 'running disagreement' with a colleague, whose sensitivity to literature is unquestionable, who sees Fanny in Jane Austen's *Mansfield Park* as an insipid character and Mary Crawford portrayed in positive terms as a genuinely lively and attractive contrast to Fanny. But differences in response do not deny the possibility of 'negotiation' on the meanings and quality of a text, or that we are left with the relativistic position of 'all opinions are equally valid'. Further co-creations are possible, which can feed into and modify the first co-creation between writer and reader. These further co-creations of meaning come out of comparison and discussion of our reactions to the text with other readers – a mutual honing and learning process. It is Leavis's 'something in which minds can meet' – interchanges which he summarizes as 'This is so, isn't it?' . . . 'Yes, but . . .' (1972: 62). We can, by close scrutiny of 'the words on the page' and detailed discussion and comparison with others' responses, get a long way towards agreement.

It is interesting to substitute *therapy* concepts for *literary* concepts in Leavis's description of the collaborative, co-creative process of literary analysis/practical criticism (my substitutions are italicized in square brackets). The 'literary' metaphor underpinning narrative therapy is immediately clarified.

> what we are doing is to bring into sharp focus, in turn, this, that and the other detail, juncture or relation in our total response . . . what we are doing is to dwell with a deliberate, considering responsiveness on this, that or the other node or focal point in the complete organisation that the poem [*person's account of the problem*] is, in so far as we have it. [Literary] Analysis [*therapy*] is not a dissection of something that is already and passively there. What we call analysis [*therapy*] is, of course, a constructive or creative process. It is a more deliberate following-through of that process of creation in response to the poet's [*person's*] words . . . It is a re-creation in which, by a considering attentiveness, we ensure a more than ordinary faithfulness and completeness. (Leavis, 1943: 70)

Leavis did not call the processes of literary criticism and discussion 'co-creating narratives around the text', but it seems to me it is precisely that. Through conversation with another reader we co-create a potentially modified response to the text, and by this means each of us will separately co-create a rather different virtual text next time we read the work. It is a three-way co-creation: author, reader, and the second reader who discussed the text with the first reader. However, each of our virtual texts will still be different from the other's virtual text, although less so than before, and different from our own future readings. Despite closer agreements and mutually modified perceptions, there can be no single correct and final virtual text. Similarly, the conversation I hold with a person when counselling is one further co-creation of stories expanding the text of his life, towards which many others – friends, relatives, lovers and so on, all speaking within culturally influenced assumptions – also contribute through other co-creating conversations:

> The stories that persons live by are rarely, if ever, 'radically' constructed – it is not a matter of them being made-up, 'out of the blue', so to speak. Our culturally available and appropriate stories about personhood and about relationship have been historically constructed and negotiated in communities of persons, and within the context of social structures and institutions . . . the stories that persons live by are full of gaps and inconsistencies, and contradictions that contribute to a certain indeterminacy of life; it is these gaps, inconsistencies and contradictions that provoke persons to engage actively in the performance of unique meaning . . . Thus, when considering the proposition that is constituted through an ongoing storying and re-storying of experience, we are considering a process of 'indeterminacy within determinacy . . .' (Epston and White, 1992: 125)

It is through questioning that, in narrative therapy, persons are invited to break from the 'determinacy' of the stories they have co-created about their lives: 'capacity for change lies in people's ability to be in language with one another and, through the linguistic process, create and develop the realities that have meaning for them and through which they continually reorganise their mutual living and develop self-descriptions that provide "new and empowering accounts of ourselves instead of disabling ones" ' (Anderson, 1997: 118, quoting Shotter, 1991). Questions reveal clues, which further questions can assist the person to identify as unique outcomes. These unique outcomes can then be examined in detail by the person through her responses to further questions, and she can decide on their significance as they are revealed, established and explored in detail – through questions. In response to such questions the person may come to tell a more rich and experience-near story and, in response to questions, may make choices for the present and future in the light of this enriched story. This is narrative co-creation, and I believe that this is what is happening when my own counselling works for persons – even when, as sometimes occurs, the details of sessions have faded for the person and she simply thanks me for 'listening'.

The therapist's part in the co-creation of narratives

In my counselling I attempt to become fully engaged in encouraging, through questions, deconstruction of neglected story-elements. It is this detailed expansion of unique outcomes, not their simply being recalled, which enables them to 'ripple longer than old ideas' (White, 1989: 97). They are pumped up until permanently visible and, once enlarged, they are scrutinized for what they mean for the person. They are then, through questions, linked to other deconstructed unique outcomes, and so gradually a sub-plot is told. There are further echoes here, for me, of my training in literary criticism and my past as an English teacher, when I attempted to assist students to enhance their readings of poetry and fiction through *scrutiny of significant detail* in the text. (Leavis's pioneering literary journal was called *Scrutiny*.) A line of poetry or even a single image may be exhaustively examined for meaning and significance in relation to the rest of the poem – after which the reading of the poem becomes different, more complete, richer. The virtual text changes; the exploration of detail has led to an enriched response to the poem as a whole. When I am engaged in detailed exploration of unique outcomes in a person's self-story, I am contributing to their understanding of their experience becoming different, more complete, richer. For persons, the 'virtual text' of their lives – the interconnected map of memories which comprises their sense of their lives – changes: therapy has led to an enriched apprehension of their experience.

When I am involved with persons in co-creation of enriched stories, I try to make the process unequal, with the major role going to the person. But a story told in therapy can never be created by the person alone. Therapists of any persuasion holding conversations with persons are contributing to the co-creation of narratives and are doing so by every look, word and action. A mute nod carries a message of 'Yes – that's significant' which co-creates an emphasis of meaning at that point. Even the absence of a reaction is an implicit message: 'You haven't said anything worthy of a reaction yet.' If I think I see a moment of hesitation as a person asserts that she knows her husband loves her despite his continual affairs, *any* reaction of mine is influential: if I have a neutral or blank response I am inviting her to ignore the significance of what she has just said, implicitly ignoring its possible inherent contradiction. My message is 'I believe you.' If I look a little puzzled my message is 'Do you really mean this?' and my implicit invitation is 'Do you want to consider that statement?'

A therapist who believes that dreams indicate significant information will ask about them, and the person's dreams will become more important to him – they will be remembered and pondered, and become part of his narrative. If a therapist believes that many problems are self-created by a person not thinking clearly, then the direction of sessions will predispose the person to become sensitized to his thought processes. Therapists who encourage persons to become more conscious of the nature of their feelings will increasingly be told stories centred on feelings rather than on thought processes. 'It has interested us for some time that psychological problems seemingly appear, change shape, and disappear as therapists' vocabularies and descriptions change' (Anderson and Goolishian, 1988: 375). I represent to myself that many persons who consult me are 'living thin self-stories' or 'captured by dominant cultural assumptions', whereas some years ago I saw many persons as 'out of touch with their true selves' or 'denying their feelings'. The stories which persons co-author with me are now quite likely to embody social constructionist and postmodern perspectives. I cannot prevent my therapeutic assumptions influencing persons' stories; my responsibility is to be aware of this and to make this clear to the person.

By my part in co-creating re-tellings I am influencing those stories. I inevitably bring my own ideas, beliefs, values and positions into the therapy room. It is important for me to be aware of this rather than believing, on the one hand, that I am 'neutral' or, on the other hand, that the assumptions underlying my work are global truths which it must be beneficial for the person to accept. My assumptions relate to my own life experience and the influences of my reading, thinking, circle of friends, training and all the multiple factors that have contributed to making me who I am at the moment when, on this particular day, at this particular time, I am attempting to assist this person. I am, for example, a white, middle-class male of my generation, and my view of persons and the world has been influenced by these factors in ways often invisible to me. My politics are liberal left, so I do not invite persons to consider the harmful effects of liberal-left ideas in the production of their problems; though, holding liberal-left views, I do believe that considering the nature and sources of racism, gender stereotyping and unacknowledged power politics may have a beneficial effect.

I must aim for my questions to be transparent in form and intention, not clever-tricky or imbued with hidden assumed expert knowledges; their purpose must be explained to the person; I must check out with the person that he is finding them acceptable; and the person must be aware that he has a choice of whether or not to respond to them. I must try to ask them tentatively, respectfully, conversationally, and out of a genuine interest in the person's conception of her experience and the meaning she assigns to that experience. They must comprise my share of a sensitive and genuine human interchange and engagement with life. Paradoxically, I must utilize my inevitable power position to ask questions which, among other functions, promote my disempowerment in relation to the person.

A sequence of questions

Below is an example, from my work, of a unique outcome being 'drawn down as it passes across the screen' (White, 1997a) and, through questioning, brought fully to the attention of the person, who is then invited by extended questioning to consider its significance for him by 'plotting' it into the story of his past, present and future. The dialogue is not verbatim but is written up from very detailed notes jotted during the session. I attempt to reproduce the content and tone of the conversation, but omit awkwardness of phrasing, repetitions and sections where the topic is left behind for a while. I summarize exchanges which might otherwise identify 'Joel'.

Joel, a 28-year-old technician, had spent several years in the Far East earning a good wage and sending most of it to his wife in England, who was caring for their two small children. Unlike some members of the foreign contingent he resisted temptations to have sexual affairs. On his return, his wife unexpectedly told him that she wanted a divorce, as she had met another man whom she wished to marry. A near-suicidal depression had followed but Joel recovered to some extent, and at the time of coming to therapy had found happiness in a new relationship, with Sara. A year before meeting Joel, Sara had left a man who subjected her to physical violence. Joel found it difficult to keep regular work, partly because recurring depression affected his confidence and energy, when he would phone in sick. In the first two counselling sessions he discussed stresses unrelated to his new relationship, but in the third session he took up this theme. The couple was largely financed by Sara, in whose house they lived. Despite Sara's protestations to the contrary, Joel was afraid she despised him and would soon end their relationship. This prospect terrified him, but the more she tried to reassure him, the more convinced he was that she was actually covering up her real attitude.

1 *Joel:* She's going to get fed up with me soon. I'm just living on her charity. I'm useless.
2 *Martin:* What does *she* say about all that?
3 *Joel:* I'm trying to get work. But she's critical of me – says I'm putting 10 per cent into the house and she's putting 90 per cent. So she resents me. Ten per cent against 90 per cent. I'm just a 'kept man'.
4 *Martin:* What exactly did she say when she talked about your 10 per cent and her 90 per cent?
5 *Joel:* I suppose . . . well . . . she said it was all right. She said I'm trying to get work and all I can give is what I get from the dole, but she's working and so she can put more into the household.
6 *Martin:* Thinking back on what she actually said, was she being critical or was she being reassuring?
7 *Joel:* Reassuring . . . she was trying to reassure me . . . but probably she was just trying to let me down lightly. She resents it but she pretends it's OK. Not much of a man, am I? My life's in a complete mess, I don't know where I am about . . . [*other problems he had discussed*] . . . and all I'm giving Sara is hassle. I'm so confused. I'm tired all the time yet I'm not doing anything to make me tired, except late night, early morning discussions. It would finish me if she said it was over. There are times when I think Sara *would* be better off without me – when everyone would be better off without me [*cries quietly*].
8 *Martin:* [*after waiting for Joel to recover equilibrium*] Late night, early morning discussions?
9 *Joel:* Yes. Often Sara and me will lay awake in bed till early in the morning discussing things.
10 *Martin:* Discussing things . . .?
11 *Joel:* Sounds ridiculous. The meaning of life, that sort of thing. Loving things. What life's all about. She gets me thinking.
12 *Martin:* I'd be really interested to hear a bit more about those discussions, if you feel like telling me . . . if they're not too private?
13 *Joel:* No, it's OK. Well, we've always done that. We go to bed quite late anyway and usually we'll start talking. About anything and everything. She's quite religious – not church – but quite religious about the meaning of life. We get talking in bed. We do talk in the daytime but that's usually about practical things and what I ought to do about . . . [*various problems*]. Our discussions in bed are different.
14 *Martin:* Is this something either of you did with your previous partners?
15 *Joel:* [*grins wryly*] No! Her bloke wasn't into anything like that – he used to bash her about until she got out of the relationship – and my ex-wife couldn't care less about all that sort of thing.

16 *Martin:* If Sara was in this room now, and I asked her what it was about you that made it possible for her to have late night conversations about the meaning of life with you, what would she say?

17 *Joel:* Sorry?

18 *Martin:* If I was to ask Sara what it was about you as a person that made it possible for her to have these discussions about life with you, what would she tell me? What would she say about you? How would she describe you?

19 *Joel:* I suppose she'd say I was interested in things.

20 *Martin:* Things . . . ?

21 *Joel:* Things like what life's all about.

22 *Martin:* How might she describe you as a person – what would she be seeing in you compared with her 'ex', which make those conversations possible?

23 *Joel:* [*thinks for a few moments*] She'd say I'm thoughtful . . . sensitive even . . .

24 *Martin:* What other qualities would she tell me she sees in you – about late night discussions and generally? What does she love in you? What do you give her? What difference have you made to her life?

25 *Joel:* Bloody hard questions.

26 *Martin:* I know. That's why I asked them!

27 *Joel:* [*grins, then thinks*] I'm caring. I really care for her and she sees how much I care for my kids. I'm honest – she knows she can trust me and that I'll say what I mean and that I won't ever deceive her in any way. She knows I'm really concerned for her and I'd never willingly hurt her. She hasn't had that before. In fact she's said some of that.

28 *Martin:* Is she an honest person or a dishonest person?

29 *Joel:* [*surprised*] She's dead honest.

30 *Martin:* So you can believe her. So if I've got it right, you've given Sara emotional security . . . ?

31 *Joel:* Yes . . .

32 *Martin:* . . . and she has discovered in you qualities of integrity, compassion, sensitivity, openness to ideas about life and human existence?

33 *Joel:* Yes.

34 *Martin:* . . . and she loves those things in you?

35 *Joel:* Yes.

36 *Martin:* Are those qualities common in men or are they rare?

37 *Joel:* Rare.

38 *Martin:* What other evidence has she seen of those qualities in you?

39 *Joel:* She knows I care about my kids.

40 *Martin:* How does she know that?

41 *Joel:* [*talks in detail about his relationship with his children*]

42 *Martin:* How about when you were abroad?

43 *Joel:* Well, I didn't know her then.

44 *Martin:* I mean, what you've told her about how it was for you, when other men were having affairs?

45 *Joel:* I didn't have affairs . . . I was faithful to my wife . . . most other men were getting all the sex they could. They used to say I was a wimp for not getting sex.

46 *Martin:* Does Sara know what that was like for you? Standing out

against your mates at that time because you had different values and beliefs?

47 Joel: I think so. I have talked about it.

48 Martin: Did Sara find these qualities in her previous men?

49 Joel: No. The last one was a right bastard. He slept around, as well as being violent to her.

50 Martin: What does all this tell you about yourself as a man contributing to the life of a woman?

51 Joel: I'm a different sort of man . . . I've become different . . . she loves me for those differences.

52 Martin: I have this vision of you both lying warmly in bed together, as the light gradually fades at the window and the night darkens. You're talking quietly and closely about important issues concerning life and human existence, as traffic sounds fade and the stars come out one by one. I think that that picture will stay with me for a long time.

53 Joel: [He nods, looks down for a while, then looks up quietly and calmly] Yes.

In so far as this written up extract represents what actually occurred in the session, it shows that initially I attempt to invite Joel to consider evidence about Sara's attitude to his financial contribution to the household (1–6). He is so set in preconceptions about her attitude that his memories of her reassurances are simply quoted by him as more evidence that she is resenting him and pretending to be reassuring. The dominant story is too powerful to be re-storied through this element. In any case, he might be right – for all I know, Sara might indeed be resenting his lack of contribution while reassuring him out of kindness. The clue at 5, where he quotes Sara saying that his contribution is acceptable as it is proportionate to his income, does not in fact turn out to be a unique outcome; it does not hold meaning for Joel, so I do not pursue the point. Instead, I pick up on a clue in something he says as an aside in 7. He mentions for the first time in our sessions that he has late night, early morning discussions with Sara. This is intriguing, but might also have been misleading as a clue – perhaps they lie awake discussing money matters, or arguing about his not working? By implicit questions (8, 10) I invite elaboration, which comes in 11, and more fully in 13. Clearly, these are not trivial discussions, but are mind-and-feeling-stretching discussions about important life issues. They relate to Sara's 'spiritual' interests, which she is able to share with him and which he clearly respects and takes seriously. The clue does turn out to indicate a unique outcome – and my questions are then designed to move Joel's focus away from his self-condemning vicious circle of damning himself through his view of himself through Sara's eyes as a kept man no matter what she says, to a different storyline which carries contrasting meanings. The 'late night, early morning discussions' become the starting-point for an invitation to talk about his perceptions of Sara's perceptions of him in a different context from the financial issue.

At 14, I ask a generalized 'landscape of action' query related to the past. The format of the question implicitly invites Joel to make a connection between the contrast of past and present for both of them, not just for him or for her as individuals. The *unity* of experience of the couple is emphasized, as a contrast to Joel's previous statements expressing his sense of their individual differences in economic contributions. Joel's reply (15) continues the theme of common differences in 'landscape of action' between the couple as they are now, and their experiences in the past with different partners. At 16, I move to landscape of identity/consciousness, continuing the 'circular' theme of his perceptions of her perceptions. My question at 16 is rather awkwardly put; it is inviting Joel to tell a story very different from his ingrained self-condemning dominant story – I am in effect challenging him to see whether he might think well of himself by his reflecting on his perceptions of Sara's view of him. Understandably, he does not grasp the question and so I repeat it more explicitly (18). His responses are hesitant at first, and generalized, and so once again I re-phrase my questions more explicitly (19–22). From now on he manages increasingly to imagine himself as seen through Sara's eyes and to acknowledge aspects of his identity which the dominant story had masked from him (23–35). I expand these landscape of consciousness/identity questions in 37–51. I ask politicizing ('externalizing internal discourses' or 'deconstructing modern practices of power') questions, inviting him to consider how he has defined himself in relation to the kinds of behaviours and attitudes found in many men (36, 46, 50). These are not 'abstract' questions; they are rooted in his actual experience as Sara's partner, and in his perception of her experience as his partner. All these questions around one particular unique outcome, incorporating landscapes of both identity and action, linking it with the past and the present, are designed to *embed* his new awareness that in those aspects of thinking and behaviour where he has chosen to be different from many men, he has in fact contributed uniquely to the life and happiness of the woman he loves and who loves him. I do not need to draw lessons or ask overt questions around 'What matters most – this or equal financial contributions?' It is enough to have encouraged the telling of a new story-strand of past/present, action/consciousness/identity. In the imagery of my contribution at 52, I offer a summarizing symbolic representation of what White, in discussing his concept of spirituality, has called 'epiphanies of everyday life' (White, 1997a) and, quoting the poet David Malouf, 'little sacraments of daily existence' (White, 1996: 47–8). The image of Sara and Joel in bed discussing the meaning of life late into the night was the starting-point of the discussion around unique outcomes. Such 'epiphanies' are moments which represent significant meaning for us, often non-dramatic or 'ordinary', but magical – perhaps what Wordsworth called

> . . . that best portion of a good man's life,
> His little, nameless, unremembered acts
> Of kindness and of love.
> (*Tintern Abbey*, 1798, ll. 33–5)

By returning to and re-presenting, as evocatively as I know how, the situation of Joel and Sara discussing 'the meaning of life', I offer Joel a visual/emotional image which he can, if he wishes, weave into his self-story as a reminder of his identity in Sara's eyes. I do this precisely so that the significance of these intimate moments does *not* stay one of Wordsworth's 'unremembered' acts, but plays a full part in solidifying this more self-valuing sub-plot of his life.

Summary

In narrative therapy, questions are asked in ways that are designed to be respectful, conversational, part of a dialogue and demonstrating a genuine interest in persons' accounts of their experience. These questions invite persons to explore their past, present and possible future, and in so doing to tell new 'sub-plots' of their lives by identifying unique outcomes and then linking them into meaningful sequences. Questioning allows unique outcomes to be explored in detail for meaning and to become embedded in the person's awareness. 'Deconstruction' (detailed critical examination) of culturally influenced assumptions which bear on persons' problems is also a function of questioning. The co-creation of persons' stories through therapist questioning creates a moral responsibility for the therapist to be fully open with persons on the aims of questions and the nature of the assumptions which inform them.

6 *Therapeutic Documents*

'Therapeutic documents' encapsulate new knowledges, perspectives and preferred changes which have become part of the person's enriched but still perhaps slightly fragile view of her remembered experience. They may take many forms including letters, statements, certificates and creative writing. Although usually in writing, they may also consist of or include visual elements.

Two examples of therapeutic documents

A letter reinforcing a deconstructing conversation

Bill, aged 28, saw himself as a failure and was apprehensive about his future. He left university in his first term because he felt stressed and isolated, and returned to live with his parents. He then successfully completed a course in management at a local college, took a well-paid post as a management trainee and gained swift promotion, but after three years in the job had experienced a return of extreme stress reactions, and resigned. He was living with his parents again, and they had suggested therapy. The letter was sent after one session, when no further sessions had been agreed.

Dear Bill

Just a few thoughts following our conversation today.

I was impressed by the swiftness of change in your mood since you rang to make the appointment, with your decision to leave your job producing a sense of calm and lightening of mood. Perhaps you are someone who can recognize when a situation is not right for them, and act on that knowledge, even if it means some degree of self-doubt, or even a temporary sense of failure. So many people I see in my work are influenced by ideas widespread in our society about 'toughing it out' or 'keeping on going' or 'facing up to responsibilities' which, although admirable in many circumstances, simply do not usefully apply in all; sometimes a tactical retreat is actually part of an overall advance. After all, your earlier retreat from your undergraduate course where you were unhappy and stressed, resulted in your taking a course where for several years you were happy (if a bit bored at times) and where your life could revolve around what really mattered to you – your music as creative leisure, your friendships, and your love life! If you'd stuck it out at university you might have just become increasingly ill through stress. I know from what you said that you're worried about whether this 'retreating' might become a pattern, with depression and anxiety combining to knock you off balance. If you decide to have more counselling we could look at this and perhaps work out some counter-strategies to these two subtle enemies which try to undermine your life.

I liked the way in which you were able to look at some of the ideas I raised – and then in effect say 'no, that's not right' (such as when you pointed out that the job itself had not been beyond your capabilities, but that the conditions of doing it had created stress by denying you lightheartedness). Counselling is particularly useful when people firm up their own ideas by *disagreeing* with the counsellor!

You know you can ring for another appointment if and when you want to. But if I don't see you again – good luck and best wishes.

Sincerely

Martin

An end-of-counselling certificate

I sent a certificate to Donna, a 13-year-old who had recovered from post-traumatic reactions, when counselling ended. A detailed description of Donna's counselling follows later in the chapter. As the certificate shows, documents can echo White's claim, about externalization but equally applicable here, that narrative practices can 'free persons to take a lighter, more effective and less stressed approach to deadly serious problems' (White, 1989: 6). However, there are many occasions when a more direct, 'serious' and straightforward format and tone are appropriate. For a full account, with many examples, see the final two chapters of *Narrative Means to Therapeutic Ends* (White and Epston, 1990) and White's updated paper 'Therapeutic documents revisited' in White (1995a).

Therapeutic documents in re-storying

Richer stories coming out of examined experience can slip away as thin habits of thinking and of self-story-telling attempt to reassert

```
* * *

Anglo-Australian Trauma-bashing Society

* * *

This is to certify that
DONNA RICHARDSON
has developed successful strategies to defeat
the false friends of
REPEATED INTRUSIVE MEMORIES
and has learned to call on help from her true friends of
HAPPY MEMORIES
LOVING FRIENDS AND RELATIVES
RESOURCEFULNESS
OPTIMISM
and in so doing
has been able to turn away from Over-Anxiety
and re-learn how to live a full and joyous life.

Date: 11th November 1994
Signed
Martin Payne
(English Representative, Anglo-Australian Trauma-bashing
Society)

* * *
```

their previous dominance. Persons sometimes say that, by the time they get home after a session, the discoveries they have made start to blur. Summaries, reminders, affirmations and records in permanent written form can assist persons to reinforce and keep in mind newly told sub-plots of their lives.

There is, however, a danger that the physical permanence of a document might make it a brake or a limitation, conveying a sense that this is the final definitive statement, which could close down opportunities for further thought, discovery and re-storying. To counteract this, timing is very important. I often introduce documents when the person has taken part in re-storying conversations which have already assisted her to perceive and describe aspects of

her life in richer and more helpful ways. At this stage, some consolidation in more 'fixed' form than the evanescent spoken word
can serve as a launch-pad for further conversations deconstructing
the up-to-then dominant story. I also introduce documents when
the person has temporarily slipped back into a dominant story and
then tentatively moved away from it again – a document is a
'marker' to help her keep the new story alive.

I have to resist the temptation to use documents inappropriately,
and prematurely, as 'statements of the positive'. Too swift and too
emphatic an exploration and recording of achievements and successes can produce a sense of unreality if the person's perception of
where she is with the problem are not in step with this. Affirming
documents are unhelpful if the person's descriptions of elements of
an alternative story are still too new to be fully felt as real. No part
of narrative therapy, including the use of therapeutic documents, is
intended to be jollying-along encouragement or 'top-down'
reassurance. White and Epston remind us that a therapist does well
to keep pace with the person or, if anything, stay a little to the rear:

> For persons who experience themselves as spectacular failures, just to
> point out positives and to be generally and directly enthusiastic about
> events in their lives constitute a 'disempowering' distinction. Under
> these circumstances, the person will identify a major discrepancy
> between where he perceives himself to be in life, on the one hand, and
> where he perceives others perceive him to be, on the other. He will 'find'
> the pictures that others have of his life to be way ahead of what he
> believes to be his actual circumstances, will experience himself falling
> short, and will have his sense of failure confirmed ... Supporting
> persons from behind is not problematic in this way ... The therapist ...
> maintains a cautious attitude, so as not to catch up too quickly with
> developments in the person's life ... (White and Epston, 1990: 148–9)

I once sent a congratulatory letter to Donna, the young woman
whose end-of-counselling certificate is reproduced above, after she
diffidently said that she had coped well with an unexpected major
crisis. I interpreted her coping as a unique outcome and saw my
letter as a concrete reinforcement of what had appeared undervalued in her account. Fortunately, in the following session, after
receiving my letter, she was courageous enough to admit that she
had not told the truth – she had not coped at all well, and had felt
devastated and set back. She had softened this to reassure her
parents, who were also at the session. I suspect that my misjudged
letter added to her distress, by pointing up the difference between
what she really experienced and the version which, with the best

of motives, she had told. From this mistake I learned that therapeutic documents must be *co-created*. When written by the therapist they must incorporate unique outcomes, not clues. My letter did not summarize and reflect Donna's perceptions – it was an imposed interpretation coming out of my misunderstanding of her situation. If my letter had inhibited her from correcting her previous account, therapy might have created an ever more false and oppressive situation for her.

Therapeutic documents in the deconstruction of power relations

Therapeutic documents, whatever their form or whatever their purpose in encouraging and embedding new self-stories, are frequently political in intention. They challenge unrecognized imposed assumptions and ideas of others, whether individuals, family, peers, professional persons or the assumed truths of that interacting aggregate of people called society. By the public voice many therapeutic documents give to persons, embodying their thoughts, perceptions, beliefs and feelings as a concrete record, they can form a counterbalance to a very different kind of document – those written by people in positions of power, which implicitly diminish persons and treat them as objects. 'Official file' documents of this type include unacknowledged, invisible paperwork and/or computer entries, such as casework or medical records (White and Epston, 1990: 125–7). These documents are not always available to the person, who may not even be aware of their existence. If they are officially available, they may be difficult to access, and persons may feel inhibited from asserting their right to see them.

White has described his own ethical priority to show or give copies of all his notes and paperwork to persons he is assisting (1995a: 47, 167–8). The counselling profession as a whole is not immune from 'secret file' practices. An article in *Counselling* reviews the ethical and legal arguments for keeping notes on work with 'clients' over various periods of time, without ever addressing the issue of who owns the notes ('client', counsellor or both?), and there is no mention of showing or giving 'clients' the notes, or copies, throughout counselling or when it ends (Easton and Plant, 1998). An article on referral letters in *Counselling* does state that the 'client's' permission must be obtained before a referral letter is written, but then becomes hesitant, with nervously qualifying wording: 'Good practice, *if appropriate*, dictates that you and your client discuss the form the referral letter will take, and you *can* provide the client with a copy for her/his records' (Warren-Holland, 1998, emphasis added).

Therapeutic documents in narrative therapy are deliberately subversive of these kinds of practices where they exist in the fields of mental health, social services and other institutional contexts.

> The practices associated with these *alternative* documents contrast with those associated with [official types of] file. Whereas the file has a narrow readership of professional experts, the news carried by the award is more widely available to the community. Whereas the file has a significant, if not central, part in rituals of exclusion, *the award* is more often associated with what Bryan Turner (Turner and Hepworth, 1982) refers to as 'rituals of inclusion'. Awards of various kinds, such as trophies and certificates, can be considered examples of *alternative* documents. (White and Epston, 1990: 190–1, emphasis added)

White and Epston distinguish between these secret official documents and quite different types of official documents which are open, public and celebratory, such as certificates, diplomas and other confirmatory awards. Narrative therapy uses therapeutic documents within this social tradition, borrowing from it the aim of celebrating and validating achievements through witnessing to family, peers and community. As a former teacher in further education I recognize this; it fits with my experience of seeing young people who have left school with few or no formal examination successes blossom enormously in confidence and belief in themselves once they gain vocational or academic qualifications. The certificates and diplomas representing those achievements are precious to them – they show them to each other and to friends and relatives, scrutinize the typeface and paper quality, and sometimes have the award framed and put on a wall at home in a prominent display of pride.

Therapeutic documents in work with children

Some of White and Epston's most appealing and moving writing are their descriptions of work with children and their families. The use of therapeutic documents is often important. Documents in which the child's perceptions and knowledges are taken seriously, and cooperatively re-written with or by an adult, have a self-empowering effect during therapy, and a final 'award' document can be a literal 'souvenir'. In 'Fear busting and monster taming: an approach to the fears of young children' (1989: 107–13), White describes a 'ritual' which he encouraged parents to undertake, designed to assist their child in relation to his night fears. Drawings, photographs, notes and certificates played a major part:

> The parents are to obtain a photograph album and label it the 'Monster and Worm Catching and Taming Album' or the 'Fear Busting Album' and take pictures of their child . . . undertaking the various preparations for monster taming . . . [and] take photographs pertaining to any other more fearless aspects of the child's life style that emerge . . . I usually show the child examples of the 'Monster Taming and Worm Catching and Taming Certificate' and the 'Fear Busting Diploma' . . . membership is so exclusive that, try as they might, it is unlikely that they will find any of their friends, relatives or class mates who have either a Monster and Worm Catching and Taming Certificate or a Fear Busting Diploma . . . (White, 1989: 110–11)

Mark, aged 6, overcame his fears after only one session:

> At the next appointment, two weeks later, Mark was beaming and Marjorie [Mark's mother] looked happy and relaxed. Mark, carrying his 'monster box' and Fear Busting Album, detailed how he had caught and tamed his fears . . . we reviewed the Fear Busting Album together and Mark was presented with his diploma. On the follow-up, Mark was 'fear-free' and relatively care-free. Marjorie reported that he had not had any relapses, was even more confident and that they were both much happier. (White, 1989: 112)

In 1987 David Epston and four colleagues published a moving account of their work with Hayden, a Maori boy fatally ill with cancer (reprinted in Epston, 1989: 29–44). Therapy started when Hayden was aged 10 and continued until his death four years later. Therapeutic documents played a major part in the work. Epston wrote to Hayden summarizing some of their exchanges; Hayden wrote back; Epston wrote, with Hayden's agreement, a letter to his parents summarizing a family session about Hayden's stealing from his parents; Hayden's parents prepared an 'honesty chart' to be put above the boy's bed and filled in according to how he came through some secret 'honesty tests' they would set him; Hayden wrote to Epston about his success in these tests. Epston's paper ends with two documents written after Hayden died, by a social worker and Hayden's mother. In this way he extended therapy beyond Hayden to persons who had been close to him by these persons writing documents witnessing to their thoughts on Hayden's life and death.

Therapeutic documents in narrative work with a young teenager

I offer the 'story of therapy' which follows primarily as an example of how therapeutic documents may be used in narrative therapy. Although therapeutic documents are my focus, the reader might also like to identify other narrative therapy practices in this account. I took Donna's age into account in some details of therapy, but I might have taken a very similar approach with an adult experiencing this kind of problem.

Donna, aged 13, had been diagnosed by her doctor as experiencing 'post-traumatic stress disorder'. Eighteen months before, Donna had been a passenger in her father's car when he lost control because of another driver's error, and crashed. Donna had been quite badly injured, and she retained some visible but unobtrusive scars on her neck. Her father's injuries had been life threatening. He was in hospital for a long while and needed many months of follow-up treatment. For a year and a half after the accident Donna told nobody about the distressing psychological reactions she was increasingly experiencing. Finally a school friend, worried about the differences she had noticed in Donna, had told Donna's parents about these observations, and the matter came into the open.

I wondered whether, even before Donna met me, a letter might be helpful to her. She had suffered a major trauma, experienced frightening reactions, and coped with these by not talking about them. Now the 'secrets' were out, and she had been referred to a 'therapist' for 'treatment' – it would be natural for her to feel nervous and to wonder if she was going to have to re-live the accident all over again by describing it. My letter was not perhaps a therapeutic document in the strict sense, as therapy had not even begun, but was nevertheless a concrete, re-readable statement. It was intended to make contact, reassure her about counselling, set a friendly and informal tone, and unobtrusively initiate certain ways of conceptualizing and talking about her problem characteristic of narrative therapy:

Dear Donna

I have just arranged with your parents for you all to come to my house on Wednesday evening next week. I thought you might like to know what we will be doing together.

Basically, the idea is for you to talk about the ways in which your accident is still distressing you, and for me to try to help you to overcome the bad memories which are invading your life and making it hard for you to feel safe. Among other things, I might suggest you do some drawing and writing at home – but only if this feels OK for you (and despite being an English teacher many years ago, I won't mark your writing or bother about the spelling!). Nasty events quite often affect people for some time afterwards, and this can be quite frightening, but it's perfectly normal for this to happen and with a bit of help you should be able to defeat these unpleasant thoughts and memories.

I look forward to meeting you soon.

Yours sincerely,

Martin Payne

At the first session Donna gradually settled and, sometimes prompted by her parents, responded to my invitation to tell me what was happening in her life. She felt dominated by memories of the accident and by physical and emotional reactions associated with those memories, including flashbacks; sleep disturbances; fear reactions to anything reminding her of the accident, such as flashing lights on police cars; extreme anxiety about her father's safety even if he was in an adjacent room; irritability; difficulty in concentrating; indifference to previous leisure interests; fear of even short journeys; continuous obtrusive memories of the accident; and continual obtrusive fretting thoughts about it. Donna had been afraid that talking to her parents about these reactions would cause them unnecessary distress, at a time when her father was recovering slowly from his serious injuries and when her mother was worried about his recovery. The longer she had kept the reactions secret, the worse they became – so in turn the more she feared revealing them. Her school-work had suffered, she had behaved irritably and 'on a short fuse' with friends, and disturbed sleep had made her continually tired and lethargic.

I congratulated Donna on her skill and consideration in building a defensive wall around herself to contain the thoughts and to prevent them from invading her parents' life as well as hers. But perhaps that wall had now become a prison? Donna nodded. I asked her to identify which reactions were most distressing, and she said that the intrusive memories, thoughts and flashbacks were worst. I asked if anyone had discussed with her possible reasons why these reactions happened, and she said that nobody had done this. I then invited her to consider the idea that people generally find the more an experience is repeated, and the more familiar it becomes, the less frightening it is. She agreed that this was so. Did she also agree that *thinking* about something worrying, making it familiar by going over it in imagination, usually helped her to cope with it? Yes, that made sense to her. I then suggested that her reactions might have been friendly in intention – attempts by her mind to help her to come to terms with the accident, so that in the end familiarity would make the memories less distressing. The trouble was that this event had been so unusually terrifying that her mind had made a mistake; instead of helping by 'familiarity breeding contempt', the repeated memories and images had kept the accident alive for her and had the opposite effect to what her mind was aiming at. Did that make sense to her as a possibility? She said that it did.

Yvonne Dolan (1991: 14), writing of post-traumatic stress reactions in a different context, makes the point: 'Flashbacks can be seen as an unconscious attempt to desensitize through repetition; however, this apparent desensitization attempt is . . . rarely successful. Instead, the survivor needs additional help and support from external rather than just internal resources.' I asked Donna whether there were any contrasting, happier thoughts or images which sometimes entered her mind and pushed the unwanted thoughts and images away. She couldn't think of any examples, so I asked if she could tell me of any thoughts and images which, if they *could* do this, might be helpful in reminding her of happier events and safe places, as opposed to her thoughts and images of danger and fear. For the first time in the session Donna became quite animated. She mentioned a recent school trip to Italy, which she and her friends had very much enjoyed, and an evening when various members of the family had fun together. I invited her to tell me more about these times and, by persistently showing interest in the concrete details of these experiences, assisted her to describe them at length with vividness and precision. The trip to Italy had been particularly enjoyable and, she now remembered, had for quite a lot of the time banished the bad memories.

I suggested that this might be evidence that bad memories were vulnerable to the power of friendship and of family love, and that this might be a clue to how Donna might exclude them in time. By her deliberately making good memories more vivid and powerful, bad memories might find less and less space for themselves. It was just an idea – I could be wrong – but might it be worth an experiment? Donna agreed that it might. I asked if she had taken photos on her trip to Italy – yes, she had, she said. Right – I was going to request her father to pay for big enlargements of the three which most represented her good memories of the trip. Would Donna clear part of a wall in her bedroom and perhaps get a large pinboard? My suggestion was that she arrange her Italy trip photos on the wall, and look at them each night before going to bed, really concentrating rather than just glancing at them, to bring back and keep alive her memories of that good time when bad memories had retreated. In addition, I would like to suggest she write a short description of the evening when the family had fun together, making her account as vivid as possible – and this account could also be displayed. If on any other occasions she realized that the bad memories were absent, even for a short while, it might be a good idea to represent these on her wallboard too, in any way she chose. Donna seemed pleased at these suggestions and her father undertook to help with the practicalities. I also suggested that she might like to select a small object strongly associated with feelings of safety and security, and have it with her at all times – when unwanted memories and thoughts started to invade she could hold this object tightly and it might have some power in preventing the intruders from entering any further. This was an adaptation of a technique described by Yvonne Dolan (1991: 92–4).

At the second session, a fortnight later, Donna said that she had created her display and was enjoying looking at it. She had chosen a tiny, cuddly, toy dog given to her by her grandfather as her object of safety and now carried it with her. On one occasion she had found her intrusive thoughts vanished more quickly than usual. She also realized that she had developed a way of preventing the intrusive thoughts and images from interfering with her school work: when her concentration lapsed because the thoughts started to intrude, she did not waste energy in fighting them but took a break, then came back to the work later. However, she was still finding a problem with bad temper and irritability, particularly with friends, although they understood and made allowances. I said that perhaps the intrusive thoughts and memories were like *false* friends – they claimed to be trying to help her by repetition/acclimatization, but in fact were tormenting her. What did she do about friends who turned out to be false? Had she ever had to face this? Yes, she said, this had happened to her. She had not tried to renew those friendships but had just moved on, making other friends. When her false friends had tried to 'get at' her she had faced them out, and in the end they had stopped. For the rest of Donna's therapy the externalization of her distressing reactions as 'false friends' became a central image, and the technique of ignoring false friends, while building and drawing on real affection and friendship, became a metaphor for her fight against intruding memories.

Three weeks later Donna reported some encouraging changes. Her concentration had improved and she had enjoyed writing an English essay on a topic unrelated to the accident. She was far less fearful when her father was out of sight and had stopped following him around the house. She had read a horror novel alone in her room and, despite her parents' worries that it might arouse fear reactions related to the accident, had enjoyed the story without any ill effects. She had been less irritable. Because of these encouraging signs I suggested that Donna might like to complete a short questionnaire before the next session, which could be repeated at different times over the period of her therapy to form a record of her progress, as the questionnaire incorporated a 'scoring system'. She could keep a copy of this document for her display board and I would keep a copy for my notes. The questionnaire was my simplified adaptation for Donna of Horowitz's 'impact of event scale' (Horowitz et al., 1979, in Scott and Stradling, 1992: 177). She awarded herself points on a scale from 0 to 3 according to the degree to which she judged she had, that particular week, escaped from 15 listed possible reactions to the accident. These included avoiding things which reminded her of the accident, pictures of it popping into her mind, feeling guilty about it, dreaming about it, and feeling as if it had only just happened. Donna brought two completed copies to the third session, three weeks later. She had scored 62 per cent which, I reminded her, would have been a 'good pass' if the score had been an examination result.

At the fourth session I said that I was going to ask one of her parents to take part in a dialogue with me. I had prepared a version of Michael White's training exercise where an 'Investigative Reporter' interviews a 'Problem', with an 'Observer' listening

(White, 1995b). I was to act the part of a 'false friend', Miss Nastyfears, and Donna was just to listen, in the role of 'False Friend's Resister'. Questions Donna's father asked Miss Nastyfears, as he enthusiastically played the 'Investigator', included:

- What was it about Donna at that time which you took advantage of?
- What knowledge and skills possessed by Donna were you aiming to undermine?
- What parts of her life has Donna always succeeded in keeping away from your influence?
- What special skills, knowledge and qualities have you found in Donna that have limited or defeated your attempts to make her life miserable?
- As Donna continues to build on her discoveries of how to get you out of her life, what sort of a future do you see for yourself?

Donna was listening to a re-storying of her experience, with the 'Problem' testifying to the difficulties it was finding in trying to dominate her life. Afterwards, Donna and her mother said that they had found the 'interview' revealing and helpful in bringing out evidence of Donna's courage, endurance and progress. Looking back on the session now, I realize that I missed an opportunity to reinforce the impact of the 'interview' through documents. Tape recording the session would have added verisimilitude to the 'Investigative Reporter' and given Donna a means of re-storying by listening to the tape, and a transcript might have made a useful addition to her display.

At the next session Donna's parents described a distressing setback. Their solicitor had arranged for them and Donna to be seen by a psychologist, who had asked Donna many persistent, probing questions about the accident. As Donna described the events she had re-experienced their terror. Donna's mother, hearing full details of the accident for the first time and seeing her daughter's extreme distress, had become so upset that she had had to leave the psychologist's consulting room. Post-traumatic reactions had now started to affect her and she thought she might now need therapy herself. Indeed, these reactions continued over the next two or three weeks, after which she began therapy with one of my colleagues.

I realized that the interview had probably been arranged in connection with Donna's compensation claim. Clearly, the family had not known Donna would face such intrusive and detailed questions, and had not had the opportunity to prepare for the ordeal. Donna claimed that, although upset at the time, she had not been affected by the interview once it was over, and that since then she had been getting on well with her normal life. As described above, I misjudged the situation and wrote a congratulatory reinforcing letter – only to discover, in the sixth session, that Donna had in reality reverted to protective behaviour towards her parents. She had experienced a very powerful return of some of the reactions which therapy had been assisting her to exclude, including extreme irritability, and had become very upset and tearful over minor misunderstandings with friends. I was painfully aware that my 'therapeutic letter' might well have added to her stress by the unintended irony of its positive tone. Much of the session was spent in discussing how 'Secrecy' was an ally of the 'False Friends', because people who cared for Donna needed to be sure of what she was actually feeling and thinking.

Donna used the next session to discuss an issue concerning difficult relations with a friend. At the end of the session her father remarked on how much this topic contrasted with the topics of earlier sessions. Donna had not even mentioned the accident or its consequences – she had discussed a pressing but 'normal' concern. This matched what he and his wife had noticed recently: Donna had made great progress in overcoming both the original effects of the accident and the re-activation of those effects resulting from the interview with the psychologist. He felt that the work we had done before the psychologist's session must have laid a firm foundation for Donna's recovering from the setback. A session was agreed for four weeks' time, but a few days before the appointment Donna's mother rang to say that Donna was so much better in all respects that they all felt no more counselling would be necessary. I wrote to Donna, expressing my pleasure at her progress. The letter ended:

> I enclose a Certificate. It's light-hearted – but it has a serious purpose, which is to remind you and the False Friends that you have found ways of overcoming your problems. The reason for the Australian reference on the Certificate is that I use methods developed by an Australian therapist, Michael White.
>
> You *may* from time to time have setbacks, with unhelpful memories returning and producing some difficulty for you, but I'm sure you will deal with these well and come through. You can always come back for a follow-up session if this does happen – but it may not.

> You and your parents were a pleasure to work with and I wish you all the best for the future.
>
> Sincerely,
>
> Martin Payne

Donna's certificate is reproduced on p. 129.

Writing to apprehend experience

As a teacher of English, before I ever thought of becoming a counsellor, I discovered that talking and writing about puzzling, painful or worrying aspects of life could be helpful to people. Writing, in particular, could be therapeutic, although at that time I did not use that word to describe what I observed. When students chose painful or confusing experiences as topics for writing, they sometimes not only 'discovered' what they had experienced through putting it into words, but, in the act of shaping and controlling this material, of storying it, found that they felt better. I vividly remember an essay by an evening-class student, in response to the deliberately vague set title 'A day that changed my life', where she chose to describe how she had been sexually assaulted many years before. It was a powerful and very personal piece of writing and I felt privileged to read it. At the end of the essay she wrote that she had never told anyone of the incident, let alone described it – and that she now felt a great sense of release. I also found that students' descriptions of joyful or satisfying events often appeared to reinforce their pleasure in these experiences.

Talking is ephemeral unless recorded, but when experience is put into writing persons create a permanent entity. They hone it until it expresses what they have discovered they mean; they read and reread what they have written; they show it to an audience, even if the audience only comprises the teacher. They know that what happened to them is now 'on record'. As a teacher I always gave choices – I would never urge or even invite persons to write about painful or traumatic events in their lives. As White says of therapy with persons who have been abused, 'There is an entirely significant distinction to be drawn between distress and traumatisation'

(White, 1995a: 87). I am dubious about the idea of 'catharsis' through writing, although emotion certainly often accompanies the struggle of putting painful experiences on to paper. I am inclined to believe that the act of writing changes the meaning of the experience for the person retrospectively, by enabling them to recall detail in ways that are more 'experience-near'. When a person writes, events are recalled, sifted, prioritized, organized into sequence and encapsulated into words on the page. Memories are concrete, no longer amorphous. The written description takes on its own 'reality' and comes to represent the events to the person, displacing the unstructured memories which preceded the writing. The new association of past events with the 'safe present' when the account is written can detach the events from their place as a malign presence-from-the-past in the person's self-story. In therapeutic writing, this detachment from the effects of past events can be enhanced by persons including unique outcomes and deconstructed ideas in the narrative, so that the story they write is richer than their pre-storying memories. I now frequently encourage persons to write about their lives as well as to talk about them, and many have said that they find the results helpful.

Persons sometimes produce writing on their own initiative:

Jenny was feeling increasingly undervalued by her husband, who in her perception was giving excessive attention to a woman friend of the family. She did not suspect a sexual affair but felt hurt and abandoned because he appeared indifferent to her own need for time with him, and talked about little but this friend. Jenny defined the problem she brought to counselling as her 'jealousy'. She had tried to overcome this, partly by contact with the friend and attempting to help her with her problems. She could not reconcile her perception of being neglected and undervalued with what appeared to be an innocent and supportive relationship, and she was feeling angry, confused and self-blaming. Her husband refused to come to joint therapy, saying firmly that it was her problem and that she had to sort herself out. He had angrily called her reactions 'irrational jealousy' and had lectured her on the connection between these reactions and her unhappy childhood, explaining that this past history had made her over-sensitive and suspicious.

In therapy, deconstructive questioning led Jenny to take the view that her experience of unhappiness and insecurity as a child should, rather, have led her husband to be aware of the legitimacy of her vulnerability. Instead, he used it as a basis of accusation, assuming a power position of 'psychological expertise' from which to deny the impact of his actions and to 'interpret' and dismiss her feelings. As a therapeutic document, I gave Jenny a copy of Gass and Nichols's paper 'Gaslighting: a marital syndrome?' (1988, discussed in White, 1995a: 51–2), which describes this kind of predominantly male behaviour. Jenny began to identify other hurtful behaviours by her husband, which had become 'invisible' to her by their frequency and familiarity, and which contradicted her dominant story of his being loving and considerate towards her. At the end of a session in which she talked of how fragile these new perceptions felt, how quickly they became vulnerable to her husband's insistence that there was something 'wrong with her', I suggested she might think of persons, living or dead, who could have recognized the genuineness of her despair and the legitimacy of her anger – a 'support team' or 'nurturing team' (White, 1995a: 104–7). This idea appealed to her, and we agreed to discuss it in the following session.

At the start of the next session, Jenny took out of her bag three long letters which she had decided to write to three persons, two living and one dead, to ask them to be members of her 'nurturing team'. In the letters she described her situation, the conclusions she was reaching about it, and her dilemmas concerning what actions she might take. She did not actually intend to post the letters to the living persons, and she did not feel the need for a 'support team meeting' – one of the options I had mentioned. The three persons' presence in her life was now an invisible but powerful supportive force, and writing the letters had been enough to confirm her new perspectives and to increase her determination to find ways of bringing about change.

A few weeks later she left her husband, taking her child with her, and moved to a rented flat. At this point I gave Jenny, as a therapeutic document, a copy of White's 'Migration of Identity' chart (White, 1995a: 102). This chart represents in the form of a graph how, typically, women who have separated from abusing men move from initial euphoria to a low point of doubt, when they are tempted to go back to the man, and then gradually return to knowing that they must stay separated. I had observed this sequence in other women who discussed their feelings on leaving abusive men, and I wanted to offer Jenny an opportunity for solidarity with these women – a sense that, if a reversal of feeling should occur, she had moral support from others who had faced similar conflicts. A few weeks later she did indeed experience a reversal of feeling, including the invasion of powerful doubts about her new perception of the way her husband had been treating her. She discovered that looking at the chart gave her a perspective on these doubts and prevented her from taking a precipitate decision to return to her husband. She also, without any suggestion from me, produced another written document symbolically representing her emergence from 'non-identity', when under her husband's influence, to her new state of knowledge and conviction. Jenny then came across evidence which appeared to confirm that the relationship between her husband and their friend had after all been more than friendship, and in her final session she acknowledged both the pain and grief of this discovery, and its validation of her perceptions, feelings and convictions.

Safeguards

LITERACY   It is essential to check that persons have sufficient literacy to feel comfortable with writing, especially since people who have minimal or few literacy skills are often reluctant to reveal this. I have developed various ways to approach this issue, such as saying 'Some people like to produce a short piece of writing at this stage, perhaps a few notes, or a list of their thoughts. It helps them to remember what thoughts they had in their counselling. Others don't like the idea of writing, or they just don't have the time for it. What do you think about this idea?' Persons can easily reject the suggestion of writing by implying that they find the idea impractical or unappealing. I then say something like 'Right – fair enough – but what if you told me roughly what you are thinking and then *I* wrote some notes, checking out that I'd got it right? How might that feel?' Sometimes a person willingly chooses this alternative, resulting in therapist-produced documents which the person nevertheless 'owns'.

HESITATIONS AROUND MECHANICAL SKILLS   Some persons are nervous about 'showing themselves up' to an 'educated' therapist if their mechanical skills are poor. I always assure them that if they decide to let me read their document I would not at all be interested in aspects like spelling, punctuation and grammar, which I think are over-rated, but only in what they 'say'.

PURPOSE   I do not conceive person-produced documents as therapeutic through any process of 'release' or 'catharsis'. They are permanent records of new knowledges and achievements, and their purpose is to consolidate, reinforce and perpetuate the self-story incorporating these new elements. This does not mean that emotion is always absent in their production; often persons find the process of writing to be moving. Sometimes they affirm that writing has helped them to feel 'released' or 'free from a burden' and when this happens I believe and respect their statement. But I have an unspoken reservation that such results may be temporary if the writing has not also assisted them to revise and consolidate the *meaning* of the events they describe. Because of this I do not encourage persons to engage in writing of a directly emotional nature. I encourage them to write about what they *think* rather than what they feel.

AVOIDING RE-TRAUMATIZATION Sometimes persons who have had experiences of terrifying situations, abuse or violence wonder whether writing detailed accounts of these events might be helpful. They ask if it might 'get it out of my system' or 'help me to come to terms with it'. I face a dilemma here. I have no right or wish to deny persons the opportunity to create writing which they feel could be helpful to them, and I have known instances when persons have found release from the effects of past memories through writing about them. Nevertheless, I fully identify with White's view that 'the notion of healing practices based on the imperative of returning to the site of the abuse in order to re-experience it is a highly questionable notion and, as well, danger-ous . . . [this] can reinforce for them the dominant meanings that inform the self-destructive expression of the experience of the abuse. And, this can contribute to renewed trauma' (White, 1995a: 85). My practice is to be cautious. I do not say 'No, don't do it, it could be dangerous.' I ask the person where he gained the idea that such writing might be helpful, and discuss with him the meta-phorical nature of the 'getting it out of the system' phrasing he is using. I usually find it possible to gain agreement that 'getting it all out' metaphors are implicit comparisons with poisoning, implying the need for something harmful to be neutralized or ejected. But are memories, images in the mind, actually the same as poison? Is writing about traumatic experience really an equival-ent to 'getting poison out of' the body? If not, what are the differ-ences? Perhaps bad memories could equally well be described as 'painful wounds still in the process of healing which need to be left alone'? Might writing about painful events 'feed' them rather than 'starve' them, and make their memory even more powerful and threatening? If the person does decide to go ahead and write about the traumas he has experienced then I suggest some safeguards, adaptations of Yvonne Dolan's precautions for persons verbally describing their abuse (Dolan, 1991: 27–8). These measures might include choosing a 'symbol of the safe present' to represent and evoke safety in the present time, and having it to hand while writing. Another possibility, to prevent flashbacks from taking over, is for the person to choose a distinctive object in the room where he is writing. If his memories become too painful, he can focus on this as a 'lifeline anchor' and draw himself back to the present.

CONFIDENTIALITY   I make it clear that I have no assumption that I will see the person's writing. If he does ask me to read it, I assure him the document will be confidential. Sometimes persons produce a piece of writing which is too long to read in the session, so I assure them that it will be locked in my filing cabinet, and if their name is on it I suggest this be removed or blocked out as an additional security measure.

FLEXIBILITY   Persons often produce documents significantly different in format, length and purpose from what we have discussed. I assure them that, to me, this variant is a sign that the writing we discussed was not geared to their needs – and I express pleasure in their taking the initiative.

RESPONDING   I spend time discussing documents which persons have written. I do not assume that the act of writing is enough in itself to be therapeutic. Follow-up is needed to assist the person to reinforce and confirm the discoveries she has made through the process of writing. If I have read the document I tentatively state what it 'said' to me and invite the person to explain, amplify or simply to re-tell some of the meanings of the document for her. If I have not read the document, perhaps because it is too personal or private for the person to share, I do not of course ask questions about content. I invite her to talk about what writing the document has meant to her, what differences it has produced in her thoughts and feelings, and if there are any ways in which this writing might have paved the way for her life in the future.

Avoiding top-down stances in therapist-produced documents

In my experience, therapist-created documents present particular difficulties in terms of 'authorship'. They need to be produced with particular care in order to maintain 'therapist de-centring' (see Chapter 9) and to represent the person's thoughts and perceptions rather than the therapist's. Even the originators of narrative therapy sometimes appear to have difficulty in avoiding a rather 'therapist-centred' tone or approach when writing documents. David Epston describes sending 'letters of prediction', in which he outlines the changes and developments *he* anticipates in persons' lives, asking them not to open the letter for several months – but he actually expects them to give into curiosity and open the letter anyway, which then becomes 'a prophesy which may fulfil itself' (White and Epston, 1990: 95). Epston assumes and hopes that persons will 'cheat'. But what if they leave the letter unopened as requested, and what if Epston's 'expert' predictions then turn out to be only partly true or not true at all? What would that make them feel? How would that assist them? In a therapy which values transparency it appears inconsistent to depend on tricking persons for a therapeutic document to be effective. Perhaps this is a residual influence of the 'paradoxical injunction' techniques in strategic family therapy, when persons are requested to follow a course of action in the belief and hope that they will actually do the opposite (Haley, 1987: 76–84).

In writing therapeutic documents, I need not abandon forms of language which express my own assumptions and positions, but my vocabulary needs to match the person's own perceptions of what has come out of therapy. I can all too easily become patronizing and condescending unless I embody in documents only such elements of her self-story as the person has already recognized. To take externalizing language as an example: persons often continue to refer to themselves as anxious, or to describe themselves as having anxiety. In writing a therapeutic document I use the vocabulary of my approach to therapy, and externalize problems, but a person will see no discrepancy between her saying 'I'm not anxious any more', in a session, and my writing, in a therapeutic document, 'Jane has defeated anxiety.' On the other hand, if I include a sentence like 'Jane has successfully opposed the attempts of internalizing discourse to recruit her into a career of self-blame' then, unless this reflects very detailed, transparent and clear discussions in our sessions, she will feel baffled and imposed upon.

Co-creating person-produced documents

Some persons are not very confident in their ability to express themselves in writing, and seek my help in the mechanics of producing a document. The balance between facilitating the person's own thoughts and expressions on the one hand, and imposing the expression of these thoughts on the other, when assisting the person to put them into writing, is extremely delicate. It is quite difficult to avoid supplying phrasing or vocabulary when a person is struggling to articulate new ways of thinking and perceiving. Therapy vocabulary, which may have been helpful to the person in provisional verbal interchange, can be stilted and remote from her own personal expressions when writing, but my therapist power position may make it very hard for the person to refuse 'helpful' suggestions. Obviously, a document virtually written for the person by myself and just containing my ideas would be 'top-down' and disempowering. The process of consultation about what she wishes to express, and in what words this might best be expressed, needs to be sensitive and tentative.

But perhaps a degree of 'therapist-speak' is almost inevitable – we all tend to take on vocabularies expressing concepts which are newly meaningful to us. I like to think that when I assist persons to produce documents, and their writing ends by incorporating some narrative therapy terminology, the persons are not having this imposed upon them but that the language represents and expresses their freshness of discovery.

An example of how such a balance may be achieved, in work by White, comes in an article by four members of a group with the self-chosen title 'Power to our Journeys'. This group consists of persons who, according to the article,

> have been recipients of mainstream psychiatric services for varying lengths of time, have had admissions to psychiatric hospitals, have been subject to various treatments, and have all been assigned various diagnoses over this time. The people who have diagnosed us have mostly settled on the diagnosis of schizophrenia . . . We get together once per month and invite Michael White to join us to keep a special record of our conversation and to ask questions that assist us to express our thoughts on various issues. After each of these meetings he puts together

our ideas in a document which serves as a record of our evolving knowledges and the development of our skills of living. These documents are a powerful resource to us in our work to recover our lives and in assisting us to deal with crises. (Brigitte, Sue, Mem and Veronika, 1996: 26)

After describing how members of the group have been 'silenced' over many years about their experience of voices and visions, the authors describe how they are now been able 'to speak of the troublesome voices and visions in a forum that contributes to a powerful exposé of their purposes and their operations . . . by meeting together to extend this exposé and to further pool our knowledge and skills, we have all been able to further change our relationships with the troublesome voices and visions so they become less dominant in our lives' (1996: 26). There are moments in this article when the actual authors' 'natural' expression is clear:

At times this very silencing has contributed to a sense that we might be going mad.

Some of us became homeless for years, just going from place to place. There were friends and relatives who managed to hang in, but we didn't know how to help them.

It is not that we still don't have hard times. We do.

At times we feel like larrikins, and the feeling is just great.

Despite these moments, much of the article appears to be written in narrative therapy vocabulary and in White's own prose style. Perhaps he wrote it on behalf of the group, checking it out with them, in the same way that he writes documents recording their meetings – 'putting together our ideas'? His 'voice' is often present in the rhythm of sentences, and in the vocabulary: 'assigned various diagnoses', 'similar projects to reclaim their lives', 'assist us', 'evolving knowledges', 'recover our lives', 'so they become less dominant in our lives'. It shows in the consciously externalizing language: 'a powerful exposé of [the visions' and voices'] purposes and their operations', 'change our relationship with the troublesome voices and visions'. If the article was literally written by the four group members White appears to have been such a powerful influence that their own personal styles of expression have been rather submerged. Whatever the method of composition, at a superficial reading the piece could appear to demonstrate an imposition, where the persons' own style of writing has been marginalized. Parts of the article read like White's own papers:

> It has been important for us to experience our work to reclaim our lives from the troublesome voices and visions as a struggle against injustice. These voices and visions are oppressive, and since our work on revising our relationship with these voices and visions addresses issues of power and control, then this relationship is a political relationship. This political understanding provides us with strength, as it keeps us in touch with the fact that we are not just on a personal journey, but also on a political journey. (1996: 29)

> It has been proposed elsewhere that the libraries of psychiatric hospitals be obliged to include the sort of alternative texts that might be created by collections of the sort of therapeutic documents that we provide here, and that these be placed alongside the more formal psychiatric texts. These alternative texts just might be more helpful to people who are struggling with troublesome voices than the standard texts. (1996: 30)

Perhaps White might have done rather more to encourage these four persons to write in their own register. But this would have presented them with an enormous task – to express their ideas through vocabulary which was both their own, and yet adequate to convey and embody concepts which have been developed in the vocabulary of narrative therapy and which became influential in their group sessions. I think that the 'White-echoes' are inevitable – perhaps reflecting the many conversations the group has held with him, where he offered them opportunities to tell alternative stories to describe their experiences. What could be more exciting for persons than discovering vocabulary which both expresses and encapsulates new directions and discoveries in their thinking? In my opinion, the article demonstrates an *integration* of the writers' own natural expressions, and therapist-influenced expressions which have been absorbed into their evolving self-stories – aspects which they refer to as 'Solidarity', 'Determination' and 'Authoring' of our own lives (Brigitte et al., 1996: 31–3).

Examples of therapeutic documents

I offer below some therapeutic documents from my own work. I do not see this selection as comprehensive or the examples as 'ideal'.

They are certainly not offered as a substitute for reading the relevant chapters in *Narrative Means to Therapeutic Ends* (White and Epston, 1990) with their rich variety of examples.

Arthur's graph of panic's retreat

Arthur, an engineer, had been increasingly affected by panic attacks, which appeared to have no logical explanation or origin. Almost worse than the attacks themselves was this sense of irrationality and arbitrariness, which resulted in his feeling at the mercy of events. To gain some sense of power over the attacks he decided to study them. He kept a record of them and noted their relative intensity, their duration and the life events associated with them, in the form of a graph with daily entries. After a few weeks he identified situations in which they were more likely to occur, and developed strategies for anticipating them and 'seeing them off', which his beautifully produced graph, with its colour codings and mathematical precision, showed to be increasingly effective. They were less powerful, less frequent and lasted for shorter times. Arthur produced a statistical analysis of the attacks' waning power which in turn appeared to become a self-fulfilling prophesy, and the attacks finally disappeared. Arthur's document is not reproduced here because in its final version it was about two metres wide!

Witnessing through publication

In this instance I have permission to use the person's real name and circumstances. Wendy had a little boy of two, David, but her second son, Andrew, had been born without life two years after David's birth. She brought several issues to counselling, one of the most important being her continuing grief for Andrew, and the stresses produced by well-meaning but unhelpful attempts by friends and relatives, who did not conceptualize Andrew as a 'real person', to try to encourage her to 'get over it and move forward'. For Wendy, Andrew was her second child, now 'in eternity', and people's dismissing his reality was profoundly hurtful. In our third session Wendy mentioned that she had been on a creative writing course, that she had had poetry published in a local newsletter and had written a poem which had reached an advanced stage in a national poetry competition, and a play for radio. I did not need to encourage Wendy to write therapeutic documents – she was already doing this. In putting her writing into the public domain she is not only witnessing to her own life and beliefs but is making a contribution to the lives of others. Several short books, sometimes combining prose and poetry, have followed, including what she sees as her most significant exploration of the theme of re-kindled hope for another child after the loss of her son Andrew, *Rocky Start* (Webb, 1997), which describes her fragile pregnancy with her third son, Peter. Wendy continues to write, with the proceeds going to appropriate charities, despite an exceptionally busy life. I quote a poem from *Rocky Start*.

Birthday Joy

No birthday cake, no party hats,
To mark time's passage. Lustreless
The backdrop of our tinselled fate.
One solitary candle's glow.

The joyful tryst, of two from one,
Foils consummation; cloyed in death.
No birthday cake, no party hats,
To mark time's passage, lustreless.

Discarded wrappings wrap no gift;
Empty the box of birthday joy.
Timeless nativity was birthed,
Simply to immortality.
No birthday cake, no party hats,
To mark the lustrous snuff of time.

Two light-hearted/serious certificates

The certificates displayed here were 'presented' to persons – both adults – in their final sessions, with an explanation that, although the certificates were quite light-hearted, they had a serious purpose in celebrating the person's successful fight against problems, and in serving as a reminder of these victories. The 'Australian' references were explained by my paying tribute to White and Epston as originators of the 'award' idea.

Practical issues

Five years after *Narrative Means to Therapeutic Ends* (White and Epston, 1990), White returned to therapeutic documents in a follow-up essay 'Therapeutic documents revisited' and addressed the amount of time and energy it takes therapists to encourage or create documents (White, 1995a: ch. 8). White makes a case for

* * *

ANGLO-AUSTRALIAN SOCIETY OF ANXIETY AND
DEPRESSION BASHERS

This is to certify that
GEORGE FITT
has demonstrated the ability to
recognize
face up to
fight
and defeat
EXISTENTIAL ANXIETY
and its ally
IRRATIONAL DEPRESSION
And has put in place
Strategies for Recognition and Early Massive Attack
should these enemies dare to attempt further invasion

* * *

Signed
Martin Payne
(UK representative, AASADB)
March 1995

* * *

documents *saving* therapist time. He refers to David Epston, who asked persons how many sessions of good therapy, which would otherwise have taken place, they thought each letter had represented for them: 'was the receipt of the letter as valuable to you as a whole session of therapy, or half a session of therapy, or did it subtract from your experience of therapy?' (White, 1995a: 200). On average, persons thought receiving one letter was as useful as four and a half sessions of therapy.

> So . . . our response would be, 'How could a decision *not* to engage in this practice be justified?' After all, even if one of these documents took one hour of a therapist's time to prepare, then, considering that the average duration of an interview is one hour, by my calculations the

---

ANGLO-AUSTRALIAN SOCIETY FOR THE SUPPRESSION OF DEPRESSION

This is to certify that

HELEN WARTON

has demonstrated outstanding ability in the following skills:

- The identification of Depression and Panic
- The ability to recognize the appropriateness of Self-care
- The capacity to leave an Impossible Situation rather than remain subject to it
- The ability to recognize who might help, and to call on help
- The ability to tell Depression to get out of her life
- The ability to insist that Panic leave her alone
- Recognition of an appropriate pace of escape from Panic and Depression's power in her life
- Recognition of evidence that she is escaping from Panic and Depression's terrorization
- The ability to build on small successes until they grow huge
- The ability to recognize that out of Resistance has come increased Strength, Resourcefulness and Courage

Date of Award: August 1997

Certified by: M.E. Payne
(UK Representative, Anglo-Australian Society for the Suppression of Depression)

---

therapist has saved three and a half hours of their own time, or three and a half hours of agency time! (1995a: 200)

I find this argument flawed. Unless some or all of the time I saved could be ring-fenced for administration, including writing therapeutic letters, new persons would keep starting therapy at closer intervals than previously, since each person would be averaging fewer sessions than those seen before the introduction of therapeutic documents. I would soon be overwhelmed with all the additional therapeutic letters and documents needed for the increased number of persons – and since I am contracted to a fixed number of appointments per week I would find quite the opposite of 'saving three and a half hours of my own time'. With regard to private work, I do not feel I could charge persons for the time taken to write documents, and in any case this would probably put my fees out of their reach.

Perhaps a more helpful answer to questions about how to prevent therapeutic documents consuming inordinate time is White's suggestion of brief, person-produced documents, which he calls 'simple translations' and 'statements of position'. These, he claims, 'are not at all time consuming – in fact they require the investment of a bare minimum of '"non-contact time" from thera- pists' (1995a: 201). 'Simple translations' comprise conclusions reached by persons in a session, checked out and recorded in note form by the therapist during the session itself then written up into a summary; 'statements of position' are similar, but are written up by the person with the therapist's assistance. I must admit to remaining unconvinced: my production of such documents has usually taken at least an hour. The production of 'statements of position' for a number of persons a week would need considerable commitment outside 'contact time'.

My experience is that the only way to produce therapeutic docu- ments is to accept this as a commitment to the persons I see, and write them in my own time. They are a really useful contribution to counselling, but I feel the practical difficulties involved are not satisfactorily addressed in White's essay. I am left with a degree of guilt that, by not producing and encouraging documents as often as I would wish, I am not entering fully into narrative practice for all the persons who seek my assistance.

Summary

Therapeutic documents produced by the therapist, or by the person with appropriate precautions against imposition of therapist ideas or re-traumatization, can provide permanent expressions and reminders of progress, discoveries and new perspectives. They can celebrate and affirm change and achievement, and assist the person's escape from the imposed 'expertise' of others. Letters, statements, certificates and many other formats may be used, including non-verbal as well as written or typed documents, chosen according to the person's age and situation. One result of producing therapeutic documents appears to be the satisfactory completion of counselling in fewer sessions than would otherwise have been needed.

7 Telling and Re-telling

A person's telling and re-telling sub-plots of his life to a range of people in addition to the therapist, and hearing the responses of these others, can be a powerful means by which these sub-plots become confirmed and influential in the person's life and identity. This chapter outlines and discusses some methods of encouraging this process.

Examples of telling and re-telling

The following examples are of sessions where processes of telling and re-telling were undertaken in different ways, according to the resources available. I present the accounts without initial explanation, so that the reader can come to them freshly, as if an unbriefed observer. After the examples, I discuss the principles underlying telling and re-telling practices, then return to the examples to give descriptions of how these overall principles find expression in the varied circumstances of the sessions.

Gemma and Sara
I am working one to one with Gemma, and it is the third session. At the first session Gemma had unexpectedly brought her friend Sally with her, and also to subsequent sessions including this one. Her friend's presence had not been explained by Gemma, but I had welcomed Sally and given her a chair out of Gemma's line of vision. Then, and in the two subsequent sessions, Sally had quietly listened. Gemma mentions that between sessions the two friends hold discussions on the problem she brought to therapy, but that she still doesn't know what to do about it. We explore the issues further, with Sally listening. Towards the end of the session I invite Sally to pull up her chair and contribute to the conversation. I ask her questions around her knowledge of Gemma's history of dealing with the problem she has brought to therapy. What instances can she recall of Gemma's capacity to stand up to this problem, to live a full life despite it and to tackle similar issues? Sally's friendship

with Gemma is longstanding, and she has plenty of examples to give. I ask her what Gemma might say if questioned on Sally's role as a staunch friend. What qualities in Sally, in Sally's opinion, has Gemma valued and been able to recognize she can call on? What does this say about Gemma's capacity to recognize where she can seek appropriate assistance? What might this suggest about Gemma's ability to trust, and to be open and honest with, herself and others? Sally, perhaps not quite grasping this rather complex series of questions but answering them in the way _she_ finds meaningful, says that Gemma probably knows that she, Sally, had faced a similar problem in her own life, and had found a way through it, so perhaps this gives Gemma hope? I invite the friends to tell me more about their between-session discussions. Sally says she thinks Gemma wishes to take a particular step towards resolving the issue which brought her to counselling, but although this possible solution has been discussed between them, she hasn't heard Gemma talk about it in the therapy room. Gemma agrees that this step is indeed what she really wishes to consider and discuss – she hadn't mentioned it because she thought I might think the idea unwise. The three of us discuss the idea in some detail, trying to work out its possible outcomes, both the dangers and the potential advantages. We agree to meet again in four weeks' time, and meanwhile the friends will discuss the idea further. The session has taken 50 minutes. At the next session Gemma reports that she decided to risk putting her idea into action, and that she and Sally discussed how she might go about this. She acted, the outcome was entirely positive, and she is feeling happier than for years.

Rose and Richard

I am talking with Rose and Richard, who are married. My colleague Mary Wilkinson is sitting in a corner, out of the couple's line of vision. She is listening, and occasionally taking notes. A filing cabinet, a computer and a printer on a table take up most of the rest of the room's space. A cassette recorder is recording the session, and 35 minutes have passed since the session began. I invite the couple to turn their chairs so that they can see Mary too. I hand each person a notebook and pencil in case they would like to take notes, then invite Mary to join me in a 10-minute discussion of the conversation which has just taken place, while Rose and Richard listen. Mary does not 'interpret' what she has heard, or offer explanations for what the couple has revealed about their lives, relationships and conflicts. She talks of what has been particularly striking for her in their story. I respond to her comments and add some of my own, still with the couple silently listening. I ask Richard and Rose to turn back to face me, and invite them to comment on the conversation they have just heard. They do so, talking with each other as well as with me. After a further 10 minutes I ask them to move the angle of their chairs once again, then invite Richard, Rose and Mary to join me in a brief discussion about how we have all experienced the session. I know from previous sessions that the couple are comfortable with the cassette recorder, so I focus on Mary's presence: had they found this as acceptable as they anticipated when I suggested it at the previous session? Had a third person's listening made them inhibited or self-conscious? Both say that they had been comfortable with the situation, and that Mary's and my comments and conversation had been interesting and thought-provoking. I stop the recorder and give the cassette to the couple to take away; the session has lasted an hour.

Mark and Chris

A male therapist is quietly talking with Mark and Chris, a heterosexual couple, in a large therapy room. The interview began almost an hour ago. High on opposing walls are two video cameras supported by metal brackets, and changing pinpoint red lights show that the cameras are active alternately every couple of minutes. The whole width of one wall is taken up, above waist height, by a 'one-way' screen. Mark and Chris know that there are people behind the screen listening and watching, and they are familiar with this situation. On the other side of the one-way screen is a smaller, windowless observation room where several therapists are listening to the consultation by means of a loudspeaker system. They see the therapist relax, sit back in his chair and stand. He looks at the screen and says, 'Can we change round now, please?' For a few minutes things are a little disorderly, as the team members move from the observation room into the therapy room, and sit in a circle. The therapist and the couple have moved to the observation room. The group members begin to discuss what they have observed, with Mark, Chris and the therapist watching and listening behind the screen. The therapists do not 'interpret' the interview they have witnessed or offer explanations for what the couple has revealed about their lives, relationship and conflicts. They do not offer 'encouraging praise'. Instead, they talk of what has been particularly striking for them in the persons' story. Sometimes they relate what they have heard to episodes in their own lives – one woman says that the couple's determination to find a way of sorting out their differences reminds her of how her own parents came through a bad patch in their marriage, and went on to have a happy life together. Another observer briefly reveals the history of his struggle to understand that some of his behaviours, which he had seen as expressing love for his partner, had in fact been quite controlling. This memory helped him to see how painful it was for Mark to face similar issues in his conversation with the therapist, and he had been struck by his success in doing this. Three of the group outline questions they might like to ask the couple in order to gain a clearer idea of what certain experiences had meant for them. Others ask these colleagues what led to those particular questions coming into their minds, and in what ways did their colleagues envisage that answering these questions might be helpful to the couple? After 30 minutes or so the therapist enters, saying it is time to change round again. Soon the team is behind the screen again and the therapist, Mark and Chris are back in the therapy room. The observers hear the therapist invite Mark and Chris to comment on the discussion they have just heard, and, if they wish, to respond to some of the questions posed by members of the group. They take up this invitation, and also talk about their reactions to the echoes of their story in the observers' lives. After about 20 minutes the therapist looks at the screen and says, 'OK – can you all join us now, please?' The observers enter and everyone forms a circle. The therapist invites a discussion of ideas and reactions around the process of speaking, listening and sharing which they have just experienced. And what about the technology – the cameras and the one-way screen – were these OK or did they feel obtrusive and get in the way of spontaneity? Chris and Mark say that they found the whole experience absorbing and helpful, and affirm that the cameras and screen had not felt artificial or obtrusive. They really appreciated the team's involvement, comments and questions. Several persons talking about the couple's reactions to their problems, and commenting on their attempts to overcome them, had been affirming. They had both felt a sense of connection with the observing team despite the screen – or rather, *because* of it: if the team had been present in the therapy room this might have been distracting or inhibiting. After about 20 minutes the therapist draws the discussion to a close. He fetches the video cassette containing the recording of the whole process, and gives it to the couple to keep. The time from start to finish has been about two hours.

Telling sub-plots of self-stories

To repeat ground already covered: persons often tell self-stories of sadness, pessimism, confusion, pain and defeat. With the therapist's assistance they can begin to tell a modified story, and to include previously invisible, forgotten or dismissed elements which form the basis of a wider, more helpful perspective. The linking of these elements through questioning encourages persons to build them into 'sub-plots'. Once persons have begun to re-tell their stories to incorporate these sub-plots they come to recognize that these richer stories describe their lives more fully than their previous versions.

In the early stages of therapy, re-tellings are usually just to the therapist, in co-created dialogue. When articulated in conversation with a counsellor, persons' sub-plots fall into structures and sequences, but at this stage their stories are fragile. Having responsive *audiences* to a story brings a powerful additional dimension to the process of re-storying. To borrow from the language of the Internet: it is outside the therapy room where 'real life' occurs. Practices of telling and re-telling bring 'real life' into the therapy room, and also take what has happened in the therapy room out into real life – not just leaving it to the person to make these connections but providing specific contexts for this as part of the process of therapy. Recording the whole session can be an effective means of widening the audience for the story, and increasing the number of 're-tellings' heard by the persons.

Recruiting an audience for tellings and re-tellings

Questions inviting persons to identify people whom they might tell of their discoveries, to whom they might like to reveal their newly discovered unique outcomes and sub-plots, have always played an important part in narrative therapy. Recently, however, White has organized situations where a team of 'outsider witnesses' are, with the approval of the person, invited to attend sessions to listen to the person in conversation with him, and to comment on this conversation. A process of telling and re-telling, hearing and re-hearing, is established by these means, and the focus shifted from the single therapist as audience, to a larger group, sometimes including or consisting of people significant to the person in her real life, who will still be in the person's life when therapy has ended and the therapist is a fading memory (White, 1995a: ch. 7; 1997b: ch. 4). One aim of therapist-organized telling and re-telling is for the therapist decisively to move aside – to 'decentre' – so that the person's own real-life relationships increasingly form the context of her self-discoveries and so that these relationships, not the relationship with the therapist, are affirmed as 'therapeutic'. Therapist decentring is discussed more fully in Chapter 9.

Re-told self-stories 'become' life

White insists that the therapist has a crucial role in encouraging exploration of the *meaning* for the person of the discoveries she is making through telling and re-telling:

> *People are explicitly consulted about these subplots of their life* . . . Do they see them as positive or negative developments, or both positive and negative, or neither positive or negative? . . . In this work, *these subplots of people's lives are actually experienced* by those who consult us. In the course of the work itself, *people live these subplots.* Or, if you like, people's lives are embraced by these subplots. These subplots are not stories about life; they are not maps of the territory of life; they are not reflections of life as it is lived. *These subplots are structures of life, and in fact become more constitutive of life.* (White, in Hoyt, 1996: 43–4, emphasis added)

White does not take the extreme relativist position that since all experience is subjective, and all knowledge relative to time and circumstance, persons cannot know any truths about their past, or that all versions of the past are equally valid (or invalid). The past cannot be recalled in full, but we can do far more than shrug it off as unknowable, giving all 'versions' equal status. Our past did happen – we actually lived it and are actually influenced by our remembered version if it. We can resurrect and expand our knowledge of our past and our present – and when this has been firmly established in our awareness, we can choose to move from ways of thinking and acting which have been bounded and limited by our former dominant stories and step into different ways of thinking and living. These changes are *built* on the past; they are not unprecedented changes out of nowhere. Jenny's escape from a marriage which had become unsatisfactory (Chapter 6) was facilitated by her accessing knowledges that were already part-recognized. She told

her story, heard it re-told by myself in summarizing and paraphrasing responses, was encouraged to re-tell it in a more experience-near way so as to include aspects she had not brought fully
into awareness in the previous telling, and heard my further
responses and summarizing. With this process being repeated over
several sessions, the new story became rich enough for her to *act* in
accordance with it. A person's 're-authoring' her life, through the
processes of narrative therapy, can result in her beginning to *live* or
perform her new story, not just narrate it as a contrasting description.

Principles of telling and re-telling

Persons are encouraged to 'embed', develop and enrich their
evolving self-stories by:

- Telling them to a variety of people in addition to the therapist.
- Hearing their stories reflected back to them in ways which
  demonstrate others' interest, respect and wish to understand.
- Telling them again to other audiences.
- Hearing the stories as perceived by this audience.
- Continuing to re-tell and re-hear, re-tell and re-hear.

By these means, a person's self-story becomes a multiple story –
or, rather, it becomes a *multi-plotted* story capable of further enrichment and development in the context of the person's life outside
the therapy room, both now and later when therapy has ended. The
tellings and re-tellings in the therapy context, or arising from this
context, are launching pads for confirmatory and exploratory
tellings in the future, and these future tellings and re-tellings will
flesh out existing plot-lines and create further new self-story sub-
plots. Telling and re-telling in therapy is a logical enactment of the
most basic assumption underpinning the narrative way of working: 'we believe that persons generally ascribe meaning to their
lives by plotting their experience into stories, and that these stories
shape lives and relationships' (White and Epston, 1990: 79).

The examples reviewed

I now return to the examples of 'telling and re-telling' in various
settings with which I opened this chapter. I discuss them in the

reverse order of their earlier presentation – this time moving from the more complex to the simple. By this sequence I hope to demonstrate that practices developed and practised in a family therapy context may be realistically adapted, 'pared down', to more modest settings.

Mark and Chris

This description is of a half-day session during an intensive training course in narrative therapy given by Michael White at the Dulwich Centre, Adelaide. I have invented Mark and Chris, and the responses of this fictional couple and the team are also invented, but they are typical of actual sessions in which I took part. In this instance the team behind the screen consists of therapists.

White describes the development of this way of working in 'Reflecting teamwork as a definitional ceremony' (1995a: 172–9) and in 'Re-membering and definitional ceremony' (1997b: 3–116). Having observed that many team techniques in 'the culture of psychotherapy ... are informed by the discourses of pathology' and are designed to demonstrate therapists' belief in their own 'expertise', he began experimenting with alternative team formats which would seek to avoid 'unwittingly [contributing] further to the very forces that provide the context for the problems' (White, 1995a: 173–4). He was strongly influenced in his development of a format for this procedure by the anthropologist Barbara Myerhoff's description of a project spontaneously developed by a community of elderly ex-European Jews in Los Angeles (Myerhoff, 1986: ch. 11). These people had counteracted their sense of isolation and 'invisibility' in the wider social context by 'inventing a culture' where their history and their present circumstances were vigorously and emphatically made visible to themselves and the outside world by being 'told' in various formats. 'Tellings' included long dialogues between individuals, an invented ceremony uniting religious and secular elements, and a public parade in the full glare of media publicity to protest against the death of a member of the community who had been hit by a bicycle on a sidewalk, followed by a group meeting uniting young and old. The elderly Jews created a large narrative painting round the wall of the main room in their community centre, depicting their history; and took part in a university art and cultural festival, where their contribution was filmed and shown on television. Myerhoff suggests that these 'definitional ceremonies' allowed them to gain an increased sense of identity and pride within their own community of elderly Jewish immigrants (1986: 269); but also, and crucially, that by 'bearing witness to their own story' to the wider community they brought about important changes in their recognition by that wider community: 'by enacting their dreams publicly, they have altered the world in which they live' (1986: 284).

> Myerhoff calls attention to the critical role that the 'outsider-witnesses' plays in these definitional ceremonies. These outsider-witnesses are essential to the processes of the acknowledgement and the authentication of people's claims about their histories and about their identities, and to the performance of these claims. The participation of the outsider-witnesses in definitional ceremonies gives greater 'public and factual' character to these claims, serving to amplify them and to authorise them. (White, 1995a: 178)

In sequences of therapy such as that described in the example of Mark and Chris, White creates a parallel to the 'definitional ceremonies' described by Myerhoff about a very different context, but a context that was also about self-definition, and about the affirmation and confirmation of persons' knowledges about their lives. Through persons telling and re-telling their stories to the team of 'outsider witnesses', listening to their reactions, then telling the outsider witnesses of their reactions to those reactions, persons are led through a 'definitional' experience which is witnessed and affirmed. Myerhoff's explanation of the benefits gained by the elderly Jews through their publicly visible 'ceremonies' can also be used to describe the results of telling and re-telling in narrative therapy:

> As a result . . . something has changed externally; through their self-display, their commentary has persuaded outsiders of their own truth . . . [they] have managed to convey their statement to outsiders, to witnesses who then amplified and accredited their claims . . . A self-fulfilling prophesy and then some: the reality created by [their] imaginative statements is not limited to their own minds and beliefs but has become true for . . . non-members. As a result, the real world has been brought into conformity with imagination, by means of imaginative statements. (Myerhoff, 1986: 284, slightly adapted)

The role of the outsider-witness team
When briefing the outsider-witness reflecting team, White emphasizes that its role is not to bring expert knowledge to bear. Its members should avoid hypothesizing about or interpreting the person's behaviour, advising, analysing or congratulating. Rather, their aim should be to acknowledge the person's problems and

struggles and by so doing to 'provoke people's fascination with certain of the more neglected aspects of their lives' (White, 1995a: 180) – in other words, to raise possible unique outcomes. Team members may choose to speak of ways in which the person's story resonates in their own lives, and to share these echoes – not as self-focused revelation, reminiscence, moralizing or example-giving, but *in the service of assisting the person.* 'Decentred sharing is facilitated by outsider-witness group members when they join with each other over explorations of the history of the experiences [evoked] in response to the therapeutic conversation . . . to do this in ways that honour what it was that evoked these images of their lives – that is, the expressions of the persons who are seeking consultation' (White, 1997b: 103).

The aim is to create a sense of 'linking' or 'joining' with the persons through the acknowledgement of problematic or hopeful elements common to many lives; to assist the persons by reinforcing their 'richer' self-story, now at the stage where new sub-plots are being integrated into it, by sharing memories of situations in the therapist's life, or in the lives of people she has known, which have a resonance with the person's story. One result of this sharing is to 'de-centre' the therapist. A therapist's recollection of her own experience in this context can modify assumptions by the person that therapists stand apart from the struggles and problems of life, or that they have any special, learned, superior, expert knowledge with which to overcome them. Team members are briefed to be alert to any situation where members may, because of the power of the personal memory evoked, begin to cross the boundaries of sharing their own memories with a focus on the person, and slip into emotional self-revelation, self-disclosure, disguised advice-giving or using their own lives as moral examples. If this does happen, or appears to be about to happen, other team members have a responsibility to bring the discussion back into focus, perhaps by asking their colleague questions like 'What is [the person's] experience teaching you about these powerful memories?' or 'How did what [the person] said about his mother and father's relationship trigger these memories of your own parents?'

The novelty and originality of this witnessed definitional ceremony makes it difficult to give a precise name to the outsider-witness team's contribution. It is part reflecting back of the person's story, part discussion, part inter-member questioning, part sharing of personal experience, part musing on possible questions around meanings for the person of elements in his story, part tentative 'floating' of unique outcomes. But because the focus is always on the person's story, which is being considered from many angles and thereby 'enriched', perhaps the best definition is simply White's own term – it is a *re-telling*:

> the outsider-witness group is invited to respond with a re-telling of the stories told and of the knowledges and skills expressed. At this time (the second stage), the persons who are at the centre of the ceremony participate as an audience to these re-tellings . . . In these re-tellings, many of the significant expressions of life that would otherwise pass like a blip across a person's screen of consciousness, and disappear off the edge into a vacuum, are pulled down into the story-lines of their life. But, more than this, the re-tellings of the outsider-witness group encapsulate the first telling, but exceed the boundaries of it. In this way, these re-tellings contribute significantly to the generation of rich descriptions of the stories told and of the knowledges and skills expressed. (White, 1997b: 94–5)

The video recording of the session, kept by the persons, extends the therapy forward into their lives. In watching it they see and hear themselves telling their story, and may realize that there are some elements which were *not* told – and then integrate them into the story. They again hear and see others commenting, and may have further thoughts about those comments, which they can share with each other, if a couple, and perhaps with trusted friends and relatives. If each person has been rather absorbed in their own thinking and feeling in the session, they have an opportunity to re-hear their partner's contribution, and to reconsider the therapist's questions and the team's commentaries.

Setting and conditions

Cultural expectations need to be taken sensitively into account when inviting persons to take part in definitional ceremonies. Before undertaking a counselling project with the Aboriginal community in South Australia when the input was to be informed by narrative therapy approaches, great care was taken to include therapists from the Aboriginal community in the team, and to consult Aboriginal organizations and communities about ways in which narrative therapy elements, including definitional ceremonies, could be made culturally appropriate (McLean, 1995).

Mary Wilkinson (1999) has suggested that the social context of Michael White's work with *white* Australians, where in general people readily engage in friendly conversations with strangers, facilitates those persons' agreement to share accounts of their lives

and concerns with others in therapy and to listen to others discussing how the expression of these concerns creates echoes in
their own lives. By contrast, in England where I practise, and
where the culture of reticence is strong, persons at an early stage
of therapy often spontaneously say that they very much value the
assured privacy of one-to-one conversations in the therapy room.
Persons are sometimes very surprised, even dismayed, at my tentatively floating the idea that others might be invited to a session
or sessions, even others close to and trusted by them, let alone a
person or persons they have not previously met. A full explanation
of the nature and purpose of the proposal often brings agreement,
but by no means always, and of course it is crucial to offer a choice,
to make sure that the person recognizes this choice is genuine, and
to respect his decision. When the person does not agree for outsider witnesses to be invited I nevertheless attempt to widen the
therapy context, at an appropriate stage, by asking questions about
whom in his life he might like to tell about his discoveries. I may
also take on something of an outsider-witness role by commenting
on his story and the positive echoes it creates for me in my own
life. These actions fulfil some of the functions of outsider witnessing, but unfortunately do not diminish the risk of my remaining
over-centred compared with when a wider range of people takes
part.

Getting a number of people to come to sessions, and organizing
tellings and re-tellings by all those present, may sound dismaying,
unrealistically time-consuming and difficult. The example of Mark
and Chris describes an ideal context for such procedures: a family
therapy centre with an international reputation. Such a setting is,
of course, out of reach of most counsellors who work with individuals and couples. However, there are less ideal but still effective
ways of applying the principles of telling and re-telling.

Richard and Rose

There were physical restrictions to the setting, but the essentials for
telling and re-telling were nevertheless present. The room was just
big enough to accommodate a couple and two therapists. There
was, of course, no one-way screen but Mary sat quietly out of the
persons' line of sight. By careful timing, I was able to include the
four stages of the process within the hour allowed for the session.
After my initial interview with the couple, Mary took on the role of
an outsider witness, and I shifted my role, becoming a second outsider witness in this team of two therapists discussing the couple's

story. We both bore in mind the functions of the team at this stage of the session, and our dialogue resembled, on a smaller scale, the interchange between team members in the example of Mark and Chris. We included personal memories, and tentative questions, relating to the persons' story. In the third stage of the session I discussed the team exchange with the couple, and in the closing moments all four of us talked about how the session had worked for us. There was no video equipment, but a sound recording was made for the couple to take home, listen to, and discuss in their next session with me.

Gemma and Sally

In this session a fortuitous circumstance became a powerful resource for telling and re-telling. I had been surprised, at Gemma's first appointment two sessions before the one described, when two women arrived. Often persons brought friends or relatives for moral support, usually leaving them in the waiting room but very occasionally bringing them to the therapy room. Sometimes such an accompanying visitor has put unwanted pressure on the person, and is attending to censor their story or to inhibit them, and this possibility needs to be dealt with. More usually the person is comfortable with the visitor's presence and, when reassured, I would welcome the visitor, provide a chair out of the person's line of sight, then more or less pretend that they were not there. I now think this reflected a negative, therapist-centred assumption – that the person was there to talk with *me*, and that the person they invited to accompany them should quite literally take a back seat! Sally and Gemma taught me an overdue lesson that a person accompanying someone to counselling at their request is important to that person, and has their full trust. Such visitors' importance in and knowledge of the life of the person can be a useful *resource* for the person and the therapist, and calling on their services in the session is a swift route to therapist de-centring. I agree with Harlene Anderson's (1997: 86) assertion, in a book published a year or so after the session I describe here, that:

> Friends are often intimately involved in our problems and our attempts to solve them . . . perhaps because of professional ideas about matters such as confidentiality and boundaries, we often forget or dismiss our clients' friends. To me, however, it only seems natural to include in therapy conversations people who are significant in our clients' lives, with whom they are in conversation, and who are resources to them and to me.

My invitation to Sally to pull up her chair and join in the conversation was spontaneous. She had listened with concentrated
attention, sitting still, in silence – she had never shifted in her chair,
coughed or in any way obtruded. I suddenly wondered if such
sensitivity might indicate the potential for an active role. I doubt if
I would have taken this 'risk' if I had not read White on definitional
ceremonies – and then suddenly thought that Sally might be
invited to perform the role of outsider witness, by joining with me
as a team-of-two. She was not a therapist, and my taking part in
outsider-witness teamwork had always been with therapists – but
did that matter? My experience in White's training sessions had
been that, when taking on the role of outsider witness for the first
time, I had sometimes lapsed into misconceived contributions, but
these had been counteracted by other members of the team. By
leading the discussion and asking Sally specific questions I facilitated her making appropriate contributions. The responsibility for
the session was mine, and it was important to honour the specific
practices developed in this therapy, and their rationale. An unstructured free discussion might have been quite useful to Gemma, but
it would merely have reproduced something like the discussions
the friends already held in private.

The fact that Sally was Gemma's friend immediately produced
benefits. She was able to contribute by responding to my invitation
to comment on Gemma's story in the session, but also by extending this commentary into the rich field of her knowledge of
Gemma's life outside therapy. In doing this Sally brought into focus
a strand in Gemma's thinking which she herself had not volun-
teered in the therapy room, and which proved the key to her overcoming her problem.

Recording sessions electronically

Recording sessions is extremely useful in telling and re-telling, but
not essential. It needs to be approached carefully, especially when
suggesting it to individuals. At the first session persons are vulnerable. They have come with pressing concerns which they wish to
voice; they have walked alone into a strange room with a stranger
whom they may see as some sort of authority figure, and who in
reality *is* in a power position which can never quite be counteracted.
Explaining the purpose of recording, and asking whether it is
acceptable to record the session, faces persons with an immediate

and inappropriate distraction from their concerns, and also a dilemma – if they feel uncomfortable with the idea it is difficult for them to say so in case they offend, and if they accept, despite misgivings, they will find it difficult to trust me and to relax into the session. I need information coming out of the session itself to know whether offering to record is appropriate to the person's circumstances. Her problem may concern a bullying or insensitive partner who does not know she is coming to counselling, in which case having a cassette of our session in the house, which the partner might find and play, would constitute a threat. Parents who wish to talk about problems with their teenagers' behaviour may be uneasy about the possibility of the recording being discovered. I usually wait until the second session to raise the issue of recording, asking the person to think about it and give me an opinion next time. Occasionally a person agrees then changes his mind, but most persons do like having recordings made, and soon forget the machine once the session is under way. The recordings belong to them – if I wish to keep a copy I ask their permission, and give the same safeguards regarding confidentiality as for written documents.

Recruiting members of the wider community as outsider witnesses

The audience for re-telling can occasionally be widened to people beyond the therapist team and the person's actual acquaintance. White has described how he arranged for a little boy who faced his problems bravely, and who came to sessions in a miniature fireman's uniform, to visit the local fire station. There he told a fireman about his struggle, and heard about how firemen also learn skills with which to face danger. In another instance, White arranged for a teenager, who had been competing with a temptation to take drugs, to talk with a famous local athlete, who gave of his time generously and who, it emerged, had faced and overcome a similar problem in his own youth. A child bullied at school was given the opportunity to listen to White interviewing a group of children with similar experiences, invited to come to a therapy session for this purpose (White, 1997a). In all these instances, White was careful to brief the outsider witnesses on what might be helpful for the person – he did not leave the content of the meetings to chance.

Obviously, a therapist will take care to choose an outsider witness whose experience is relevant, who can provide a listening and a telling that will be potentially helpful, and who on all available evidence is someone of integrity. The idea needs to be thoroughly aired with the person seeking assistance so that the therapist does not break confidentiality, since some information about the person will need to be given to outsider witnesses or their meeting with the person will be counterproductive. The therapist's briefing of the outsider witness will concentrate less on details of the person herself, than on what the outsider witness's own experience and knowledge might contribute to the person in assisting her to build another dimension to her story. Once the two people have met, the person may find that she is comfortable to reveal further information about herself and her problem, but that is then her own decision.

White stresses that his development of practices for facilitating 'telling and re-telling' are not complete – they are 'work in progress' – and that he anticipates that much creative thinking in this area will take place among narrative therapists (White, 1995a: 177; White, 1997a).

Summary

When persons have begun to identify helpful, previously untold sub-plots of their lives, the process can be assisted by the therapist organizing situations where people other than the therapist make a contribution. Sessions may take the form of definitional ceremonies where outsider witnesses listen to the person's story, share their reactions to it with each other while the person listens, and then listen to the person's reactions to their reactions. Sometimes these contributions include memories of personal experiences triggered by the person's account, offered as potentially enriching reinforcements of the person's story. Relevant people from the wider community may also be invited to play a part. The therapist encourages all contributions of outsider witnesses to be in a spirit of respectful, engaged interest.

8 *Narrative Therapy in Practice*

To draw together some of the ideas and practices described in this book, this chapter describes the work I undertook with two persons. There are common elements in the stories, but the ways in which I used narrative therapy differed and I hope that these differences illustrate the flexibility of this way of working.

Issues of therapist/person gender

There may be a lack of gender balance in two extended accounts of a male therapist's attempts to assist women. I do not believe, or wish to imply, that men are the best therapists for women, that women are more frequently affected by problems than men, that men can cope with life better than women or that men are not so deserving of therapy as women. I have selected these particular stories of therapy because I believe that they illustrate some narrative approaches with particular clarity. However, assumptions and behaviours based on my location in men's culture may have unwittingly affected my work with these women, or my descriptions of this work, and I urge readers to be alert to this possibility. I hope I have avoided triumphalism, which I see as typical of men's culture. I am painfully aware of many instances, arising out of my limitations of skill and imagination, when my narrative work has fallen well short of assisting persons in ways which they would call successful. For this chapter I have chosen examples which the persons concerned regarded as successful practice because I think examples of how narrative therapy *can* work are more useful than examples of how therapist limitations can get in the way.

Two contrasting means of assisting persons to 're-write' self-stories

These accounts illustrate contrasting means by which past experiences may be re-described, previously neglected or unseen sub-plots emerge, and the 'thin' overall self-story become 'richer'. These contrasting means are: (a) by the person's accepting the reality of memories comprising the dominant plot, but recalling parallel, previously hidden memories which modify the overall self-story; (b) by the person's recognition that the memories which comprise the dominant plot are themselves incomplete or distorted, and substituting a more 'experience-near' account. Clara's therapy illustrates example (a). It was important, I felt, to respect the *accuracy* of the dominant plot-line in her story. But it was not the *only* plot-line possible. Towards the end of therapy I encouraged Clara to take part in 're-membering conversations' (White, 1997a; 1997b: 22–92; Chapter 9, this volume). In 're-membering', people significant to the person in the past and in the present are recruited into their story, as witnesses to the person's experience and identity, by being either metaphorically or literally invited into the therapy room. Clara's significant people could not actually be invited to a session but their 'presence' was evoked by her responding to my invitation to reminisce, and to examine the meanings for her of those reminiscences. In assisting Ruth to tell her story I was drawn into using approach (b). Through responding to my questions, Ruth discovered that her dominant story was an *inaccurate* representation of what had happened. The dominant story was subjugated as a more powerful plot-line emerged which she found both revelatory and helpful.

Some of the practices I have described earlier in the book are not present in these examples, but I think they do both describe a process of encouraging sub-plots of life to be recognized and magnified so that they become woven into overall self-stories which the persons found richer and more helpful than the dominant stories they initially brought to counselling.

Clara

Clara came to counselling for eight sessions over a period of four months, with varying gaps between sessions. In the first session there was no question of eliciting a full description of her situation – she was too tearful to say very much. I did learn that for several years Clara had been a nurse, on a hospital surgical ward, but had given this job up despite loving it because increasing depression and stress had finally made it impossible for her. For about a year she had enjoyed her present job as a senior hotel receptionist, which brought her into contact with people without the distressing aspects of nursing, but recently she had begun to find even this work extremely stressful because of a return of depression, fatigue and lack of energy. At times she could hardly bear to go to work at all. This was mysterious and frightening for her, as there was nothing in her current personal life to account for it. She had been happily married to her second husband, David, for many years and he and her two sons by her first marriage got on well. On leaving nursing she had seen a psychotherapist a few times, who told her that her problems arose from a lifelong habit of trying to please people. Clara accepted this 'expert assessment' and thought her over-pleasing came out of a feeling, imbued in her from childhood, that she was not worth much. She saw herself as clumsy, not very bright, not very attractive, and a bit of a failure. Could she learn to stop over-pleasing, she wondered? I said we could certainly look at this idea, but meanwhile I was curious about how she had held down such a demanding job as nursing in a surgical ward – how had she kept depression and stress at bay for so long? And how had she managed to cope with the busy and responsible post she now held – how had she prevented depression and stress from ending this career too? Clara said that she had just fought them off when a nurse, but in the end there had been no alternative to leaving. Her doctor had prescribed antidepressant medication, saying that she might need to keep on this for about five years. Gradually she had begun to feel better. Certainly she had been able to enter into her new job with energy and pleasure. However, she hated relying on pills and had stopped taking them soon after starting the job. She told the doctor of this decision two weeks ago and he immediately prescribed the same medication, which she was taking with reluctance and a sense of failure. I tentatively asked what she knew about the physiological aspects of depression, and whether she had come across the idea that, for some people, depression arose more from physical causes than from reactions to life experiences? Had she considered the possibility that when she recognized the power of depression, saw her doctor and was prescribed medication which then restored normal functioning, she might have discovered a way of attacking depression and defeating its attempts to govern her life? I promised to send her a magazine article presenting psychological and physiological explanations for depression, and we arranged to meet again in a week.

Narrative elements: Empathic listening was particularly important in this first session with a person who was extremely upset and tearful. I needed to keep in check any tendency to press ahead with invitations for a full description of the effects of the problem at this point, which might have increased Clara's distress. By doing this I allowed space for a full description of the problem to emerge when she might be ready. Naming the problem followed from Clara's own use of the terms 'depression' and 'stress' which I used as externalizing terms to lay groundwork for the possibility of Clara's later separation of the problems from her own identity. I respected her idea, gained from the previous therapist, that childhood experience might have a connection with her problems, but stayed with clues to unique outcomes, asking her how she accounted for her history of defeating depression, rather than continuing to focus on depression's successes in affecting her life. Paradoxically, a clue to a unique outcome was an echo of her dominant story. Fighting through had helped her to keep going in her employment, but had also led her to characterize taking antidepressants as failure. Through externalizing the internalizing discourse of 'fighting alone equals strong/accepting assistance equals weak', I encouraged her to re-examine these cultural assumptions. By offering an alternative perspective to the view that persons fail if they have to take pills to defeat depression, I also implicitly challenged the widely held belief in the counselling culture that taking antidepressants postpones dealing with the 'real' problems (for example, Hammersley and Beeley, 1992). By giving Clara an article presenting balanced arguments around ways of characterizing depression I attempted to counteract any tendency to impose my own views on this issue.

A week later Clara was still very tearful, despite which she talked at greater length. She described major anxieties she and her husband had faced a few years before in connection with her eldest son. She also told me that four years ago her father had died unexpectedly after admission to a hospital in another town. She had not been able to say a last goodbye to him, and working in a surgical ward where patients sometimes died had kept alive her sensitivity to the circumstances of his death. Her mother, with whom Clara had always had a far from easy relationship, did not tell her when or where her father's funeral was to take place, and indeed Clara still did not know the locality of his grave. It was soon after these events that she started to 'be depressed'. I asked Clara whether she thought that depression's invading her life at that point was puzzling or understandable, and whether her reactions to these events were natural or strange. Clara said she supposed her reactions to these events had been natural and that the depression could be related to them. I asked if she could think of a word to describe her mother's actions. This was hard for Clara and she could not think of a suitable word. I persisted: were the actions kind or cruel? Could they best be described as tactful and protective, or would more accurate words be something like insensitive or callous? Would cold-hearted be an appropriate term, or could her mother's actions be better described with a term such as considerate, forgetful or ill-judging? Clara was clear that 'cruel' was an appropriate description, and that some of the other critical words described the ways she had always experienced her parents, particularly her mother. In her childhood her parents had been grudging and resentful about many aspects of her life, in sharp contrast to a friend's parents' attitude. We agreed to look at the history of her relationship with her parents next time. I ended by sharing something I had heard the television presenter Jimmy Saville say when, in a live broadcast, he suddenly realized that the woman talking to him was crying, and she told him her son had just died. He said something like 'So all England is his grave, and the whole world is his grave, and what a lovely grave that is.' This had appeared to comfort the woman. Clara's story also reminded me of Wordsworth's lines:

> No motion has she now, no force;
> She neither hears nor sees;
> Rolled round in earth's diurnal course,
> With rocks, and stones, and trees.

I wondered whether Clara and David could invent a private ceremony to take the place of the one they had missed, and I described a ceremony devised by a person I had seen for therapy, for a loved sister whose grave was abroad. Clara said she could identify with this idea, and talked of a farewell ceremony a friend had devised for scattering his father's ashes.

Narrative elements: I continued to use externalizing language for Clara's problems. Clara began to tell her self-story, with descriptions of landscapes of consciousness and of action: her son's problems and her continuing feelings about these, her father's death and the circumstances around it, her mother's behaviour at that time and how this had hurt her. At this early stage I did not move to asking questions around clues to unique outcomes but by 'naming questions' encouraged Clara to define, and thus to clarify, both her own reactions to these events and her opinion of her mother's actions. This encouraged her to begin to tell a sub-plot of normalization with respect to her own reactions to events, and another of something like cruelty concerning her mother's action. My sharing the images of the whole world as a loved person's grave offered the possibility of an alternative story, when told in the future, to her present story of being excluded from her father's grave. Similarly, the discussion of 'invented' ceremonies offered the possibility of an alternative story, when told in the future, to her present story of being cut off from his funeral. Her devising and performing such a ceremony might assist her to move from her present, 'liminal' (intermediate) stage of grieving.

At the third session Clara looked, and said she was feeling, less distressed, and was more able to talk and think about issues in her life. She discussed mixed feelings about her father, describing some of the stern and distanced ways in which he had always treated her. Her grief for him was still very real, but now she was confident that she would in time 'discover' appropriate ways of saying farewell to him. Her main preoccupation since we last talked had been what she called her 'lack of self-esteem'. She said that she really did think badly of herself, and always had. I said I was going to ask her to do something which might be difficult – and then I invited her to give me at least three examples of characteristics which other people who knew her would say they liked in her. This *was* hard for Clara – at first she said she 'didn't know what good things anyone might say about me' – but a little to her surprise she did answer my question, after taking time to think. She was not a 'gossip', she was a careful driver, and she responded calmly to others' aggression. She was also quite independent-minded; sometimes she found it hard to accept her husband's loving protectiveness, as she had been brought up in no uncertain terms to fend for herself. We agreed to explore the history of her relationship with her parents, the influences this might have had on her later life, and the meanings this history had for her. I explained that, in my experience of working with people, their having a fresh look at the past often revealed forgotten aspects which could become helpful in dealing with present issues.

Narrative elements: Clara continued to tell her story; the brief version above does not convey the low-key, silence-punctuated atmosphere of the session. Clara's dominant story of not liking herself emerged strongly in her narrative despite the more optimistic opening of the session where she expressed a degree of confidence in finding her way forward in grieving for her father. I invited her to challenge that dominant story by asking a question about others' perceptions of her, and from this she gave four positive self-descriptions. As she was feeling less distressed than previously it appeared appropriate to suggest moving our discussions to her history in her family of origin, where she herself saw the roots of her problems. My assumption was not pathologizing: I did not believe that we should or could trace 'damage'. My assumption was that sub-plots of persons' lives always emerge, result in a 'richer description' of the past, and contribute to a helpful, 'richer' self-story. My explanation (hardly longer than its representation above) was intended to set expectations for the non-pathologizing exploration of memories of childhood in the following session and to be transparent about my approach to therapy.

The fourth session began with Clara reporting a further improvement in her spirits. Her anxieties concerning her son's past problems were in perspective, she said, and she had joined a slimming club, determined to contribute to a better self-view by improving her appearance. Some of her son's friends had mentioned how much they enjoyed coming to her house – they found its atmosphere relaxing, informal and accepting. This powerfully reminded Clara of how *she* had felt when visiting her friend's parents' house 35 years ago. She recognized that she had succeeded in her determination not to reproduce, in her own family home, the atmosphere of her own childhood home. She affirmed that this was evidence that a person could escape the influence of their parents. At my invitation, she expanded on these discoveries and what they indicated to her about her capacity to value herself.

Clara reverted to the need to be strong which had made her reject antidepressants and which she believed to have originated in childhood. At my invitation to tell me about her life as a child she grew animated and occasionally tearful. The family home had been a rented house in a deprived area of an industrial town where 'you had to be a fighter to survive'. Money was always a problem as her father's jobs had been sporadic, poorly paid and with long hours; her mother also worked, unusual at a time when men took pride in supporting their family and women were generally housewives. Her childhood was harsh, she said. Unlike her best friend, she was never kissed or cuddled, as her parents firmly maintained that showing affection and concern for a child was to 'spoil' her, and that praise was likely to make her 'too big for her boots'. She remembered vividly that successes she achieved at school were greeted with criticism or at best indifference. On the day she learned that she had been accepted for a full-time course at the local art college her mother's reaction was 'That will mean more expense for us, then.' The house was damp and cold in winter – no fires were lit. Usually no concessions to illness were made, and she remembered going to school with heavy colds and doing arduous domestic chores at home despite a headache.

I asked whether she had any memories suggesting that, perhaps in different economic and social circumstances, her parents might have treated her differently. Had they ever shown less harsh attitudes or more sympathetic responses? Clara said that she often put this kind of question to herself. She then described the single episode in her whole childhood which might fit this description, a golden memory which had stayed with her. She had been very ill one winter, perhaps with pneumonia, and certainly with a sore throat and a high temperature. The doctor insisted that she must stay off school and sleep in the warm. Her parents made an improvised bed for her in the kitchen, the least cold room. One morning she had been left alone, and developed a raging thirst. Despite feeling ill and giddy, she got out of bed, poured herself a drink of water from the tap, carried it back to her bed where she drank it, and set the empty glass on the floor. Later, her father came home for lunch and saw the glass. Clara explained why it was there, that she had been so thirsty she had needed to get out of bed to get a drink, and that she had not felt strong enough to return the glass to its place. Instead of reproving her, which was what she had expected, her father said that if he had been at home he would have got her the glass of water himself. This was the *one memory* from her whole childhood which contradicted her dominant story. Her father's words had accompanied Clara throughout her life as evidence that he loved her.

There was no such memory concerning her mother, and Clara believed that this had contributed much to her inability to value herself. I mentioned Yvonne Dolan's 'healing letters' sequence where an adult writes letters to and from the persons who were indirectly responsible for childhood sexual abuse. I wondered whether Clara might like to adapt this exercise to her own situation of emotional neglect (Dolan, 1991: 191–3)? We agreed to discuss this idea next time.

Narrative elements: Clara's story, which previous sessions suggested she very much wished to tell, had so far only been partially narrated. Although she reported the development of some recent thoughts and actions which showed that she could value herself to some extent, such as recognizing significance in her not reproducing the atmosphere of her family of origin's home, I did not attempt to build the whole session around these recognitions. These unique outcomes 'in the present' appeared a little fragile to stand against a lifetime's self-criticism. They seemed a little provisional, without historical sub-plot material to give them substance and to join with them as a whole sequence linking the past with the present. So I encouraged her to talk of her childhood. Clara's story was of almost unremitting harshness. Her description of the one unique outcome which emerged, the treasured memory of one passing remark from her father which enabled her to keep alive for 35 years the belief that he loved her, was extraordinarily moving. But it was isolated; it did not form a link in a sub-plot. It was important for me to put aside any tendency to persist in trying to elicit unique outcomes concerning her parents' attitudes and actions. Doing this would have been disrespectful, a demonstration of assumed superior knowledge. Its basis would have been 'My readings in narrative therapy show me that significant contradictions to the dominant story always exist, so if I persist, Clara will remember instances where her mother *did* show affection, and further examples of when her father demonstrated love for her.' Instead, I offered for her consideration a different means of escaping from the effects of the dominant story of her parents' emotional distancing and humiliating behaviours, a different means of re-writing her story, an imaginative letter-writing process of healing, which might eventually allow her to tell a story around the experience of having escaped the malign influences of not being loved by her parents.

In the next session I explained the 'letter-writing' therapy in detail and we discussed variants which Clara might try. She agreed to think about this and to let me know her decision next time.

Narrative elements: In suggesting that Clara might consider writing this sequence of therapeutic documents I was transparent in discussing their rationale and details, and I gave time between sessions for her to consider the idea and choose.

At the next session Clara said that she felt uncomfortable with the letter-writing idea. We abandoned it, and I moved to a different means of assisting her to reinforce the 're-writing' of her past. She had never received focused caring attention from her parents – but had there been anyone in her early life from whom she *had* received this? Anyone who had valued her and demonstrated this by their actions? Clara immediately identified two persons – her art teacher and her grandmother. The art teacher had recognized Clara's artistic talent and fostered it both in school and outside the class-room. She lent Clara books about great artists, took her to London galleries and held weekly art sessions at her own house, when the woman and the young girl drew, painted and talked. These were some of Clara's best memories of childhood – of being happy and engaged in this activity, forgetting the time and suddenly realizing it was dark and she had to get home. The art teacher had been a lovely person and Clara would always be grateful to her; without this woman's influence in her life she would not have gone to art college, or recognized that she had a talent which would give her lifelong pleasure and satisfaction. I acknowledged Clara's praise – and then asked her what the teacher had gained from *her*. What difference had knowing Clara made to this person's life? What qualities in Clara, quite apart from her talent in art, had led to the teacher's befriending her? What had the evenings working and talking, and the trips to London, meant to the teacher? What had Clara herself, her particular personality and attributes, contributed to these occasions which enriched them for the teacher, compared with painting and drawing alone, and solitary visits to galleries? These questions were difficult – she could not answer them – Clara had never thought of the relationship in this light. I asked what the art teacher might say if, miraculously, she was in the room with us now and I asked her those questions. Clara replied that perhaps she would say that Clara had contributed enthusiasm about art, and acceptance of the teacher as a friend. The teacher had probably been quite a lonely person as she lived by herself and was 'a bit of an old-fashioned lady – quite reserved with most people'. They had laughed quite a lot as well as talking seriously and Clara thought this might have been important to the teacher. I said that I had a vivid image of the two women, of different generations, talking, laughing and doing creative work together with such mutual satis-faction that time was forgotten.

Were there similar memories surrounding anyone else in Clara's early life? Yes, there were – her grandmother (her father's mother) had always been warm and welcoming to Clara. Clara remembered her as a widow with a 'man friend', an insurance salesman who had often collected Clara from her house in his shiny Morris car with slippery leather seats and taken her to her grandmother's house for a threesome tea, then brought her home again. She had also sometimes stayed with her grandmother for the weekend. Clara talked of these memories at length and I encouraged her to think about what she had contributed to her grandmother's life by her visits. Perhaps Clara could decide to keep these revived memories – of the art teacher and of her grandmother – fully alive as part of the present? Perhaps she could think of herself through their perceptions? What would the grandmother and the art teacher recognize in the present-day Clara that would make her recognizably the person they loved and valued? Clara was moved by the memories she had evoked and by the idea that these people could still play a part in her life.

Narrative elements: By abandoning the letter-writing idea I demonstrated my faith in Clara's knowing what elements of therapy might be helpful to her. In encouraging her to think of persons in her past who accepted her, by holding a 're-membering' conversation, I continued to respect her knowledge of the hurtful limitations of her parents' attitudes. However, I was not allowing one aspect of her dominant story to go unchallenged – that because her parents had not loved her very much, especially her mother, this both proved that she was unlovable, and made her unlovable, so any attention she received was due to others' kindness. My questions were firmly set in the frame of 'what did you contribute to their lives' as well as 'what did they contribute to your life?' I was attempting to assist Clara to 'say hello again' to these people (White, 1989: 29–36; 1997b: 22–5) and to bring their 'presences' fully back into her life as supportive sources of evidence that she had been loved, that she had been worthy of love, that she had contributed to their lives and that she still demonstrated those same attributes.

Clara mentioned her parents' mistrustfulness: they were introspective, generally unsociable and 'suspicious of everyone'. She took this theme up in the seventh session. She herself found trusting people difficult, which she attributed partly to parental influence and partly to being quite badly let down by some people. She disliked this trait. When I asked her to think about whether there had been persons in her life whom she had trusted, despite her parents' example, she once again spoke of her childhood friend Jeanette. Jeanette's mother once cheerfully changed some bedsheets which Jeanette had stained with an unexpected period, and Clara knew her own mother would have complained bitterly and unceasingly in the same circumstances. This incident had demonstrated to Clara that some people could be trusted – they would not automatically condemn an accidental action or use a misfortune to make someone feel bad about herself. In response to further questions, Clara talked of other people she had trusted at various times in her life and who had not betrayed that trust – her art teacher, her grandmother, Jeanette, two present-day friends and her husband. Her picture of herself as someone reluctant to trust others began to modify into a picture of someone who *could* trust but who had been let down badly by several people and so had become rather cautious.

Narrative elements: I chose not to externalize 'mistrust'. Clara remembered her parents demonstrating this attitude as part of a wide range of restrictive, ungenerous behaviours which they chose to perpetuate. I did not wish to soften this perception by any linguistic implication that this trait was an accidental attribute beyond their control. I wondered whether Clara would find it helpful to acknowledge, once she had remembered evidence of this, that she herself *could* trust. Most of the session consisted of invitations to identify unique outcomes around the capacity to trust and to thread them into a sub-plot of her life from childhood to the present.

In the eighth and final session I encouraged Clara to talk about her relationship with her husband. Despite her diffidence, I did manage to encourage her to describe, in considerable detail, her perceptions of what he thought of her when they met, what he had found attractive in her as a person, what he continued to love in her, what she contributed to his life and what all this told her about her identity. Clara was now a little more used to invitations to think well of herself through defining the views of persons significant to her, and her contribution to the session had a feeling of joyful nostalgia, self-acceptance and happiness. We agreed to end counselling with an open invitation to return should she ever wish to, but so far, 10 months later, she has not done so. A note accompanying her permission to use her story in this book says that she is 'jogging along nicely'.

Narrative elements: This session had an air of ceremony and confirmation, with the 'final part of the enriched story' being told, and linked through questioning with Clara's discoveries about the past. Depression had made an exit from her life, she was enjoying her job, and she was no longer dominated by negative views about herself.

Ruth

Ruth came to counselling with a distressing dilemma. A few months before, her 4-year-old child Tom had developed constipation, and the doctor had noticed physical signs which might indicate sexual abuse. He had referred the child for specialist examination, asking Ruth if there was anyone in or known to the household capable of child sexual abuse. In her shock, and fear for the child, Ruth said that her 32-year-old cousin Terry might be such a person. Terry or his wife sometimes looked after Tom when Ruth and her husband went out for the evening, and he had done this recently. The doctor advised her not to leave Tom alone with Terry pending medical investigation of the possible abuse symptoms. Terry was due to look after Tom the next evening, and when Ruth told her husband of the doctor's suspicions and advice he at once phoned Terry to cancel the arrangement. This had puzzled Terry and it ended by Ruth's husband explaining the reason. Terry reacted with horror at what he called the 'accusation' and the conversation ended with Terry slamming his phone down, telling his wife what had happened, then phoning other family members, including his parents, to express his outrage. Two days later the specialist gave a firm opinion that the child had not been abused and that the symptoms observed by the doctor were merely related to constipation. Ruth and her husband went to explain and apologize to Terry but found him and his wife unforgiving. Meanwhile, Terry's father had told Ruth's mother about what had happened. Terry was a general favourite, and Ruth soon found herself accused by most of the family of malicious scaremongering for naming Terry as a possible suspect when she had no shred of evidence that he could be an abuser. Even her husband started to wonder why she had suspected Terry, as Tom was looked after by several other people, including a paid babysitter they did not know very well. Ruth apologized again and again to Terry and his parents, and to her own parents, but to no avail. Everyone was full of angry resentment, and could not forgive her. This echoed many instances in the past when Ruth had felt undervalued by her parents. She was a middle child and the only girl, and Terry had been such a frequent visitor that it had almost been like having three brothers. On the whole she had got on with the boys but had often been mercilessly teased, and always sensed that her parents preferred boys.

I asked Ruth what would have happened if she had not told the doctor her suspicions of Terry, allowed him to baby-sit, and it then turned out that he was in fact abusing her child? Which was worse – to act hastily in anxiety for a child's safety or to hold back suspicions and risk a child being harmed? Ruth said that she had not thought of it like that, and clearly the second option was very much worse. I asked if she had any ideas about how to help her family to see her choice in this light. She did not think she could. In any case, the sticking point would be her mentioning Terry – she had not actually *accused* him of abuse, but he and the family did not see it that way.

There *was* a reason why her thoughts had jumped to Terry when questioned by the doctor. One afternoon when she was 14 years old, she and Terry, then aged 18, had gone to their friend Andy's house when Andy's parents were away for the day. The young people raided the drinks cupboard, and after a couple of hours listening to records became thoroughly drunk. Andy said he had a good album in his room but was not sure where, and the three went to look for it. Once in his bedroom Andy pushed her on to his bed, removed some of her clothes, and raped her, while Terry stood in the doorway watching. Because she was very drunk she could not resist.

Afterwards, still very affected by alcohol, Terry and Ruth walked back to her house. On the way, Terry pulled her into an alleyway and started to try to touch her intimately, but Ruth told him to stop and he did. Once home, Ruth went straight to bed and slept. Terry told her parents that she had a headache and they accepted this. The events of that day had never been mentioned again by Terry or Ruth, and I was the first person Ruth had ever told the story. She said she was glad she had told me, and felt a weight had lifted.

The session had run over and we had to end. I thanked Ruth for trusting me with such a painful and personal story and suggested that next time we might discuss how other abused women facing dilemmas like hers had found ways of resolving conflicts around disclosure. I mentioned a couple of books about overcoming the effects of sexual abuse which had been found helpful by other women I had worked with, including one (Dolan, 1991) which had a chapter discussing Ruth's kind of dilemma.

Narrative elements: Ruth telling her story was the main element of this session. My question to Ruth about what she would have felt had she said nothing about Terry, then found he had in fact abused Tom, presented a situation which she had reason to think entirely possible – it was only in retrospect that Ruth knew Tom had not been abused. I deliberately 'named abuse' (White, 1995a: 82–111) and used this term throughout for what *both* the two young men had done. I was transparent in acknowledging the sources of ideas for therapy which I would offer for her consideration, but which I would not impose by using them without prior discussion and permission. By this means I was stressing the element of choice for her, as part of ensuring, as far as possible, that therapy with a male counsellor would not echo the situation of male domination of the abuse itself.

In the following session we did discuss disclosure, and Ruth said she did not want to offer justifications to her family for mentioning Terry to the doctor because Terry's father had a weak heart and the shock of learning what his son had done 12 years ago might endanger her uncle's life. She was left feeling resentful and frustrated about the unfairness of the situation. We discussed whether writing privately to Terry might be helpful. The letter could invite him to meet Ruth, acknowledge what had happened 12 years ago, take responsibility for it, recognize the appropriateness of Ruth's response to the doctor and stop criticizing her to the family. If after writing the letter she felt it could not be sent, she could keep it as a reminder of her innocence in relation to her family's criticisms. Ruth liked this idea, and she also wondered whether a letter to her parents, protesting about the ways in which they had always marginalized her, might also be valuable. I suggested she give herself time to think about these possibilities, and to see whether better variants might occur to her. I gave her a modified copy of Dolan's 'Abuse Recovery Scale' to take away and complete, explaining that many women found this reassuring in demonstrating the degree to which they had already overcome the actual or potential effects on their lives of having been abused (Dolan, 1991: 32).

As she was about to go, Ruth said that my using the word 'abuse' in the previous session, for what her cousin and his friend had done, had made 'a tremendous difference' to her. She had never thought of the incident in this way and had been very surprised when I had called it this, but on reflection she agreed – it *had* been abuse.

Narrative elements: Discussing the possibility of Ruth's writing therapeutic documents was the focus of this session. There was a continuation of transparency through my full explanation of the idea's source and rationale. Ruth's own extension of the letter-writing process to include her parents encouraged me to think that introducing the idea

of documents had been appropriate. Her unsolicited comment on the
way in which my calling the young men's actions 'abuse' had changed
her perception was a confirmation of the power and importance of
naming in narrative therapy.

The third session turned out to be central to Ruth's therapy. I give
below a version of part of our conversation, based on notes written
up immediately afterwards, and although I cannot of course reproduce the exact wording I believe that the sequence, tone and
content are reasonably accurate. Ruth has confirmed this.

Martin: Yvonne Dolan writes about how some of the women she works with
find a statement of belief or reminder of truth helpful. They write a short
statement – just a few words sometimes, or a couple of sentences –
summing up what they know about who was responsible for the abuse.
They keep it with them to read or to hold on to whenever they start to get
back into old habits of thinking the abuse was their own fault. They might
write 'It was his fault, not mine' or 'Victims of abuse are never to blame.'
Something like that.

Ruth: I do think it was my fault.

Martin: Oh, sorry – I'm getting too far ahead. So you do blame yourself for
the abuse?

Ruth: I should never have got drunk. If I hadn't got drunk it would never have
happened. And I didn't do anything to stop Andy – I just lay there while
he had sex with me, and Terry looked on. I should have said something,
or fought him off. I was too drunk. We all were.

Martin: I'd like to try asking you some questions about what happened, if
that's OK with you. Would it be OK if we went over the whole way the
abuse situation came about, and took it apart in detail? I don't mean what
Andy actually did to you – I'm not going to ask about that – but the whole
circumstances and background?

Ruth: Yes, all right.

Martin: If you do find it too distressing we'll stop, OK? Let me know?

Ruth: Yes.

Martin: The three of you went to Andy's parents' house to listen to records,
and then the drink started to flow. Can you remember who thought of
raiding the drinks cupboard? Who started all the boozing?

Ruth: Andy did. He just opened the cupboard and took out glasses and lots
of bottles.

Martin: How was it that you all had so *much* to drink? Did you all just help
yourselves as you felt like it? Or did anyone pour out drinks more than
the others?

Ruth: I think Andy did it the most. He kept filling my glass and telling me to
drink up. Terry filled my glass a lot too but it was mostly Andy, I think.

Martin: What did you drink?

Ruth: I don't know. All sorts of stuff – I thought a lot of it tasted terrible but
I still drank it. Probably vodka, whisky, that sort of thing, plus some beer.
We drank all afternoon.

Martin: Was this something you often did, or was it unusual?

Ruth: No, no, I'd never done anything like that. I was only fourteen, I didn't drink. I suppose I wanted to show I was grown-up. I didn't say no, anyway.

Martin: Terry and Andy would know that you weren't used to drink.

Ruth: Yes.

Martin: And there were two of them and one of you. Two young men about twenty and one girl of fourteen. What about them?

Ruth: Sorry?

Martin: Were they used to drink?

Ruth: Well, they went to the pub quite a bit with their mates. I suppose they did drink quite a bit, yes. They were used to it, I suppose.

Martin: Have I got this right, Ruth? Two young men know the effects of too much booze. They spend a whole afternoon in a house where nobody is going to interrupt them, plying an inexperienced 14-year-old girl, cousin of one of them, with a mixture of spirits and beer to the point where she's totally zonked out of her mind?

Ruth: Yes, that's right. But they were drinking too – they were drunk too. I should never have got myself into that situation.

Martin: Terry was your cousin. One of the family. Almost like another older brother.

Ruth: Yes.

Martin: Does a young man owe a duty of care and protection to a young female relative or is it OK for him to do nothing when she looks as if she's getting into a dangerous situation?

Ruth: He should protect her.

Martin: Maybe the 'cousin' bit is irrelevant, actually. Maybe all men have a responsibility of care for women? Perhaps we all have a duty of care for others? What do you think?

Ruth: Yes, we do.

Martin: Did Terry give you care and protection?

Ruth: No, he didn't. He joined in. Well, he didn't actually do anything to me, he didn't have sex with me, he just – he watched.

Martin: Still, he *was* your cousin. Maybe that does make the whole thing feel a bit different? Watching his friend rape his cousin?

Ruth: I can remember . . . [*she describes some details of the abuse, and her memories of hazily seeing Terry standing in the doorway watching*].

Martin: He didn't try to stop Andy?

Ruth: No.

Martin: Did he protest in any way?

Ruth: No. He just went along with it.

Martin: So he condoned it. Even encouraged it? By failing to protest, to stop it, to get help, to protect you in any way, was he also responsible for it? Or was the whole thing down to Andy?

Ruth: No, I see what you mean. Terry went along with it so he's responsible for it happening too even though he just watched.

Martin: Maybe abuse can include *not preventing* a sexual attack, or not even trying to prevent it?

Ruth: Yes. It can.

Martin: So abuse can certainly consist of willingly watching someone being sexually assaulted – being a part of the whole situation?

Ruth: Yes.

Martin: Can you just remind me – did you know Andy well?

Ruth: Quite well. He was Terry's friend and I'd met him quite a lot. He came round with Terry a lot.

Martin: Had you ever been alone with him?

Ruth: Well, yes, I had. He was OK – I quite liked him.

Martin: In all the times you'd known him, been alone with him, had he ever made you feel uncomfortable? Made a pass, or talked sexy, or anything like that?

Ruth: No. I don't think so. He'd been OK. I was young – he was about five or six years older than me. A bit older than Terry. I was just a kid most of the time he knew me.

Martin: So you had no reason at all to think that going to his house with your cousin could be dangerous? Am I right? All your experience of these young men up to that point was that they were OK, and because Terry was your cousin, almost like an older brother, you had even more reason to feel safe?

Ruth: Yes – I did feel safe – it never occurred to me that anything might happen.

Martin: Let me check this out with you, OK? All your previous knowledge of Terry and Andy led you to believe that they were trustworthy. All your previous experience of Terry and Andy justified your thinking that getting drunk together was just a bit of mischief – a laugh?

Ruth: A laugh, yes.

Martin: So though Andy kept on filling your glass you actually had no reason to feel worried. Getting drunk together really did feel like silly but innocent fun, not dangerous. You had no reason at all to suspect that going up to Andy's room with him and Terry would be anything but what Andy said – an innocent search for an LP. It was only at the point when Andy pushed you on to the bed that you could have started to worry, and by then it was too late. Andy was a physically mature man and you were an inexperienced 14-year-old girl who had been made drunk – possibly deliberately – by two men you had no reason to distrust. Is that a fair description?

Ruth: I never thought of it like that. I never thought they might be getting me drunk deliberately.

Martin: Well, we don't know whether it was planned – maybe that's going a bit too far – it *might* have been on impulse. But still, I wonder if they *were* actually as drunk as you? You were so drunk that you had to go to bed when you got back home, but Terry was able to talk to your parents and say you had a headache. He couldn't have been plastered if he did that. He did stop touching you in the alley when you told him to – about the only thing Terry did which sets him a little bit apart from Andy, perhaps. So he was in control of himself. And as a man myself I can think of something that shows Andy may not have been as drunk as you thought – that he *was* in control of what he did. Being totally drunk makes it really difficult for a man to have sex. Shakespeare says that drink 'adds to the desire but takes away from the performance', something like that. Maybe the very fact that Andy fully raped you shows that he was much less drunk than you thought at the time and since?

Ruth: So what you're saying is that they were responsible for it all along, not me?

Martin: I'm saying that, yes, but I'm inviting you to look at the *evidence*, not just think it because it's what I think.

In a later session Ruth told me that she now had a quite different view of what the young men had done to her, and that she accepted it was they who were to blame, not her. This freeing from guilt and self-blame, and the re-examination of Terry's role in the assault, enabled her to be even more firmly convinced that she had been justified in naming him to the doctor, and strengthened her capacity to resist her relatives' attempts to make her feel guilty at this.

Narrative elements: I began by offering the possibility of a person-created therapeutic document designed to reinforce Ruth's awareness that she was not to blame in any way for the abuse she suffered, but at once discovered that I had been premature. She *did* to an extent blame herself. My conviction that victims are never responsible for their abuse gave me confidence to deconstruct the whole sequence of events in order to allow an alternative story to emerge compared with the one which had dominated her memory. My technique was far from perfect – I used too many leading questions, and statements disguised as questions – but on the whole I checked out landscapes of action and consciousness with her and invited her to confirm or refute my redescriptions. I attempted to present an attitude of 'This is so, isn't it?' and to invite a response, if appropriate, of 'Yes, but . . .' (see p. 117). I needed to bear in mind that my power position as therapist might make it difficult for Ruth to reject or disagree with what I said or implied, but her saying that she did feel responsible for the abuse showed that she would not hesitate to put me right when necessary. In this reconstructed dialogue, Ruth and I are co-creating a re-telling, based on information elicited from and checked out with her, in which specific focused detail accumulates to a sub-plot which was there all the time but which had not been recognized by her because it had not been told. At the end of the sequence she asks me my view and I give it – thereby transgressing one of the traditional 'golden rules' of counselling, where the 'proper' response would be to turn the question back on to Ruth by saying something like 'What do *you* think?' My reason for this openness was to be transparent; to allow my congruence to be visible; not to deceive or play games with her; not to step out of my own responsibility to take and state a firm position *at this stage of our conversation*. Had Ruth asked me for my view earlier I would have promised to give it, but would first have invited her to take part in the close 're-storying' examination of events. In any case, she actually knew my view already – it had been implicit in my premature invitation to her to write a 'statement of belief', but at that point it had no resonance for her. It would certainly have been both unethical and ineffective, at that point, for me to have 'argued a case'. That would have been a potential imposition. My comment at the very end of this sequence invited Ruth to consider the meaning for her of the evidence she had produced in response to my questions.

After the third session Ruth's counselling moved away from issues around the sexual abuse and her dilemma about disclosure, and for a further four sessions became primarily centred on her past and present relations with her parents. She allowed me to take away and read a long and moving letter to her parents which our conversations stimulated her to write, explaining how all her life she had been hurt by their clear preference for her brothers and their favouritism, marginalizing and lack of fully focused caring. We discussed her guilt at not being able to love them as much as she wished, and her guilt at thinking she might have been responsible for some of their marital stresses by disappointing them by her gender. At the end of counselling Ruth said that she felt different, good about herself, able to see the various mistreatments and injustices from her family clearly, and also able to recognize the secret strengths which had helped her to come through the experiences she had described.

Ruth: postscript

I sent Ruth a copy of this account to check that it matched her memory of our work, and she wrote to confirm that it did. She added that reading it had been an important experience for her. The first reading had been rather upsetting, but a second reading had been an affirmation: 'as I was reading it I crossed out the names of Terry and Andy and in my head replaced them with the original names . . . *having it in black and white* with correct names in my head made me feel really strong and as if I could face anything. Thank you for this maybe unintentional way of making me feel strong about myself' (emphasis added). She writes of recent improvements she initiated in her relationship with her parents, and of some significant self-discoveries which assisted her to decide on very important changes in other aspects of her life, saying 'since my sessions finished it made me look at everything in a different light . . . I hope you may be able to help anyone else with this story . . . My life really is good now and I know things have worked out for the best.' I *had* unintentionally provided her with a detailed therapeutic document! In her turn, she has provided me with a further example of the relevance, power and importance of such documents. Her letter is evidence that when persons re-tell and, as in this instance, re-read significant but unsuspected sub-plots around their recognition of unique outcomes, these sub-plots continue to be influential in *all* areas of their lives, not just in the specific problems they present to the therapist.

Narrative elements: By means of deconstructing conversations Ruth's overall self-story became enriched. The story she told herself concerning the rape was no longer a 'thin' description of self-blame for an event 'which happened because she was not careful enough and got herself drunk' but a 'rich' story – more corresponding to the multi-stranded actuality of the events – of her cousin and his friend's outrageous betrayal, deceit, insult and abuse, imposed on her and entirely their responsibility. Through co-creating this revised story she was able to absolve herself from guilt, and thereby to free herself from the effects of the young men's abuse on her self-view. The sub-plot of which this revised narrative then became an important element was, broadly, of escape from the restrictions of her family of origin towards the creation of a life where she is accepted and loved, and knows she deserves to be.

Summary

Clara and Ruth were both affected by self-stories in which, in different ways, parental and family actions and attitudes had created problems of identity. Clara's view of herself was largely negative. Ruth had to an extent escaped the influence of her family of origin's marginalization but was carrying self-blame for being sexually abused by her cousin and his friend. Deconstructive therapy assisted each of these women to re-examine the past and to identify elements which they had not taken into account in the stories by which they had represented that past to themselves. Clara allowed into her life memories of persons who had loved her and to whose lives she had contributed, and Ruth recognized that the responsibility for her abuse lay wholly with her attackers and not at all with herself. These changed and enriched stories then gave the past new meaning for both persons, and promoted enriched senses of identity – Clara could accept that she is valuable and lovable, and Ruth could move strongly forward into the rest of her life without guilt about the past.

9 A Fresh Look at Assumptions in the Therapy Culture

Chapter 2 outlined some ideas in recent Western thought which inform narrative therapy. This present chapter takes up the theme again by reviewing some proposals made by White for post-structuralist challenges to some widely accepted assumptions in the 'therapy culture'. Recent narrative therapy practices coming out of these challenges are then outlined. Implicit in the distinctions made in the chapter is the proposal that whatever differences of philosophy and practice exist between diverse traditional therapies of the counselling culture, such as person-centred, cognitive-behavioural, psychodynamic and other humanistic approaches, an overarching and clear distinction needs to be made between all of these and therapies informed by postmodern and, in particular, post-structural assumptions.

In offering a summary of some recent innovative aspects of narrative therapy I am not claiming expertise in knowledge of traditional and established therapies. I am conscious that there may be elements of oversimplification or misrepresentation in the generalizations concerning traditional therapy against which I set narrative ideas and practices. I hope readers will allow for this and bring to bear their own knowledges in order to critique the chapter.

The post-structuralist challenge

Narrative therapy does embody some ideas which counsellors new to it may find perfectly familiar, and congruent with their own assumptions and ways of working. I believe that its emphasis on the *primacy of the person* is likely to be such an idea. Despite his historical use of masculine pronouns to refer to persons, I suggest that Carl Rogers's implicit statement of person-centred values largely matches the values of narrative therapy:

> How do we look upon others? Do we see each person as having worth and dignity in his own right? If we do hold this point of view at the

verbal level, to what extent is it operationally evident at the behavioural level? Do we tend to treat individuals as persons of worth, or do we subtly devalue them by our attitudes and behaviour? Is our philosophy one in which respect for the individual is uppermost? Do we respect his capacity and his right to self-direction, or do we basically believe that his life is best guided by us? To what extent do we have a need and a desire to dominate others? Are we willing for the individual to select and choose his own values, or are our actions guided by the conviction (usually unspoken) that he would be happier if he permitted us to select for him his values and standards and goals? (Rogers, 1951: 20)

Different assumptions

Apparent similarities can, however, be deceptive. Even if narrative therapy embodies similar values to many other therapies, it is informed by a *postmodern/post-structuralist* way of thinking and working which poses important questions for traditional coun-selling. Activities such as encouraging a full description of the problem and exploring the person's history have different aims and meanings in narrative therapy from apparently similar elements in many other therapies; these elements are part of a different process and they arise from a different way of conceiving therapy. Many of the counselling culture's valued, taken-as-read assumptions and beliefs stand in direct contradiction to those of post-structuralist therapy. I suspect that even the sympathetic and interested reader may feel movements of impatient rejection, and may experience some difficulty in grasping these underpinning assumptions and holding them in mind.

I can identify with such reactions. I find White and Epston's writing and presentations exciting, thought-provoking, stimulating, bracing – and sometimes uncomfortable. I can discover that, despite all my efforts, I have not really understood the radical nature of this therapy, and that my thinking is still to an extent governed by pre-conceptions arising out of the discourse of my original training – the kinds of beliefs about the aims of therapy and the nature of human life it embodied, deriving from many taken-for-granted Western dominant ideas. Discomfort also occurs when I think I have grasped an idea about narrative ways of working and then discover that I have represented it to myself inadequately or mistakenly. This is more than uncomfortable – at times it is infuriating! The power of preconceptions to distort the unfamiliar and to ease it unknowingly into an existing mind-set has been demonstrated to me time and again in my attempts to understand where narrative therapy 'comes from' and what White and Epston are really proposing. However, it encourages me to know that I am not alone in this, even among therapists who associate themselves with narrative therapy. Writing in the *Dulwich Centre Newsletter* Daphne Hewson (1991: 5) admits: 'I've found that it takes some time for me to notice just what it is that Michael White and David Epston are saying when I read their writings or attend their workshops. I sometimes think I have the idea, but when I get back to my own therapy room the sign-posts to the next step or question don't seem as clear as they were when Michael or David was talking about it.' Clearly, enough people find difficulty in grasping ideas informing narrative therapy, and sometimes misrepresent them, to make White feel that occasional re-statements and clarifications are necessary:

> *Ken:* I've heard it said that you are opposed to the use of labels and to the use of medications.
> *Michael:* Now that's interesting. I've heard the very same opinion about my position on these matters.
> *Ken:* Well?
> *Michael:* From time to time I hear things about what I have said that I haven't spoken of, and from time to time I read accounts of my thought that do not relate to what I think . . . (White, 1995a: 116)

> The narrative metaphor is often referred to in conjunction with other metaphors that are commonly used in family therapy literature and practice: specifically, metaphors of system and pattern. It is very often assumed that the narrative metaphor can be tacked on to these other metaphors, and the narrative metaphor is often conflated with them. Because the metaphors of system and pattern on the one hand, and the metaphor of narrative on the other, are located in distinct and different traditions of thought, this tacking on and conflating of disparate metaphors simply does not work . . . (White, 1995: 214)

> There are interpretations of narrative therapy that read it as a proposal for a recycled structuralist/humanist psychological practice. This reading takes narrative therapy into the discourses of psychological emancipation, and casts it as a liberatory approach that assists persons to challenge and overturn the forces of repression so that they can become free to be 'who they really are' – so that they can identify their 'authenticity' and give true expression to this.
> This casting of narrative therapy is in direct contradiction to the tradition of thought and practice that has informed its development – that is, the tradition of poststructuralist thought. (White, 1997b: 217)

For a long while I conceived narrative therapy as an approach similar to Rogers's, as it shares the assumption that persons have the capacity to overcome their problems out of their own know-ledges and experience, especially problems brought about by the effects of internalizing others' perceptions. I assumed that narrative therapy, since it shares this person-centred stance, would engage with assisting persons to regain a sense of themselves as 'the persons they know themselves to be'. I saw it as a kind of person-centred _plus_ way of working (Payne, 1993). It was disconcerting, in reading White with more attention, to find that this view of narra-tive therapy is simplistic and wrong. White assumes that 'human nature' and 'the self' are not innate essences at all but are socially constructed, whereas person-centred therapists assume a perma-nent, essential self, and an objective, real entity called human nature (Mearns and Thorne, 1999: 16–19). I was also unprepared for White's firm statement that, although persons re-live various aspects of experience in his sessions in a way that is 'strongly emotive', and 'the feeling responses of all parties to the therapeutic interaction can be very intense' (White, 1995a: 20), he does not 'work with feelings' and does not wish to:

> I do not regard my position as an academic or intellectual one. But this doesn't mean that I feel compelled to join the dominant 'feeling dis-course' of the culture of psychotherapy, to practise in ways which are specified by this discourse, and to talk with people about the experiences of their lives in the contemporary ways of speaking about such things that are prescribed in and sanctioned by this discourse. I do not respond at all well to the various incitements to 'fit myself out' with the responses that are called for by this 'feeling discourse'. (White, 1995a: 87)

I had assumed that White and Epston had simply developed some creative and original practices which achieved the aims of traditional therapies in different, perhaps more positive, less path-ologizing ways. I was therefore rather jolted to realize that they did not share many of the _aims_ of therapy which I took for granted, which had underpinned my training and which had been rein-forced by conversations with other counsellors, articles in coun-selling journals and books about counselling. In an interview with Lesley Allen, White is explicit:

> _Lesley:_ I can understand how helping young women to identify and chal-lenge the various practices of self-subjugation [to anorexia nervosa] would be freeing of them.
> _Michael:_ Yes. _Not freeing them to be truly who they really are,_ but, in fact, _freeing them from_ the 'real'. And I would hope that the sort of con-siderations that we are discussing here might assist us to resist the

great *incitement* of popular psychology to *tyrannise ourselves into a state of 'authenticity'* – that these sort of considerations might open up certain possibilities for us *to refuse 'wholeness', to protest 'personal growth', to usurp the various states of 'realness'*. To open up the possibilities for us to *default,* and to break from the sort of *gymnastics* that *regulate* these states of being, that make all of this possible. (White, 1995a: 47–8, emphasis added)

White was calling many of the accepted aims of therapy 'tyrannical'. How could I reconcile this with the qualities of warmth, humanity, optimism and joyous engagement which struck me in his accounts of his work and which are so evident when watching video recordings of his sessions? What is there left for counsellors to do, I wondered, if they are not to be engaged with assisting persons to discover who they really are, to move to authenticity of being, to achieve personal growth, to become 'real' or 'whole'? Even more disturbing, from a therapist whose ideas I found engaging and whose methods I was trying to use, this passage appeared to dismiss something I had thought essential in order to be an effective counsellor. One of the criteria for applying for accreditation with the British Association for Counselling, which represents a broad spectrum of approaches, is 'evidence of serious commitment to ongoing professional *and personal* development such as regular participation in further training courses, study, *personal therapy* etc.' (emphasis added). Yet here was White saying that the idea of personal growth is a reflection of '[mental] gymnastics' from which I could 'default . . . and break'. I was forced to ask myself – *should* I be breaking from these attitudes, these 'gymnastics'? Could these taken-for-granted assumptions of the counselling culture really be characterized as the product of popular psychology's 'tyranny' reflecting 'hierarchies of knowledge'?

A post-structuralist critique of humanism

The humanist philosophical tradition in Western thought has put 'the individual', *perceived as an independently functioning entity,* at the centre both of study and of values. Post-structuralism and social constructionism, however, give full ethical and conceptual weight to social and cultural influences on persons' perceptions, identities and behaviours, and emphasize the social results of human interaction as worthy of study, as contributing to human life and as the basis of ethical choices. 'The self' is conceived as socially constructed from moment to moment, not as a permanent core entity. Rogerian therapy and others which focus on the individual as a self-contained dynamic unit are in the humanist tradition, and the terms of language through which these therapeutic processes are traditionally described and embodied are the dominant discourse of therapy. White pays tribute to the humanist tradition for being of assistance to persons in 'the support that [they] have drawn from it in challenging the various acts of domination they are being subject to, and in the significant role that it has played through its employment by the various human rights movements that have challenged different forms of discrimination and oppression' (White, 1997b: 254). Nevertheless, he sees these dominant humanist assumptions of the therapy culture as significantly *limiting*. Informing his comments is a view that since these ideas embody essentialist and structuralist concepts of humanity, which are questioned in postmodern/poststructuralist thinking, and which are no longer convincing, the time has passed when it was thought possible 'to know and speak of the "truth" of who we are – of the essence of our being, of our human nature' (White, 1997b: 220). In addition, humanist ideas incorporate and represent widespread and popularized social and cultural assumptions which reinforce the power of social institutions with a vested interest in influencing persons to see themselves in deficit terms and therefore needing the help of experts. Since persons are influenced by Western culture to believe that they need to change, grow and improve, they are encouraged to think that this must be their aim, undertaken in ways advocated by these experts:

> There is an ever-rising clamour of claims and counter-claims about the nature of the true self, and of proposals and counter-proposals for how this might be set free. It is everywhere that these claims and proposals are echoed – in the popular magazines, in the burgeoning self-help literature, in the selling of consumer products, in media advertising, in the promotions of the self-improvement industry, and so on . . . But this great lament is not just a preoccupation of popular culture. Foucault links the elevation of this will to truth with the success of the professional disciplines in the production of the great meta-narratives of human nature and of human development, those that inform the universal theories about life that are held to be true regardless of culture, class, gender, race, circumstance, place, era etc. This will to truth has inspired the development of formal systems of analysis of human life that make possible the interpretation of it and its reduction to formal categories . . . (White, 1997b: 222)

A 'triumvirate' of limiting assumptions

In the final chapter of *Narratives of Therapists' Lives* (1997b), White discusses, with many references to the writings of Michel Foucault, three interrelated assumptions which he believes permeate most mainstream psychological theories, and which he believes have become limiting assumed truths, or dominating assumptions, in traditional therapies. These three assumptions are the 'will to truth', the 'repressive hypothesis' and the 'emancipation narrative'. A 'triumvirate' is White's word for these three dominant assumptions which share joint power over the counselling culture (White, 1997b: 224).

Dominant assumption 1: the 'will to truth'
White refers to Foucault's analysis of how, in Western culture, the central philosophical question has become 'What is the truth of what we are? . . . the essence of our being, of our human nature. This has become a paramount concern of both professional and popular culture' (1997b: 220). In the post-structuralist and social constructionist traditions which inform narrative therapy 'What is the truth of who we are?' becomes a non-question. Post-structuralist thinking does not conceive human beings as possessing universal inner essences or one essential human nature unrelated to cultural circumstances. So the quest for 'who we truly are' is futile. 'Who we are' is a *variable*, not a sometimes hidden constant to be sought and defined. In the post-structuralist tradition the issue becomes 'how is it that the knowledges and practice of culture inform our modes of life and thought. It is through post-structuralist enquiry that we can break from the mission to discover something about "given" nature . . .' (1997b: 223).

Dominant assumption 2: the 'repressive hypothesis'
White cites Foucault's view that since Western cultural assumptions include the belief that we 'have' essential natures, but that these are hidden from or lost to us, Western cultural assumptions also need to define a culprit producing this estrangement – and this culprit has been identified as a psychological mechanism called 'repression'. White, summarizing Foucault, proposes that the repressive hypothesis has led to widespread assumptions that:

(a) the mechanism of repression conceals our true natures from us;

so

(b) this obscuring of our true natures prevents or inhibits our growth and actualization;

so

(c) this prevention or inhibition of growth and fulfilment produces illness and leads to 'the frustration of our authentic needs and deepest desires'.

As White (1997b: 221) expresses it:

> It is repression that hides from us the truths about who we are. Repression is not once guilty, but doubly so . . . it is also the force that frustrates the expression of truth. It is repression that keeps us from personal fulfilment . . . that stands in the way of us achieving a life that is true to our human natures. And, more than this: in that the frustration of our authentic needs and deepest desires leads to all manner of maladies, repression is thrice guilty.

Dominant assumption 3: the 'emancipation narrative'

White writes of Foucault's conclusion that, in Western dominant modes of thought, the answer to the question 'How can I understand who I truly am despite the obscuring of this truth by repression?' is 'Through liberating the self from the forces of repression' (1997b: 221). Working towards liberating the self from repression is the *emancipation narrative* informing therapies which urge this solution to this assumed problem, the 'many modern knowledges and practices of the self and of life . . . that are all in the service of living a life that is free of repression. These include the knowledges of human "needs" and practices for the fulfilment of these needs' (1997b: 221). White has cited Maslow's 'hierarchy of needs' (Maslow, 1954) as an influential example of this humanist concept. Maslow, a white, middle-class, American male, proposes a scale of *universal* human needs ranging from basic survival to self-actualization, and implies that only persons who are 'self-actualizing' are 'healthy'. White argues that Maslow's hierarchy is shot through with an unrecognized, culturally determined, individualistic and simplistically binary (healthy/unhealthy) view of human well-being which is quite limited and arbitrary in its value-laden assumptions – even dangerous: 'It is chilling to consider the sorts of actions that can be justified according to modern need discourses' (White, 1996: 51). Maslow's hierarchy, based as it is on individual self-actualization, makes ethical choices irrelevant, devalues roles within social organization, assigns no value to spiritual experience and sets up near-impossible standards of personal perfectibility for persons to aspire to.

White stresses that he is not calling humanist ideas bad or wrong, but claims that their *effects* contribute to a blocking-off of urgent and relevant questions concerning the influences of culture and society on human life. 'Just after the end of the Second World War there was great outbreak of *needs* – including for children to have their mothers constantly at home to look after them instead of working, and for men to return to the jobs those women had been doing!' (White, 1997a). He also sees these assumptions as diminishing possibilities for asking ourselves questions about our lives as they are lived in the present, as they encourage the aim of life to be conceived as moving away from present 'personal limitations' to a better future where our 'true selves' may emerge (White, 1997a). These aims for therapy and for life present themselves as 'liberating' but are in fact diminishing and entrapping:

> The joining of claims about nature, repression and psychological emancipation powerfully ties persons to the reproduction of our culture's 'truths' of identity in their pursuit of liberation – *persons are ever more tightly bound to their subjectivities through their efforts to liberate themselves* ... Under poststructuralist analysis, it turns out that it is not repression that obscures the truth, but that it is the *repressive hypothesis* that actually obscures the fact that persons are being incited to reproduce the subjectivities that are specified by the [essentialist, structuralist, modernist, individualist, assumed] 'truth' (of human nature). (White, 1997b: 224, emphasis added)

Effects on therapy of the assumption triumvirate

The triumvirate constrains our opportunities to explore with persons their own contributions to 'the shaping of their lives' through re-assessment of how the meaning they give to their experience has permeated the situation they present in therapy. Therapists who keep within the framework of assumed 'individual dynamics' become 'unwitting accomplices in the reproduction of the dominant and culturally sanctioned versions of identity, of the popular and revered forms of personhood, of the most familiar and mainstream subjectivities' (White, 1997b: 227). If as therapists we go along with these culturally sanctioned versions of identity and their individual-needs-focused bases, we are accomplices in encouraging persons to *fit into* these psychological concepts of persons seeking and needing 'personal development' and so on. These concepts do not disturb, challenge or confront social and cultural stereotyping, and do not challenge or confront the local or cultural/social political power forces influential in the construction of the problems the person has brought to therapy. By encouraging and reinforcing an *internalizing* and *pathologizing* way of seeing the problem, we become complicit in encouraging persons to define their problems in terms of 'past influences which have damaged me and mean that I need to be cured in order to change' rather than as 'one account I have given myself of my life which can be set against other, more experience-near accounts'.

White gives no examples in this spare and closely argued Conclusion to his book, but perhaps the following (based on White, 1997b: 217–35) may illustrate the point. If a counsellor is captured by the triumvirate of assumptions when counselling a child referred because of his emotional reactions to being bullied at school, he may be tempted to see the problem in terms of the child's low self-esteem and his needing to develop skills in physical and emotional self-defence. He may be tempted to wonder whether the boy's extreme degree of distress is partially caused by his 'denying' his feelings about the situation, and whether the therapist might therefore encourage those true feelings to find full expression in the therapy room. He may wonder whether the child's not 'standing up to' bullying is related to a degree of immaturity, which itself 'invites' bullying, and whether through an accepting relationship with himself the boy might begin to move towards a more mature capacity to defend himself and to discover ways of coping with bullies. If this is what the therapist thinks, and if this governs his counselling approach, he is blaming the victim and defining the situation in terms of the boy's assumed and imputed immaturity, inadequacy or pathology. A narrative therapist, taking a post-structural and social-constructionist stance, would think it appropriate to ensure that the school prevents the bullying; for the bullying children to be offered therapy in order for them to address their behaviour and to change it; for the victimized child to be given assistance to recognize that he has not been to blame for the bullying; and for counselling to assist him to understand that he has *no* responsibility to 'develop new personal capacities' to overcome the problem, such as learning to fight back or to 'stand up for himself'. If his parents are urging this latter course then the therapist would invite them to address the cultural discourses permeating this perspective on the problem, which are preventing them from honouring their child's refusal to be drawn into a vengeful and violence-reciprocating stance. Counselling may assist the child to feel better about himself, of course, but *not* by providing him with a process of improvement or growth based on the assumption that he has invited the bullying and been inadequate in resisting or overcoming it. The recognition, condemnation and addressing of power issues is the key, assisting him to develop a clear perspective on what he has been subjected to, and a clear recognition that his distress and sense of powerlessness are appropriate and inevitable given the imposition of bullying. His newly told sub-plot will not be around weakness, failure and the need to improve fighting skills but around recognition of the reality of terrorization and injustice and the results they produce on persons' identities. I offered a similar narrative process under different circumstances to Ruth (see Chapter 8).

Another illustration: a man whose peer subgroup discourse has recruited him into thinking that all women are fair game for sexual exploitation has given a meaning to his experience which needs challenge from a therapist, not crudely and confrontationally, but in ways which invite him to examine his assumptions and beliefs (Jenkins, 1990). If a therapist engages with the man in terms of the man's liberating himself from repression and working towards growth and self-actualization, such opportunities are lost – and the man has an excuse for ducking out of responsibility since his actions are being attributed to impersonal mechanisms and causes, a deficit 'within' him, such as the influence of an unhappy childhood, which needs to be addressed in terms of elimination followed by personal growth. Therapy will not be working towards the man's facing the harm he has done, accepting responsibility for it, recognizing then separating himself from the cultural influences which have affected his attitudes, and working towards restitution and a monitored, changed way of life. Instead, 'The therapeutic context becomes one for the challenging of repression, and for reproducing the "truths" of human nature' (White, 1997b: 227). A woman who has experienced subjugation by this man, whose fear of his actions may have induced a degree of paralysis of will, and who has been persuaded by him to attribute blame to herself when his violence erupts, will have the meaning of these experiences *reproduced* by a therapist who attempts to assist her through a hypothesis incorporating 'repression' and the man's assumed need to grow and actualize. It will also be replicated by a therapist assumption that she herself needs to address limitations in her own bravery or self-esteem. Such 'therapy' joins with and confirms oppressive and victim-blaming practices and turns a blind eye to the relational power politics which have produced her situation – both local, the man's actions, and social, the validation of his actions by his subgroup and by the wider cultural influences permeating that subgroup's values.

In his arguments concerning the constrictive influences of the triumvirate of ideas on therapy (and I offer only a very compressed and simplified version above) White stresses that if we allow ourselves to be dominated in our thinking and constrained in our work by assumptions of the will to truth, the repressive hypothesis and the emancipation narrative, we are not only closing down options for persons who consult us, we are also making our own ethical practice more difficult, and diminishing choices for our *own* lives for the ways in which those lives can enrich and be enriched by the work we do. My understanding of White's argument is that ethical choices cannot be made if we believe impersonal processes beyond our control are at work in us, such as repression; and that if we see our own lives principally in terms of deficits to be made good, we may be confining ourselves to a certain self-focused fretting around our assumed innate inadequacies. The triumvirate of assumptions, in White's view, narrows the range of therapists' own creative capacity to re-examine the bases of their work by deconstructing the dominant stories of the therapy culture's discourse. Rather than presenting therapists with opportunities for 'stepping outside the boundaries of what is familiar and known' and 'challenging the limits of our thought, [the three assumptions] confine therapists to a reproduction of, and a confirmation of, all that which we are already familiar with and already know ... the door is closed on opportunities for our work to become something that it wasn't, and for us to become other than we were' (1997b: 225–6). 'Taking these norms, rules and laws of human nature as a foundation for our work, as therapists we exempt ourselves from consideration of personal ethics ... When therapy is about releasing human nature from what binds it, when it is about the recovery of authenticity, there is nothing to be monitored' (1997b: 228). 'In practice this restricts us and the persons who consult us to deficit-centred or problem-saturated accounts of history – not just the history of the persons who consult us, but also the histories of our own work' (1997b: 230).

Questioning the 'intrinsic' value of therapy

According to my understanding, post-structuralism implicitly questions the whole concept of therapy as intrinsically valuable to anyone and everyone by promoting work on personal growth which we all need. And although I have not found this point made specifically in White and Epston, I believe that post-structuralist perspectives also challenge the view that therapists themselves need to be 'in therapy' as a matter of course, or at least to have had a very substantial number of hours as 'clients', in order to be competent to practise. These concepts are social constructs of the humanist therapy culture, a culture which itself is part of humanist Western values and consciousness. They reflect and embody the knowledge/power linkage of other social institutions of their time and place, and their intended benevolence can mask self-interest. A post-structuralist perspective can lead us to ask – how have these beliefs arisen? In whose real interests is such activity undertaken? When does such 'therapy' end? Who has ever claimed to gain, or has ever met someone who has gained, a state of actualization, or of satisfactory personal growth, or of wholeness, or of liberation from repression? What meanings are conveyed to persons by assumptions that all therapists have ongoing deficits and that therapists need to be permanently self-doubting about the possible effects of unrecognized repressions and 'unfinished business' on their competence to practise? Is not this continual psychological self-censoring an example of what Foucault described as positive power (positive in the sense of 'producing results') recruiting us into impossible tasks of continuous personal self-evaluation which we define as liberation?

Professional development

In offering a critique of the 'personal growth' dominant truths of much therapy, White certainly does not deny the validity of therapists' looking to their *professional* development. The post-structuralist position of questioning personal development towards actualization as an aim for therapy does not imply or validate complacency or self-satisfaction:

> In this work, I do come up against my own personal limitations, which I then want to explore. These are limitations with regard to language, limitations in my awareness of relational politics, limitations in my capacity to negotiate some of the personal dilemmas that we are

confronted with at every turn in this work, limitations of experience, limitations in my perception of options for the expression of certain values that open space for new possibilities, and so on.

I want to explore these limitations, by talking about them with those persons who seek my help, and by talking about them with other therapists, and through personal reflection, through reading, and so on. In exploring these limitations in this way, I can extend what for me were the previously-known limits of this work. (White, 1995a: 38)

Enrichment of life

I do not think my commitment to keeping open my thinking, examining my assumptions and attitudes, monitoring my behaviour, and widening the range of my ideas, corresponds to the definitions of 'need' which are assumed in traditional therapy. In addition, when I enrich my life through relationships with present and new acquaintances, travel, reading, music, art, conversation, countryside, thinking and other joys, I do not define this as 'personal development' in the sense that this term is used in the therapy culture. Enrichment, yes; not personal development. I have not *developed*; I am not better or 'healthier'. I am responsible for my choice to explore new ideas and to enrich my life with joyful activities, even while trying to bear in mind that my access to such enrichment reflects a life of privilege and luxury compared with most people's lives on this planet (Welch, 1990: 15). But this is quite different from assuming that persons who seek my assistance have deficiencies in personal development which are either producing their problems or stopping the persons from overcoming those problems, and it is quite different from assuming that persons need to address these imputed deficits through factors which I happen to find valuable for my own life.

In the counselling culture, it seems to me, 'personal development' has become confused with enrichment, and 'therapy' has become confused with lengthy examination and sometimes re-living of past and present experience in order to root out assumed sources of pain and distress. Many counsellors assume deficits, unfulfilled needs and potentials, both in themselves and in persons; persons are seen as finding it hard to overcome their problems *because of* these assumed deficits. They have 'unhealthy functioning', their 'growth' is inadequate or inhibited by repression, they need to become more 'mature' by talking with a counsellor over a long period of time, and forming a therapeutic relationship with her. Such assumptions are, in a postmodern/post-structuralist perspective, seen as uncritically culturally conditioned, and therapist-centred: a reflection of humanist and modernist historical positions which are now untenable.

Aims of therapy when 'promoting personal growth' is excluded

Perhaps once we cease to hold to the idea of helping persons to grow, to overcome repression, to discover themselves, to become actualized, we are left with what persons come to therapy for in the first place. I have never had a request from a person for therapy to 'promote my personal growth' or to 'help me to discover who I really am', although I have certainly been told 'I'm stuck' and 'I don't know what's the matter with me' and 'I don't recognize myself' and 'I don't know where to go from here.' To be fair, I have also never been asked to facilitate the identification and deconstruction of unique outcomes! Most persons who seek my assistance just want to sort their problems out as quickly as possible, and they hope counselling can assist them in this. Often persons attribute their problems to 'inadequacy' or 'failure' or 'weakness' in themselves – they self-pathologize, a process which traditional person-respecting therapies, which are nevertheless based on 'person-deficit' assumptions, can confirm and embed. I believe that narrative therapy is well placed to assist persons to fulfil the aims they themselves define, partly by its avoiding essentialist and deficit assumptions, and by promoting the telling of self-stories which undermine rather than reinforce self-pathologizing.

Persons' own forms of language

Hardly to my surprise, very few persons who come for counselling are versed in postmodern and post-structuralist thinking! Persons define their problems through the essentialist and structuralist forms of language which permeate most of Western culture. Although as a narrative therapist attempting to think and work within a postmodern and post-structuralist perspective I implicitly offer persons an alternative way of thinking and speaking about their lives, it is no part of my job to insist on this and certainly no part of my job to criticize or deny them their own forms of language and thought. I believe that if my work has been of assistance to persons, and if in undertaking this work I have framed it according to my own beliefs and assumptions, their thinking and language staying within essentialist and structuralist frameworks does not deny the genuineness of the differences in their lives which they are describing.

'Therapist decentring'

Perhaps the most important developments in narrative therapy over the past decade, those with most implications for re-thinking the assumptions of traditional therapy, concern 'therapist-decentring' practices, which reflect thinking about the nature of the relationship between the therapist and the person seeking assistance. In writing around this theme, White has suggested ways of defining the therapist–person relationship which by implication raise questions about one of the most cherished assumptions in many therapies.

'Therapist decentring' underpins the ethos and many of the practices of narrative therapy and finds specific and focused expression in three areas discussed below, 're-membering', 'transparency' and 'taking-back practices'. In the performance of narrative therapy these elements are intertwined, but I discuss each in turn for clarification. First, however, I offer my own understanding of the way in which post-structuralist thinking calls into question the counselling culture's 'cherished assumptions' about the relationship between the counsellor and the person seeking assistance. I have not found a direct critique of these traditional assumptions in White, but he has presented his own very different concept of issues in the therapist–person relationship (1997b: 125–44).

The relationship between the person and the therapist

In both Rogerian person-centred and narrative therapies, persons, not counsellors, are seen as the experts in their lives. Compared with the psychodynamic, behaviourist or cognitive therapist, the Rogerian counsellor is said to stand back from the process experienced by the person during counselling. Rogers frequently asserted his belief that, if the therapist provides a warm, accepting, empathic, genuine context for therapy, giving the person time and space to explore his problems, with appropriate 'encouragement' cues, that is enough; the person faces his fears, organizes his thoughts, dares to experience his 'real' feelings and moves towards change (Rogers, 1951; 1961).

Despite Rogers's respect for persons' experience as the basis for therapy, Rogerian therapy seems to me to incorporate two assumptions which sit uneasily with that philosophical position. One is the *deficiency assumption* discussed above – that the 'client' needs to grow. The other assumption, despite Rogers's calling his therapy 'person-centred', is Rogers's concept of the *centrality of the therapist* in persons overcoming this assumed deficiency. Despite their many differences, Rogerian, behaviourist, cognitive and psychodynamic therapies put the problem squarely 'in' the person. The person is believed not to have overcome, coped with or come to terms with her life problems because she is insufficiently 'clear-thinking', 'whole', 'mature', 'healthy' and so on, according to the therapist's definitions of these terms. Although Rogers rejected an expert role for the therapist, I believe it can be argued that the Rogerian person-centred tradition has nevertheless created the danger of an ideal-ized and self-venerating role for the therapist as 'the hero who liberates', in Harlene Anderson's telling phrase (1997: 32). The therapist is perceived to offer a temporary but *central* relationship to the person, without which therapy cannot succeed, *and which nobody else can be in a position to supply.* In Rogerian therapy, the counsellor's task is to promote 'growth' *by means of* this relation-ship with the person: 'If . . . I see a relationship as an opportunity to reinforce *all* that he is, the person that he is with all his existent <u>potentialities</u>, then he tends to act in ways which support *this* hypothesis. I have then – to use Buber's term – confirmed him as a living person, capable of creative <u>inner development</u>' (Rogers, 1961: 56, italic in original, other emphasis added).

This centrality of the 'therapeutic relationship' has become a given tenet in most therapies and is especially important in the person-centred tradition. Mearns and Thorne state:

> The distinctive feature about the [Rogerian] person-centred approach is that it does not just pay lip service to the importance of the relationship, but actually takes that as <u>the aim of the counselling process with every client</u> . . . the relationship is *all*-important: if that is <u>healthy</u> then the counselling outcome has the best chance of being productive. It is the counsellor's responsibility to try to create that <u>healthy relationship</u> . . . (Mearns and Thorne, 1999: 22, italic in original, other emphasis added)

> [In supervision] the presenting of 'cases' does not put the same empha-sis on the intricacy of the client's personality as would occur in other disciplines, but . . . much more attention is given to the counsellor's *appraisal of the relationship between the client and herself.* (Mearns and Thorne, 1999: 56, emphasis added)

> Mutuality is not always reached in person-centred counselling, but there nevertheless comes a time when it seems to the counsellor that the client may not require *their relationship* much longer. Perhaps the client has successfully negotiated the main stages of an important life transition, and *although the counselling relationship has not developed to the point of mutuality, the client is substantially able to take charge of his life* . . . Some-times a client has made enormous progress in counselling but finds it

difficult to imagine how he will continue *on his own*. (Mearns and Thorne, 1999: 164, emphasis added)

This view puts the therapy room at the centre of the process of therapy, and makes the relationship with the therapist the person's primary relationship in overcoming his problems during the often very lengthy period of meetings usually assumed to be necessary. By locating the context of therapy as the counselling room and by identifying the relationship with the counsellor as the means of therapy, I would argue that counsellors marginalize the person's relationships and living contexts outside the therapy room as factors contributing to the person's discoveries and decisions about her life. Such a view of the centrality of the therapist does not allow for, let alone promote, the person's overcoming problems with the help of friends, partner, workmates, mother, teachers, father, sons, daughters, other relatives, doctor, priest, informal and formal peer groups and so on. Anyone and everyone is excluded from the process except the counsellor. Yet people managed to face, think about and overcome their problems long before counselling was invented, and presumably they seldom did this on their own unless they were for some reason wholly socially isolated.

I have never heard colleagues claim that they elevate themselves above other relationships in the person's life – I am sure that the very idea would horrify them. Nevertheless, I would argue that this is precisely what the concept of a therapeutic relationship with the therapist can actually encourage. Certainly I have been told by many a person that friends' and relatives' attempts to help have been counterproductive: they are too optimistic, or give a lot of unwanted advice, or try to make the person approach the problem as they themselves might. It is tempting for the counsellor to concur – to believe that professional knowledge is needed, and a special relationship with a professional. Only in narrative therapy have I come across a questioning of this idea – a contrasting concept that the professional's role is more productive and ethical as a facilitator of the therapeutic actuality and potential of 'real-life' relationships' rather than as the provider of a 'therapeutic' relationship with the counsellor herself.

A therapist's relating to a person is not the same as providing a 'relationship which is therapeutic'

Questioning the concept of a therapeutic relationship with the counsellor is not to advocate a cold, distanced or disengaged way of relating to persons. When watching White at work it is abundantly clear that he relates with all the core conditions for therapy identified by Rogers – empathy, congruence and unconditional positive regard – powerfully in place. White *relates* in these ways, but this is quite distinct from promoting a 'relationship which is therapeutic'. As a narrative therapist I attempt to relate with warmth, acceptance and genuineness with persons I see for therapy. But I believe that persons' therapeutic relationships are with the people who are actually important to them in their 'real life', and that this is how it should be.

In my work I attempt to follow narrative therapy practice through an orientation towards the person embodying the concept of 'decentring' myself in the processes of therapy and in the person's life. Perhaps there are persons who are and always have been totally isolated and friendless, without even a single fleeting experience of acceptance or affection, and perhaps for these rare persons, finding in a counsellor the first human being who has ever been interested in their experience and concerned for their well-being, there might well be a valid degree of therapeutic reassurance and validation in the relationship itself. I have never met such a person but I hope I would recognize this situation and not shy away from its implications, both personal and professional. But short of such an encounter, I maintain a stance of not attempting to have a 'therapeutic relationship' with the person.

I will often introduce conversations which select out and emphasize past and present relationships in the person's 'real life' which may be, or may become, therapeutic. These are *'re-membering' conversations*. I also attempt to establish *transparency and accountability*, where I invite and share ideas on the ways in which we are working together and acknowledge factors in my own life, attitudes and experience which may be affecting and/or imposing limits on the assistance I can offer. These conversations decentre me by countering therapist mystique, or any idea that I am able or wish to stand aside from the continuity between myself in the therapy room and myself in the rest of my life. Through *taking-back practices* the effects on my own life of the persons' stories are fully acknowledged and honoured, and I emphasize the *two-way* nature of this relationship between myself and the person, including the learnings I gain from persons who entrust me with their problems. I see these as important elements in my work's ethical dimension. In describing them below I do not claim originality; my practice is based on White's expositions.

'Re-membering' conversations

A 're-membering' conversation (note the hyphen) is both therapist-decentring and therapeutic. Therapist decentring is achieved in 're-membering' conversations by the person's locating a source of assistance in relationships with persons significant to him, both those still in his life and those who are no longer present. I attempt to encourage the person to identify such people, whose imagined 'voices' he might call on to assist him. I invite him to describe in detail the history and nature of these relationships, and to 'reminisce'. I ask whether it might be appropriate for any of these people to join, re-join or become more active in the 'club of his life'. Sometimes I introduce this 'club of life' metaphor (White, 1997b: 22–4) in an open and specific way, and sometimes I use the general idea of people re-joining or being rejected from the person's life without specifically introducing the life-club metaphor.

By recalling people who have had a supportive or positive role in his life in the past, and imagining what comments they might make, what advice they might give or what their reactions might be to his efforts and achievements, the person can gain a sense of assistance and companionship in adversity even if these people are not literally available to him, perhaps because he has lost touch with them or if they are no longer alive. His self-story can become enriched by their revival as members of his life, and his felt identity can become enriched by a recognition of what he has meant to these people, what they have meant to him, and by inviting them back into his life as supportive 'presences'. This process of 're-membering' persons' 'presences' creates a therapeutic plot-line. The enhancement of memories associated with these people creates a linked narrative leading to the present, bringing their influence into the present. It is not a spiritual or religious exercise, and I make clear this 'non-religious' point about encouraging 're-membered' presences in case of misunderstanding. I have worked with persons with religious beliefs which include the idea of continuing existence after physical death who have found 're-membering' moving and helpful, but I have equally known this to be helpful for persons who have no such beliefs. Persons suffering from grief, especially when a long time has elapsed since the death, often find great comfort and inspiration in 're-membering' the dead person, and abandoning attempts to follow prescribed patterns of moving on or letting go (White, 1989: 29–36; 1997b: 24–39).

As well as people from the person's past, there may be people still available or potentially still available to the person whose assistance could be valuable, in sharing experiences and joining for celebration when problems have been overcome. Questions such as 'Who might be pleased if you were to tell them about this development?' and 'Who might you share these thoughts with in order to spread your discoveries about yourself more widely?' can encourage the person to call on these significant others as audiences for re-tellings, either privately or, if possible and acceptable, in the therapy room. This overcomes the restriction of tellings and re-tellings being centred only on myself, the therapist. Examples of 're-membering' conversations are given in Chapter 6 (Jenny) and Chapter 8 (Clara).

The 'club of the person's life' metaphor can also be drawn on when persons decide that they do *not* want certain people in their lives, such as abusers or intrusive ex-partners, but find difficulty in separating themselves from these people, literally and/or in their own minds and feelings. In these instances the process arising from the metaphor is an affirmation of the resolution to 'suspend' or 'dismiss' the offenders from the person's life – not in this case a 're-membering', but an 'un-membering'. The nature and history of the abusive or rejected relationship has usually been explored at this point in therapy, so a clear summary of the injustices imposed on the person can be listed, as evidence justifying the offender's suspension or dismissal. What the offending person might say, and in many instances *has* said, in his 'defence' can also be written down, together with statements from the person which expose the inadequacy of these justifications. 'It just happened' can be countered by 'You chose to do it'; 'You wound me up' can be countered by 'You enjoyed reacting angrily to my despair'; 'You imagined it' can be countered by 'I know what I saw and heard' and so on. The list of statements can be kept as a therapeutic document. In this process of *un*-membering of certain people, the *re*-membering of supportive persons can be very helpful: the person can invoke the witnessing of people whose support she values at this time of transition and confusion. Sometimes the suspension or dismissal can be put into effect by a symbolic ceremony, such as a Support Committee Meeting where the person calls on 're-membered' people to consider the evidence, and to assist her in her task by confirming that the evidence justifies suspension or dismissal. This can be an actual meeting (White, 1995a: 104–7) or it can be organized with the absent people's presence being imagined and/or symbolized. Writing a letter of dismissal can follow, either to be distributed to the Support Committee and selected friends or to be posted to the ex-member of the person's life if doing this is not potentially dangerous, and a copy of this letter, too, can be kept as a therapeutic document.

Although it is the therapist who introduces 're-membering' conversations, the conversations themselves decentre the therapist. They focus on and encourage support and validation from people who are or have been in genuine relationships with the person in his 'real life'. These therapeutic relationships can continue to play a supportive and affirming role when the counsellor has become a distant memory.

Transparency

Perhaps the concept of 'transparency' in narrative therapy has some similarity to Rogers's 'congruence'; both define a moral position concerning the therapist's determination to be genuine in relating to persons and to avoid a top-down or professionally distanced stance. Rogers's emphasis is on the therapist's being self-aware, on his maintaining a consciousness of his feelings and reactions and not hiding these from the 'client' (Rogers, 1961: 61–2). White's transparency practices are also self-monitoring, but his focus is on the impossibility, in conversations with persons, of a therapist's completely escaping from culturally and socially formed assumptions, beliefs and behaviour. Transparency is a means of promoting accountability by openly acknowledging these limiting factors to the person, and attempting to escape their worst effects through this sharing. White stresses the ethical priority of therapist decentring through openness with the person:

> this approach to accountability privileges the voices of persons, who are seeking consultation, [over] therapist's expressions that reflect taken-for-granted privilege, and that reproduce marginalisation of others. These circumstances provide opportunities for therapists to link these expressions to their location in the social worlds of gender, race, culture, class, sexual identity, and age. (White, 1997b: 205)

> there is nothing about narrative practices that exempts us from the reproduction of power relations, and [this consideration] encourages us to embrace a responsibility to structure into our work processes that might be identifying of these relations of power . . . (White, 1997b: 232)

Issues relating to my ethnicity, social class, age, gender, sexuality, enablement and all other distinctions between my experience and the person's experience must be subject to acknowledgement.

Taking gender as an example: White suggests that transparency practices can include, for a male therapist (a) in-session acknowledgement of his limitations as a man subject to and living in men's culture, and his checking out whether women are feeling the operation of such attitudes in his work with them; (b) encouraging women to check out their own experience of him as a therapist with women who might be able to identify the operation of such factors in his work out of their experiences; and (c) consulting women, other than the person he is offering therapy, who might assist him to be aware of ways in which these women experience his gender behaviours negatively, and taking these comments seriously as cautions, lessons or warnings (1995a: 165–6).

I have consulted women on the degree to which my performance in a video-taped interview demonstrated unrecognized sexist attitudes, and sought advice from a woman friend with a particular interest in issues of instituitional power. Two of my supervisors are women. However, I have much to learn, and much to improve on, in this aspect of my work. I easily fall into the subtle sexist trap identified by Ian Law as 'searching for a woman's opinion that supports my own opinion, rather than listening to women's opinions which are different' (Law, 1994: 40). I regularly check out with persons as to whether unacknowledged gender-based and culturally formed assumptions are being experienced by them, by questions, statements and requests such as the following:

- As a man, I can't know at first hand what it feels like to be a woman being 'put in her place' by men. Will you please let me know if I start to assume I know how this kind of male behaviour feels to you?
- I'm bound to have some unrecognized difficulties in understanding how gay persons experience their lives.
- Has my tone of voice reminded you of men who tried to lord it over you?
- I seem to have been saying quite a lot. Typical male behaviour. I'm sorry I've been dominating the session.
- Is what I've just said an adult assuming he knows what a teenager needs?
- It's all too easy for me to forget that I've got a job and you haven't. Suggesting you might go to the Citizens' Advice Bureau to get information was really insensitive – I should have realized you couldn't afford the bus fare into town.
- You've made me aware that when I asked what stood in the way

of your leaving your husband I wasn't taking into account that your marriage vows are very important to you. I'm sorry about that – perhaps it was a reflection of my generation's less serious attitude to those vows.

- I realize that I was thinking about your daughter in Western terms – I didn't know that in your country parents are considered responsible for their children right up till they get married. I'd really be grateful if you could tell me if I say anything else showing I don't understand your beliefs.

'Taking-it-back' practices

According to the traditional counselling perspective, the therapist offers a one-way service to the 'client'. All attention is on the person and his problems and the counsellor stands back from any sharing of her own life. This is seen as an ethical stance; the counsellor is at the service of the person and must not encourage any switching of attention away from the person and towards herself. Surely *this* is therapist decentring? White challenges us to re-think this assumption, and to recognize that therapy is *not* one-way:

> A one-way account of the therapeutic interaction is the account that is taken for granted in the culture of psychotherapy . . . the recipients of therapy are solely the persons who consult therapists, and that, if the therapy is successful, if all goes well, these persons will undergo some transformational process . . . it is understood that the therapist possesses a therapeutic knowledge that is applied to the life of the person who consults him, and this person is defined as the 'other' whose life is changed . . . exceptions to this one-way presentation of the ideal therapeutic process are invariably problematized. (White, 1997b: 127–8)

> I have an *ethical commitment* to bring forth the extent to which therapy is a *two-way* process, and to try to find ways of identifying, acknowledging, and articulating the extent to which the therapeutic interactions are actually shaping of the work itself, and also shaping of my life more generally in positive ways . . . (White, 1995a: 168, emphasis added)

White proposes that the traditional position, that the therapist should always exclude herself, as therapy is for the person, is actually person-limiting and therapist-centring:

> in that the ideal is for this person's life to change as an outcome of the therapeutic conversation while the life of the therapist remains as it was, this person is subject to a marginalisation of their identity . . . A very significant number of persons who seek therapy have arrived at thin conclusions about their lives and identities. They 'understand' that they

are bereft of the requisite knowledges or skills to address what it is they find problematic in their lives . . . these deficits are to be attended to and made good by expressions of the expert knowledges and the expert skills of the therapist . . . this status contributes significantly to the reinforcement of the thin identity conclusions . . . (White, 1997b: 128–9)

White's practice is certainly *not* for the therapist to draw the person into conversations about the therapist's problems! The two-way nature of what happens in therapy is the by-product – inevitable and valuable – of a process which is unequivocally and wholly undertaken *for the person, not for the therapist* (1995: 172–98; 1997b: 100–4; also cf. Chapter 8). 'Taking-it-back practices are not a formula for the production of a form of therapist-centredness, but are an antidote to this . . . *the expressions and the agenda of the persons seeking consultation remain at the centre of the work*' (White, 1997b: 146, emphasis added). I attempt to 'take back' to persons information about how our sessions have assisted me in my work and, often, in my life outside work. I do not express these acknowledgements in an exaggerated, effusive or 'congratulatory' way, but in a spirit of recognition of our common humanity, attempting to meet White's definition of this moral position: 'I am not expressing a graciousness. And these expressions are not grand – "you have turned my life around" – and they are not ingratiating. These taking-it-back practices are, first and foremost, expressions of an ethical commitment . . . the performance of an acknowledgement of what this work brings to the life of the therapist' (White, 1997b: 145).

Examples of taking-it-back practices

- I have shared with persons who believe in life after death that this reminds me of the comfort my mother gained from her spiritualist beliefs.
- I thanked Wendy (Chapter 6) for the new understanding she gave me about what it felt like to have people dismissing the reality of a child who had died, and assured her that this awareness had helped me in my work with another woman facing similar issues.
- When Ruth (Chapter 8) wrote to me about my using her experiences in this book, saying that she hoped her story would help other women, I replied suggesting that even if only one or two therapists working with abused women gained helpful ideas for practice from this part of the book then her hope would be fulfilled.

- I asked Martha, who had fought a hard and successful legal battle to gain compensation for an accident at her place of work, for permission to share her story with other persons facing similar institutional battles, as it had provided me both with information and inspiration.
- In several sessions with John, who was referred by his school for being abrupt and rude to teachers, I spent much time encouraging him to identify unique outcomes – occasions when he had been more calm and courteous. In the third session he simply ignored my opening questions and talked movingly of some very distressing memories from the past which were making him feel tense and angry all the time. At the end of the session I thanked him for using it for what *he* wanted, and for a salutary reminder that I should check out with persons that counselling is addressing the issues they really wish to explore.
- Jean, who was confined to a wheelchair, explored with me the apparent paradox that she wanted to be treated as herself, not 'Jean-in-a-wheelchair', but that she became angry when people did not take her disability into account in their dealings with her. This had a resonance for me in the way I react to people who ignore my hearing loss or do not notice my hearing aid, even though the hearing aid is designed to be unobtrusive. I found Jean's ideas helpful to me personally, and said so, in addition emphasizing that they would help me in any future counselling with persons who had disabilities.
- When counselling ends, I often tell persons that their coming out of the situation they first presented, and into a more hopeful way of living, gives me hope that, should I face similar situations, I shall be able to draw on the memory of their struggle and victory as a source of assistance and hope.

Other practices which contribute to therapist decentring

Many practices described in earlier chapters contribute to the decentring of the counsellor and to the avoidance of the therapy room's becoming 'a micro-world that is split off from the contexts of persons' everyday lives' (White, 1997b: 200). Encouraging persons to select out unique outcomes from their descriptions of their lives, to name them, to deconstruct them, to thread them together as told coherent sequences, and to consider what these sequences might become in the future, is itself therapist-decentring. It decentres the therapist in that it does not imply the necessity for some sort of cure or treatment by a therapist, and equally it does not imply that the person needs to change, grow, develop or actualize, or depend on a relationship with a therapist.

Conversations externalizing internalizing discourses decentre the therapist. They too encourage new plot-lines to be told – not in this case from a selecting out of unperceived unique outcomes, but from the critical examination of dominant stories in society, culture, interpersonal politics and 'real life' in all its actuality. Assistance to the person is not conceived as the therapist bringing expert knowledge about assumed 'inner processes'; so, by implication, the kind of assistance that *is* offered challenges the appropriateness of such structuralist ways of describing the person's reactions to events in his life. By conversations externalizing society's, and the person's, internalizing discourses the therapist encourages an exploratory dialogue about those very external influences (political/interpersonal, cultural, social) which have contributed to the person's getting into this kind of self-attributing pathology. By encouraging an examination and deconstruction of the person's choices for either staying with or attempting to escape from these effects, the therapist assists the person to consider different, non-pathologizing perspectives. She institutes and encourages this process but she does not assert herself as the means of its working.

For example, a person whose self-definition has included a recurring sense of failure because he did not gain such high academic qualifications as his siblings may come to feel a changed sense of identity once the therapist has engaged him in conversations deconstructing the parental, peer, social, cultural and class-based factors which have promoted success in academic examinations as a criterion of personal value, and which have been powerful in invading his own identity and self-story. Such a conversation might include questions around other ways of valuing persons, and inviting him to consider his own life in the light of these other factors and values. He *may* then choose to live his life by those values. The therapist has decentred herself by assisting him to focus on a critique of social, cultural and political influences informing beliefs which value examination success as an indicator of personal worth. There has been no looking to the therapist for a special relationship, or for a cure, or for fixing his 'deficits in thinking', 'being out of touch with himself', 'immaturity' or any other essentialist pathology needing an outside expert's attention.

Summary

Post-structuralism, which informs narrative therapy, implies challenge to many traditional assumptions of the therapy culture. It challenges dominant humanist assumptions, underlying traditional therapies, of the 'will to truth', the 'repressive hypothesis' and the 'emancipation narrative'. White's exploration of unrecognized reinforcements of therapist power and centrality in therapy raises questions concerning the aims of therapy, the nature of the self, implicit pathologizing of the person, therapist self-veneration and the relationship between therapist and person. Therapist decentring is an ethical commitment which permeates narrative therapy. It is particularly evident in conversations encouraging past or existing relationships to remain or become therapeutic; transparency in acknowledging the therapist's culturally located limitations and constraints; and sharing with persons what their contribution in counselling has meant to the therapist and to other persons she has assisted.

Postscript

This book is itself a narrative – my own selecting out of ideas and practices from the writings and teaching of White and Epston, offered in a particular sequence, described and illustrated in a particular way. Some aspects of narrative therapy have been omitted or just glanced at in passing because other elements began to loom larger as I wrote and to insist on detailed presentation.

I particularly regret being unable to make space for White's ideas on spirituality, which incorporate original and thought-provoking concepts (White, 1996). I have also given inadequate attention to White and Epston's belief that there is no distinction to be made between activities called 'therapy' and activities called 'politics'. This belief finds expression, among many other ways, in work where they and their associates use narrative ideas outside the therapy room to promote self-help among indigenous people and to assist the self-empowerment of other disadvantaged groups, including persons defined elsewhere as schizophrenic. The *Dulwich Centre Journal* (formerly *Newsletter*) carries many accounts of this and similar work; for example, 1995 (1) on social justice issues for the aboriginal community; 1996 (3) on 'HIV/AIDS, diabetes and grief' in Malawi and Australia; 1996 (4) and 1998 (2 and 3) on young people and adults working together in schools and other settings; and 1997 (4), 'Challenging disabling practices'.

Appendix: Learning Narrative Concepts Experientially

The reading/practice gap

Reading a book about an unfamiliar therapy often makes little or no difference to what I actually do in my work. The book begins to fade each time I put it down, and even if I make notes I am left with a thin 'virtual text'. When counselling, my established ways of working take over, unless I have very firmly set out to remember a new practice and be alert to when I might use it. Reading is not a very efficient way of learning for 'doing' – so how might I assist the reader to try out some narrative therapy ideas?

It seems to me that, beyond an early stage in working with a person, it is unrealistic to introduce narrative practices into other ways of working in the hope that they will integrate. This is despite parallels and resonances between narrative therapy and some other approaches, and despite the person-respecting values shared by this way of working and many other therapies. If an overall approach is not based on postmodern/post-structuralist concepts the practices will not fit; they will clash rather than integrate. When I was becoming interested in narrative therapy, I found it relatively easy to use externalizing language when discussing persons' problems, but the moment I started to invite alternative descriptions of experience incorporating already-existing, although ignored or unacknowledged experiences, actions, thoughts, attributes, relationships and perspectives, I was no longer working to Rogerian concepts – I was not encouraging 'personal growth' but was encouraging changed self-stories. I tried to reconcile my person-centred training and practices with narrative therapy (Payne, 1993), but finally had to recognize their incompatibility.

Experiencing narrative ways of working

Rather than attempting isolated aspects of narrative therapy, readers might be interested to attempt a sequence of narrative-based co-supervision for work in their present approach. I offer below an exercise to undertake with a colleague, in order to move from reading about narrative therapy to experiencing aspects of it *as supervision*. To benefit from this exercise, each participant should, as a minimum, have read this present book, and preferably also White and Epston's *Narrative Means to Therapeutic Ends* (1990). The exercise is suitable for counsellors who work in *any* approach. It is not about using narrative therapy with persons, but about experiencing aspects of narrative thinking when discussing work which was performed according to the therapist's usual way of working.

An exercise in co-supervision

The exercise, designed to take about three hours, is my adaptation of a training sequence devised by my colleague Peter Emerson, which he developed from papers by Pam Lambert and Michael White in the *Dulwich Centre Newsletter* (Summer 1989/90) (White's paper is also in Epston and White, 1992: ch. 4). The practices suggested are selected and simplified versions of narrative practices, but they derive from some of White's and Epston's descriptions and demonstrations of their work.

The instructions have the limitation of being prescriptive, and the dialogue they produce will inevitably be rather artificial and mechanical. Unlike narrative supervision as it is really practised, the exercise cannot allow for flexibility, variety, creativity and discoveries of new ways of working within the narrative concept. It focuses on a fairly narrow band of techniques. Nevertheless, I hope that taking part in this exercise will make narrative ways of working come alive.

Supervision often takes the form of counsellors discussing *problems* in their work, rather than presenting instances of work where they feel they have succeeded. This mirrors what happens in counselling when a person brings problems to a counsellor in the hope that the counsellor will produce new ideas, or even solutions. Counsellors' narratives to supervisors tend to be 'problem-saturated' with the supervisor seen as the 'expert' who may sort out the counsellor's difficulties. Such supervisions can reinforce counsellors' doubts about their competence. This exercise takes a 'supervisor' and a 'counsellor' through a *contrasting* process to the above. I do not imply that problems in assisting persons should not be discussed in supervision. However, the exercise does draw attention to the value of identifying unique outcomes in counselling practice and threading them into a self-story, or sub-plot, of competence. The supervisor encourages the counsellor to identify unique outcomes in her/his work, name them and discover personal and professional meanings which will enrich work with the person, affirm the counsellor's identity as a skilled therapist and be transferable to other counselling sessions.

The participants should *stay in their own identities*. Counselling issues discussed should be real, and the answers to the supervisor's questions should be genuine. The pace may be as slow and exploratory as the participants find comfortable, with the supervisor consulting the 'crib sheet' of questions as much as she/he wishes, with questions and answers being repeated or re-phrased if this is helpful. Timing is not crucial and the sessions may take more or rather less time than the instructions suggest.

Structure

Each colleague decides on some recent counselling to present to a co-supervisor. This should consist of one or more sessions where some or all of the counsellor's practices *appeared to be of assistance to the person*.

1 Each colleague takes a turn as supervisor and as counsellor, in sessions lasting about an hour. The supervisor (a) asks the questions below, in the form given, and then (b) encourages full and detailed answers by improvising further questions where necessary.
2 After the first session the colleagues may wish to have a short break before changing roles, and they will agree at that point whether to discuss the first session at once, or to postpone all discussion until they have gone through the sequence again, with exchanged roles.
3 Guidelines for the end-of-exercise discussion and follow-up are given below, but participants may wish to go beyond these.

Sequence of each supervisory session (S = supervisor,
C = counsellor)

1   (*15–20 minutes*): C briefly outlines the person's presented
    problem, then describes recent counselling when what C did or
    said appeared to be of assistance to the person.
2   (*30–40 minutes*): When C's account is complete, S asks the
    following, listens to C's answers, and follows with further,
    improvised questions to elicit even more complete and detailed
    answers:
    (a) Would you please describe again, in more detail, one or
        more aspects of this counselling which were success-
        ful?
    (b) What successes in past counselling paved the way for
        these unique outcomes in your recent work?
    (c) What was it in your work with this person which trig-
        gered your imagination in this way?
    (d) What do you think these unique outcomes might
        reflect about yourself as a counsellor?
    (e) What do you think these unique outcomes might
        demonstrate about your particular interviewing style?
    (f) What might these unique outcomes indicate about
        future directions in your work with this person? And
        with other persons?
    (g) What do you think the person most appreciated in your
        work with them?

Discussion points

1   Were you surprised at the evidence this interview produced of
    your competence and skills as counsellors?
2   How did it feel to have these qualities brought forth in super-
    vision, compared with discussing problems and failures?
3   Have any further memories of successful counselling been
    triggered by the exercise?
4   What have you learnt about narrative perspectives from this
    exercise which reading had not made clear to you?
5   What questions about narrative therapy would you now like to
    explore?

Follow-up

Soon after completing the exercise each 'supervisor' writes a document for each 'counsellor' of about one A4 side, perhaps in the form of a letter, summarizing the unique outcomes which appeared to emerge for the counsellor in the supervision, and the meanings the counsellor appeared to discover concerning these successes. The participants may wish to arrange a further time to discuss these documents. Did they reflect the supervision session accurately? What thoughts and feelings had they evoked in the counsellors? What influence did they, and the whole supervision, have on subsequent counselling?

References

Amis, Kingsley (1986) *The Old Devils*. London: Hutchinson.

Anderson, H. (1997) *Conversation, Language and Possibilities: a Postmodern Approach to Therapy*. New York: Basic Books.

Anderson, H. and Goolishian, H. (1988) 'Human systems as linguistic systems', *Family Process*, 27 (4): 371–93.

Barham, Peter (1984) *Schizophrenia and Human Value*. Oxford: Blackwell.

Benjamin, A. (1974) *The Helping Interview*. Boston: Houghton Mifflin.

Brammer, M. (1973) *The Helping Relationship*. Englewood Cliffs, NJ: Prentice-Hall.

Brigitte, Sue, Mem and Veronika (1996) 'Power to our journeys', American Family Therapy Association *Newsletter*, reprinted in *Dulwich Centre Newsletter*, 1997 (1): 25–33.

Bruner, Jerome (1986) *Actual Minds, Possible Worlds*. Cambridge, MA: Harvard University Press.

Bruner, Jerome (1987) 'Life as narrative', *Social Research*, 54 (12): 11–32.

Bruner, Jerome (1990) *Acts of Meaning*. Cambridge, MA: Harvard University Press.

Burnham, John (1986) *Family Therapy*. London: Routledge.

Ceccin, Gianfranco (1988) 'Address to Association for Family Therapy', *Context*, 8 (4): 7–10.

Dolan, Yvonne (1991) *Resolving Sexual Abuse*. New York: Norton.

Easton, S. and Plant, B. (1998) 'Practical approaches: clients' notes – how long should we keep them?' *Counselling*, 9 (3): 188–90.

Epston, David (1989) *Collected Papers*. Adelaide: Dulwich Centre Publications.

Epston, David and White, Michael (1992) *Experience, Contradiction, Narrative and Imagination*. Adelaide: Dulwich Centre Publications.

Foucault, Michel (1963) *The Birth of the Clinic*, trans. A.M. Sheridan (1973). London: Routledge.

Foucault, Michel (1984) *The Foucault Reader*, ed. P. Rabinow. London: Penguin.

Freedman, G. and Combs, J. (1996) *Narrative Therapy: the Social Construction of Preferred Realities*. New York: Norton.

Freud, S. (1917) *Introductory Lectures on Psychoanalysis*, trans. J. Strachey (1963). London: Penguin.

Gass, C. and Nichols, W. (1988) 'Gaslighting: a marital syndrome', *Contemporary Family Therapy*, 10 (1): 3–16.

Geertz, Clifford (1973) *The Interpretation of Cultures*. New York: Basic Books.

Geertz, Clifford (1983) *Local Knowledge*. New York: Basic Books.

Gergen, Kenneth (1992) 'Towards a postmodern psychology', in S. Kvale (ed.), *Psychology and Postmodernism*. London: Sage.

Gergen, Kenneth and Davis, Keith (eds) (1985) *The Social Construction of the Person*. New York: Springer Verlag.

Ghirardo, Diane (1996) *Architecture after Modernism*. London: Thames and Hudson.

Gilligan, Carol (1982) *In a Different Voice*. Cambridge, MA: Harvard University Press.

Gilligan, Stephen and Price, Reese (eds) (1993) *Therapeutic Conversations*. New York: W.W. Norton.

Goffman, Erving (1961) *Asylums*. London: Penguin.

Haley, Jay (1987) *Problem-solving Therapy*. San Francisco: Jossey-Bass.

Hammersley, D. and Beeley, L. (1992) 'The effects of medication on counselling', *Counselling*, 3 (3): 162–40.

Harré, Rom (1998) *The Singular Self*. London: Sage.

Hare-Mustin, R. and Maracek, J. (1994) 'Feminism and postmodernism: dilemmas and points of resistance', *Dulwich Centre Newsletter*, 4: 13–19.

Hewson, Daphne (1991) 'From laboratory to therapy room: practical questions for redirecting the "new–old" story', *Dulwich Centre Newsletter*, 3: 5–12.

Hobson, R. (1985) *Forms of Feeling*. London: Tavistock.

Horowitz, M.J. et al. (1979) 'Impact of event scale: a measure of subjective distress', *Psychosomatic Medicine* (41): 209–18.

Hoyt, M.F. (ed.) (1996) 'On ethics and the spiritualities of the surface: a conversation with Michael White', in *Constructive Therapies*. New York: Guilford Press.

Jenkins, Alan (1990) *Invitations to Responsibility*. Adelaide: Dulwich Centre Publications.

Kearney, R. (1991) 'Post-modernism', in J.O. Urmson and J. Réé (eds), *The Concise Encyclopedia of Western Philosophy and Philosophers* (1991). London: Routledge.

Kvale, S. (ed.) (1992) *Postmodernism and Psychology*. London: Sage.

Law, Ian (1994) 'Adopting the principle of pro-feminism', *Dulwich Centre Newsletter*, 2/3: 40–3.

Leavis, F.R. (1943) *Education and the University*. London: Chatto and Windus.

Leavis, F.R. (1972) *Two Cultures? The Significance of Lord Snow*. London: Chatto and Windus.

Lyotard, J.F. (1979) *The Postmodern Condition: a Report on Knowledge*, trans. G. Bennington and B. Massumi. Minneapolis: University of Minnesota Press.

Macintyre, Alasdair (1981) *After Virtue*. London: Duckworth.

McLean, Christopher (1995) 'Reclaiming our stories, reclaiming our lives' *Dulwich Centre Newsletter*, special edition.

McLeod, John (1997) *Narrative and Psychotherapy*. London: Sage.

Madigan, Stephen (1999) *The Politics of Identity: Considering Community Discourse in the Externalising of Internalised Problem Conversations* (*www.yaletownfamilytherapy*.com).

Maslow, Abraham A. (1954) *Motivation and Personality*. New York: Harper and Row.

Mearns, D. and Thorne, B. (1999) *Person-centred Counselling in Action*. 2nd edition. London: Sage.

Myerhoff, Barbara (1986) 'Life not death in Venice', in V.W. Turner and E.M. Bruner (eds), *The Anthropology of Experience*. Chicago: University of Illinois Press.

Nelson, K. (1989) *Narratives from the Crib*. Cambridge, MA: Harvard University Press.

Nelson-Jones, Richard (1983) *Practical Counselling Skills*. London: Cassell.

Opie, Iona and Opie, Peter (1967) *The Lore and Language of Schoolchildren*. Oxford: Clarendon Press.

Ossario, Peter (1985) 'An overview of descriptive psychology', in K.J. Gergen and K.E. Davis (eds), *The Social Construction of the Person*. New York: Springer Verlag.

Palazzoli, M.S., Ceccin, G., Prata, G. and Boscolo, L. (1980) 'Hypothesizing – circularity – neutrality: three guidelines for the conduct of the session', *Family Process*, 19: 3–12.

Parker, Ian (ed.) (1999) *Deconstructing Psychotherapy*. London: Sage.

Parker, I., Georgaca, E., Harper, D., McLaughlan, T. and Stowell-Smith, M. (1995) *Deconstructing Psychopathology*. London: Sage.

Parry, Alan and Doan, Robert E. (1994) *Story Re-visions: Narrative Therapy in the Postmodern World*. New York: Guilford Press.

Payne, Martin (1993) 'Down-under innovation: a bridge between person-centred and systemic models?', *Counselling*, 4 (2), reprinted in *Counselling: the BAC Counselling Reader* (1996). London: Sage.

Polkinghorne, Donald (1988) *Narrative Knowing and the Human Sciences*. New York: State University Press.

Rabinow, Paul (ed.) (1984) *The Foucault Reader*. London: Penguin.

Radford, Tim (1999) 'Baby talk shows skills with speech are in-built', *Guardian*, 1 January.

Rogers, Carl (1951) *Client-centered Therapy*. London: Constable.

Rogers, Carl (1961) *On Becoming a Person*. London: Constable.

Rosen, S. (1982) *My Voice Will Go with You: the Teaching Tales of Milton H. Erikson*. New York: Norton.

Scott, M.J. and Stradling, S.C. (1992) *Counselling for Post Traumatic Stress Disorder*. London: Sage.

Seidler, Victor D. (1994) *Unreasonable Men: Masculinity and Social Theory*. New York: Routledge.

de Shazer, Steve (1988) *Clues: Investigating Solutions in Brief Therapy*. New York: W.W. Norton.

Sheehan, Jim (1997) Personal communication.

Sheehan, Jim (1999) 'Liberating narrational styles in systemic practice', *Journal of Systemic Therapies*, 18 (3): 1–18.

Shotter, John (1985) 'Social accountability and self-specification', in K.J. Gergen and K.E. Davis (eds), *The Social Construction of the Person*. New York: Springer Verlag.

Shotter, John (1991) 'Consultant re-authoring: the "making" and "finding" of narrative constructions', Paper presented at the Houston–Galveston Conference on Narrative and Psychotherapy: New Directions in Theory and Practice, Houston TX.

Sykes Wylie, Mary (1994) 'Planning for gold', *Networker*, November/December: 40–9.

Tomm, K. (1989) 'Externalizing the problem and internalizing personal agency', *Journal of Strategic and Systemic Therapy*, 8 (1): 54–8.

Turner, B.S. and Hepworth, M. (1982) *Confessions: Studies in Deviance in Religion*. London: Routledge, Kegan and Paul.

Turner, Victor W. and Bruner, Edward M. (eds) (1986) *The Anthropology of Experience*. Chicago: University of Illinois Press.

Warren-Holland, S. (1998) 'Practical approaches: referral letters', *Counselling*, 9 (2): 96–7.

Webb, Wendy (1997) *Rocky Start*. Norwich: Wendy Webb Books. (Wendy's books may be obtained from Wendy Webb Books, 9 Walnut Close, Taverham, Norwich NR8 6YN, England.)

Welch, Sharon D. (1990) *A Feminist Ethic of Risk*. Minneapolis: Fortress Press.

White, Michael (1989) *Selected Papers*. Adelaide: Dulwich Centre Publications.

White, Michael (1993) 'Commentary: the histories of the present', in S. Gilligan and R. Price (eds), *Therapeutic Conversations*. New York: Norton.

White, Michael (1995a) *Re-authoring Lives: Interviews and Essays*. Adelaide: Dulwich Centre Publications.

White, Michael (1995b) *Externalizing Conversations Exercise*. Adelaide: Dulwich Centre Publications.

White, Michael (1996) 'On ethics and the spiritualities of the surface', in M.F. Hoyt (ed.), *Constructive Therapies*. New York: Guilford Press.

White, Michael (1997a) Personal communication.

White, Michael (1997b) *Narratives of Therapists' Lives*. Adelaide: Dulwich Centre Publications.

White, Michael (1999) Personal communication.

White, Michael and Epston, David (1990) *Narrative Means to Therapeutic Ends*. New York: Norton.

Wilkinson, Mary (1992) 'How do we understand empathy systemically?' *Journal of Family Therapy*, 14(2): 193–205.

Wilkinson, Mary (1999) Personal communication.

Zimmerman, J.L. and Dickerson, V.C. (1993) 'Bringing forth the restraining influence of pattern in couples therapy', in S. Gilligan and R. Price (eds), *Therapeutic Conversations*. New York: W.W. Norton.

Zimmerman, J.L. and Dickerson, V.C. (1996) *If Problems Talked: Narrative Therapy in Action*. New York: Guilford Publications.

Note

Dulwich Centre Publications are available from Dulwich Centre, Hutt Street, PO Box 7192, Adelaide, South Australia 5000, and in England from Brief Therapy Press, 17 Avenue Mansions, Finchley Road, London NW3 7AX. For information on distribution centres in other countries please contact Dulwich Centre Publications.

Index